About Island Press

Island Press is the only nonprofit organization in the United States whose principal purpose is the publication of books on environmental issues and natural resource management. We provide solutions-oriented information to professionals, public officials, business and community leaders, and concerned citizens who are shaping responses to environmental problems.

Since 1984, Island Press has been the leading provider of timely and practical books that take a multidisciplinary approach to critical environmental concerns. Our growing list of titles reflects our commitment to bringing the best of an expanding body of literature to the environmental community throughout North America and the world.

Support for Island Press is provided by the Agua Fund, The Geraldine R. Dodge Foundation, Doris Duke Charitable Foundation, The Ford Foundation, The William and Flora Hewlett Foundation, The Joyce Foundation, Kendeda Sustainability Fund of the Tides Foundation, The Forrest & Frances Lattner Foundation, The Henry Luce Foundation, The John D. and Catherine T. MacArthur Foundation, The Marisla Foundation, The Andrew W. Mellon Foundation, Gordon and Betty Moore Foundation, The Curtis and Edith Munson Foundation, Oak Foundation, The Overbrook Foundation, The David and Lucile Packard Foundation, Wallace Global Fund, The Winslow Foundation, and other generous donors.

The opinions expressed in this book are those of the author(s) and do not necessarily reflect the views of these foundations.

CITIES
as *Sustainable Ecosystems*

CITIES
as *Sustainable Ecosystems*

Principles and Practices

PETER NEWMAN

ISABELLA JENNINGS

ISLANDPRESS

WASHINGTON • COVELO • LONDON

ISLAND PRESS is a trademark of The Center for Resource Economics.

Library of Congress Cataloging-in-Publication data.

Newman, Peter, Dr.
  Cities as sustainable ecosystems : principles and practices / Peter Newman, Isabella Jennings.
    p. cm.
  Includes bibliographical references and index.
  ISBN-13: 978-1-59726-187-6 (hardcover : alk. paper)
  ISBN-13: 978-1-59726-188-3 (pbk. : alk. paper)
 1. Urban ecology. 2. Sustainable development. I. Jennings, Isabella. II. Title.
  HT241.N943 2008
  307.76—dc22

                                        2007026187

British Cataloguing-in-Publication data available.

Printed on recycled, acid-free paper ✪

Design by **Joan Wolbier**

Manufactured in the United States of America

10 9 8 7 6 5

Table of Contents

Acknowledgments

The seed for this book was planted a few years ago with the emergence of the UNEP/IETC Cities as Sustainable Ecosystems Initiative. While that program has been put aside by UNEP with their change of focus to disaster management, sustainable production and consumption, and water and sanitation, this book carries on the spirit of that original program to inspire long-term systemic change for urban sustainability.

Thank you to Lilia G. C. Casanova, then-deputy director of UNEP/IETC, and Steve Halls, then-director of UNEP/IETC, for driving the original initiative. We value the work of the team at EPA Victoria and all of those people involved in the Melbourne charette and the production of the Melbourne Principles. The CASE ideas are being explored and practiced in programs through ICLEI in Australia and Canada.

Thank you to Dr. Kuruvilla Mathew and the team at the Environmental Technology Centre at Murdoch University that hosted an experts' meeting in 2002 in the aftermath of the Melbourne charette, which was for both of us our first involvement in the CASE initiative.

Thank you to Dushko Bogunovich, associate professor, School of Architecture and Landscape Architecture, Unitec Institute of Technology, Auckland, New Zealand; and Robert Thayer, professor emeritus of landscape architecture, Department of Environmental Design, University of California–Davis for peer review of the first version and to Island Press reviewers for more recent feedback.

The book has gone through a few reworkings. Thank you to June Hutchison, James Mueller, Peta Mulcahy, and Karen Green for earlier editorial assistance. Thank you to Gary James for his assistance with the diagrams. We appreciate the enthusiasm of Heather Boyer at Island Press to bring this book to a wider audience and the patience of their editorial staff to guide its evolution into a book to reach out to the world's cities.

We are grateful to those who have helped with photographs, particularly Jeff Kenworthy, Tim Beatley, Peter Dixon, Jan Scheurer, New Metro Rail, Gary Burke, and Bill McDonough.

This work has been inspired by countless thinkers and practitioners in the sustainability field. We value the impact they have had on our thinking and lives. We applaud the efforts of the many people across the planet committed to bringing about positive change. We hope sincerely that this book goes some way to making their work known and inspires others to begin, or continue, to make changes in their communities, their workplaces, and their own lives.

PETER NEWMAN
ISABELLA JENNINGS

CITIES
as *Sustainable Ecosystems*

Introducing Cities as Sustainable Ecosystems

Our home city, Perth, situated on the ancient island continent of Australia, stretches out along the Swan River that flows from the hills to the Indian Ocean, and up and down the Swan Coastal Plain. There is much to be grateful for here: clean running water and good sanitation systems, relatively clean air, abundant fresh food, clean beaches, and the wide blue Swan River winding its way to the sea at Fremantle where we both live. We also enjoy the benefits of a diverse community, including rich ethnic traditions and indigenous culture. This place is home to the Nyungar, Aboriginal peoples who represent one of the oldest living cultures on Earth. It is located in one of the biodiversity hot spots of the world, where you can find hundreds of species in a small piece of remnant bush.

Yet there are signs of strain: algal blooms in rivers and wetlands, concerns about water scarcity and climate change, urban decay, car dependence and the related issues of smog and traffic congestion, sprawling urbanization, declining affordability of housing, and health problems such as rising obesity rates and mental health conditions, especially among the young. These issues are not unique. This picture could be true of most cities in the world to some extent, and many bigger cities, especially those in the developing world, are struggling to an even greater degree. The impact from our urban ways of living is being felt not just here. In a globalizing economy, our patterns of living increasingly have repercussions well beyond our city boundaries, reaching out across the planet.

Cities are the defining ecological phenomenon of the twenty-first century. From a minor part of the global economy one hundred years ago, they have become the principal engines of economic growth and the places where most of humanity dwells. Cities are growing faster than ever before. As Lois Sweet notes, "With the advent of the 21st century, for the first time in human history, half the world's population of more than six billion will be living in cities. The ways in which the urban need for food, water, shelter and social organization are met will not only determine the course of human civilization, but the very future of this planet. . . ."[1] While cities provide expanding economic opportunities in the new global economy, they are also big contributors to environmental disruption, both within and beyond their boundaries. How big a threat do cities pose to the global ecosystem? Can we make cities more sustainable?

With the trend toward globalization, cities are increasingly drawing in resources from across the globe and exporting wastes beyond their boundaries, having a disproportionate impact on natural ecosystems and the biosphere as a whole. As cities grow in population, the tendency is to expand in land area, consuming important natural ecosystems and agricultural land. Environmental and social problems within city boundaries are growing too, especially in developing countries (UNEP 2002). While the challenges are great, the possibility of transforming our cities offers hope for achieving sustainability.

There is a critical need to envision human settlements in more positive ways, first to reduce per capita impacts but then to move to a new and more exciting possibility where cities begin to be a positive force for the ecological regeneration of their regions. This requires a more symbiotic relationship between cities and their bioregions or "life-places" as outlined by Berg and Dasmann (1978) and cogently described by Thayer:

> A bioregion is literally and etymologically a "life-place"—a unique region definable by natural (rather than political) boundaries with a geographic, climatic, hydrological, and ecological character capable of supporting unique human and nonhuman living communities. Bioregions can be variously defined by the geography of watersheds, similar plant and animal ecosystems, and related, identifiable landforms (e.g., particular mountain ranges, prairies, or coastal zones) and by the unique human cultures that grow from natural limits and potentials of the region. Most importantly, the bioregion is emerging as the most logical locus and scale for a sustainable, regenerative community to take root and to take place. (2003, 3)

Similarly, a United Nations University/Institute of Advanced Studies report by Marcotullio and Boyle (2003) on urban ecosystems says, "Sustainability can only be achieved when cities are approached as systems and components of nested systems in ecological balance with each other."[2]

Many cities have begun attempts in this direction. However, these attempts have been mostly fragmented, lacking a holistic guiding framework to bring the threads of sustainability together. In this book, cities are viewed as ecosystems in themselves, with materials, energy flows, and complex information systems like any other ecosystem. The city-as-ecosystem approach is a useful way of viewing city dynamics, but the idea of Cities as Sustainable Ecosystems (CASE) goes further by examining the lessons from sustainable ecosystems to address the unsustainability of current city ecosystems. It offers solutions to our current predicament and provides a framework for action and ecological restoration within the city and its bioregion.

The central notion of the book is that the best innovations in human history have arisen by learning from and modeling natural systems. Cities need to develop this perspective.

Table 0.1 **The Ten Melbourne Principles for Sustainable Cities**

1. Vision	Provide a long-term vision for cities based on sustainability; intergenerational, social, economic, and political equity; and their individuality.
2. Economy and Society	Achieve long-term economic and social security.
3. Biodiversity	Recognize the intrinsic value of biodiversity and natural ecosystems, and protect and restore them.
4. Ecological Footprints	Enable communities to minimize their ecological footprints.
5. Model Cities on Ecosystems	Build on the characteristics of ecosystems in the development and nurturing of healthy and sustainable cities.
6. Sense of Place	Recognize and build on the distinctive characteristics of cities, including their human and cultural values, history, and natural systems.
7. Empowerment	Empower people and foster participation.
8. Partnerships	Expand and enable cooperative networks to work toward a common, sustainable future.
9. Sustainable Production and Consumption	Promote sustainable production and consumption through appropriate use of environmentally sound technologies and effective demand management.
10. Governance and Hope	Enable continual improvement based on accountability, transparency, and good governance.

Source: UNEP/IETC 2002

The ecosystem viewpoint is an inclusive one that sees humans as part of local socioecological systems, from bioregions to the biosphere, in which the focus is on relationships and processes that support life in its myriad forms, especially partnerships and cooperation.

This book explains how to pursue a path of urban sustainable development and regeneration. Its organizing principle is the ten Melbourne Principles for Sustainable Cities (see table 0.1). These principles are a set of aspirations developed at an international charette held in Melbourne in 2002 and endorsed by local governments at the Johannesburg Earth Summit later that year.

The first Melbourne Principle, Vision, affirms the need for cities to develop visions for a sustainable and equitable future. As discussed in chapter 1, these visions need to reflect a city's distinctive qualities and provide inspiration and guidance on the journey toward sustainability. The visioning process brings people together to consider what stage their city is at currently, what trends are occurring, and what they would like to see happen in the future. It provides the opportunity to ask important questions about what matters to people, what they need to sustain them, and what the role of ethics, technology and place should be. The vision statement is an expression of inspiration, hope, and common purpose, as well as a basis for developing indicators and monitoring progress toward sustainability. Using the ecosystem metaphor, the vision statement needs to express this sense of being part of a socioecological system, focusing on improving the quality of our interactions and relationships. A variety of examples are given of how cities are using ecosystem metaphors as the basis of their vision.

The second Melbourne Principle, Economy and Society, asserts that cities need to recognize the social and environmental value in their economies, which is based on the opportunities that they create, their critical role in innovation, and the special economic advantages created by being a city (their agglomeration efficiencies). Although economic globalization trends are driving the rapid growth of cities, they will become increasingly unsustainable unless they learn to incorporate social and environmental values that focus on the importance of communities and bioregions. For cities this means moving toward urban ecovillages with local economies embedded in and matched more closely to bioregional economies. Humans relate to each other and to ecosystems more effectively at local and bioregional scales. Cities can introduce or stimulate economic mechanisms at these scales—such as true costing, incentives for local innovations, complementary currencies, and green businesses—while reducing their subsidies for large-scale multinational businesses like shopping malls. In addition, the links between the economy and social capital need to be recognized fully. Social connections can be fostered through programs such as community arts.

The third Melbourne Principle, Biodiversity, recognizes the intrinsic value of biological diversity and natural ecosystems. Cities can play an important role in protecting and restoring ecosystem remnants within their boundaries and the wider bioregion. A system of linked static and dynamic biodiversity reserves from the city to the wider bioregion can be combined with the biosphere reserve concept to guide new development. Reducing urban resource use (ecological footprints) is vital to reducing biodiversity loss beyond the city boundaries. Bioregional celebrations and education raise awareness and appreciation of biodiversity. Furthermore, cities can provide labor and resources for restoration work in urban areas and the bioregion, acting as biodiversity arks.

The Ecological Footprint of a city, the fourth Melbourne Principle, measures the amount of land it takes to support the basic needs for food, water, energy, and materials, and to absorb greenhouse gas emissions and other waste. It provides a useful measure of the scale of a city's metabolism. Minimizing the ecological footprints of cities is a huge task that will require changes not only to city form and processes but also to the way that people live. Bringing consumption and production back to a local and bioregional scale can help restore feedback loops. An ecological footprint is shaped by the size of the shoe—the urban area. Hence density of development is an important determinant in resource use, particularly transport energy.

The fifth Melbourne Principle is the core theory of Modeling Cities on Ecosystems. Chapter 5 presents three models that are nested, moving from principles to practice. The first model is based on Bossel's work (1998), looking at the characteristics and strategies of sustainable ecosystems and socioecological systems as models for reshaping the structure and processes of our cities. For example, natural ecosystems use such strategies as nutrient cycling, diversity, panarchies (patterns of nested adaptive cycles), solar energy, feedback loops, and networks. Social strategies include adaptive learning, place-based communities, cooperation, and ethics embedded in emotional connections. Deploying these strategies, cities could be transformed into networks of compact, mixed-use urban ecovillages with integrated support systems, matched more closely to their bioregions. The second model shows how ecosystem succession patterns can be used to guide planning and the structuring of our cities. The third model shows how transportation priorities have shaped our cities according to the socioecological principle of travel-time budgets.

Sense of Place is the sixth Melbourne Principle, which is based on the idea that fostering a sense of place among city dwellers is vital to psychological fulfillment and developing connections that support more sustainable lifestyles. Cities that reflect a sense of place protect their natural and cultural assets; make historical and natural processes visible, designing with them not against them; restore and reflect the bioregional context and linkages; and have strong cultural and artistic practices that celebrate and inform their sense of place.

Empowerment through engagement of the community and region, together with effective Partnerships between government, business, and the community, form the essential institutional and social basis of CASE, captured in the seventh and eighth Melbourne Principles. They are necessary for cities to find innovative solutions to the issues of sustainability. This is how ecosystems work—through networks of support. Building this civic capacity is vital to making cities more resilient and creative, and making people more able to respond to feedback and take appropriate action. The emphasis on local and bioregional scales brings power back to a level at which people can make a difference and take responsibility. Cities around the world can begin to adopt partnership approaches to sustainability rather than just competing as globalization demands. For example, procurement of innovative sustainability technologies can be facilitated through cities working together to achieve economies of scale.

Sustainable Production and Consumption, the ninth Melbourne Principle, depends simultaneously on the appropriate use of environmentally sound technologies and effective demand management. Resource-efficiency improvements are important, but more than this, production and consumption need to be brought together more closely, and the role of people as citizens and not mere consumers has to be recognized. The focus for sustainable consumption is on meeting basic needs and living rich lives with fewer resources. Support systems (e.g., food production, freshwater and wastewater treatment) are designed to mimic and work with the patterns and processes of natural systems, with a focus on an integrated approach.

Governance and Hope, the tenth Melbourne Principle, identifies the link between good governance and the presence of hope in a city, especially hope for sustainability. Effective governance facilitates genuine participation and is underpinned by the political will to implement the necessary changes for sustainability. Hope also arises from deep within the social capacity of a city, welling up from many sources including arts and sustainability projects, ecological and cultural literacy programs, voluntary simplicity, neighborhood renewal programs, and the emergence of bioregional voices. Symbolic projects in cities showing leadership in sustainability illuminate new possibilities and provide inspiration. These and the many examples from the growing eco-city social movement, presented throughout this book, provide the basis for hope that humans and their settlements can find their place within the circle of life, simultaneously nourishing human individual and community needs along with the capacity of ecosystems and other life to be sustained.

The key to realizing the vision of Cities as Sustainable Ecosystems lies in the capacity of cities to synthesize the elements and strategies identified by the Ten Melbourne Principles with the wisdom to apply them in their own unique way. Ultimately, the path to sustainability is a shared one, relying on an informed citizenry and effective city governance, joined together in a global compact to ensure that urban humanity and all planetary life can coexist and thrive.

This book presents many case studies to bring some of the principles to life and inspire action. They come from across the world, from both poor and wealthy cities, yet there is a bias toward First World examples from Western countries. This reflects our roots but also our belief that it is the wealthy cities of the world that must lead the way. Some places are learning from our mistakes, but we can hardly expect poorer cities to use resources more carefully if wealthy cities continue along the path of unsustainability.

The core idea of the book is that cities need to be seen as ecosystems integrated within their wider context—communities nested within bioregions and the global biosphere. The path to sustainability lies in transforming our cities so that they are based on the patterns and processes of natural, sustainable ecosystems, achieving ecological regeneration, healthy communities, and viable economies within their bioregions. Cities work best at bioregional and community scales, not just at the global scale where much of the economy is taking them. New, more sustainable solutions can arise if social, environmental, and economic factors can be integrated more effectively at these scales. Thus, the ten Melbourne Principles need to be understood together, integrated into an idea of how cities can work better—both as human habitat and as part of bioregions within the wider biosphere.

As Klaus Töpfer said in a 1999 address to the World Council of Churches, "By acknowledging our rightful place within nature, we are accepting our responsibilities for its well-being, just as we take responsibility for the well-being of members of our families and friends. It's a matter of drawing a large circle, not just around your house, or your city or even your country, but around all life on Earth."[3] The CASE idea is based on the hope that humans and their settlements can play a positive role within the circle of life, nourishing both community and bioregional needs, and ultimately contributing to the restoration of vital ecological processes at all scales.

CHAPTER 1 | Vision

PRINCIPLE 1
Provide a long-term vision for cities based on sustainability;
intergenerational, social, economic, and political equity;
and their individuality.

*Elaboration: A long-term vision is the starting point for catalyzing positive
change, leading to sustainability. The vision needs to reflect the distinctive
nature and characteristics of each city.*

*The vision should also express the shared aspirations of the people for
their cities to become more sustainable. It needs to address equity, which
means equal access to both natural and human resources, as well as shared
responsibility for preserving the value of these resources for future generations.*

*A vision based on sustainability will help align and motivate communities,
governments, businesses, and others around a common purpose, and will
provide a basis for developing a strategy, an action program, and processes
to achieve that vision.*

Visions to Inspire

The path to sustainability starts with the development of long-term visions. According to
Steven Ames, the Iroquois idea of the Seventh Generation offers a useful model for community visioning:

Among the teachings of the Iroquois Confederacy, a centuries-old confederation of six
Native American nations, is the idea of the Seventh Generation. "In our way of life, in our
government, with every decision we make, we always keep in mind the Seventh Generation
to come," says Chief Oren Lyons, member of the Onondaga Nation and spokesman for the
Confederacy. "It's our job to see that the people coming ahead, the generations still
unborn, have a world no worse than ours—and hopefully better."

This practice of bringing the abstract and distant future into present-day reality is a powerful lesson. Indeed, the extent to which we are able to give something of value to the world may be measured in how much we have considered the long-term future in our current decisions and actions. Perhaps, someday, governments everywhere will think as instinctively about the Seventh Generation as do the Iroquois peoples. Until then, their teaching offers us a noble standard from which to judge our effort. (Ames 1997)

This was the core message of the landmark report from the World Commission on Environment and Development, *Our Common Future* (WCED 1987), that development had to meet the needs of current and future generations. Visions are about dreams, imagination, passion, and creativity. Long-term visions can inspire action and guide decision making. Viewing our settlements as ecosystems and living communities provides us with a direction and points to strategies for change.

Visions have always been at the foundation of good politics. The biblical saying "Without vision the people will perish" (Proverbs 29:18) has been the basis for many political programs wishing to catch the imagination of the people. Sustainability is the latest vision of global politics, but it now needs to be integrated into every city.

Many cities have made attempts in this direction, some using the ecosystem metaphor to guide them, but mostly these visions are fragmented, failing to bring together all the necessary elements and not based on broad community ownership. The Melbourne Principles provide an overarching vision, but every city needs to formulate its own vision, responsive to the needs and particularities of place within global aspirations for sustainability, equity, and peace.

The development of a vision for a city provides the basis for setting goals for action plans. The vision statement needs to recognize the constraints of a community. It should also define the ecological, social, and economic characteristics and values that the community has identified as crucial for sustainability, along with community priorities for short- and long-term action. This provides a guiding framework for future decision making.

Sustainability is not some fixed, perfect state but rather an evolving one that responds to changes in ecological processes as well as changes in human culture and institutions. Thus, community visions need to be revised regularly to reflect these changes.

Some vision statements, such as the Earth Charter, present alternative views of progress. Launched officially in June 2000, the Earth Charter is a document that was formulated by thousands of people in seventy-eight countries over the course of twelve years. It calls for a compassionate, just, and sustainable world. The Earth Charter was endorsed by local governments at the Johannesburg Earth Summit in 2002. Cities need to formulate vision statements that incorporate principles such as those expressed in the Earth Charter and the Melbourne Principles. Later in this chapter, examples are given of several city vision statements.

The Visioning Process

A vision needs to be developed through a community visioning process—an inclusive and participatory process that brings together people from across the community and empowers marginalized groups to contribute. Ames (1997) describes community visioning as "a process through which a community imagines the future it most desires and then plans to achieve it. . . . Encouraging local communities to dream is the beginning of building a better world."

Community participation is integral to the success of the visioning process, as the US Environmental Protection Agency recognizes:

> Community participation is key. Bringing people together, including business, industry, and education, along with children, planners, civic leaders, environmental groups and community associations, allows the vision to capture the values and interests of a broad constituency. Brainstorming ideas from the entire community results in a synergistic effect which can bring out a myriad of ideas that reflect the values and interests of the community as a whole.[1]

The diversity of ideas that such a process will generate, along with the ownership people have over the vision, provides the basis for genuine sustainability.

Community visioning processes in Oregon in the Pacific Northwest of the United States have attracted worldwide attention. Steven Ames, a planning consultant who has worked with communities and institutions in visioning processes throughout Oregon, has compiled a community visioning guide and given many presentations reflecting on his experiences. Ames argues for the importance of asking good questions. During his early work as an activist he observed that people cannot be forced to change, but he hypothesized that by asking people salient questions positive change might emerge. From his experiences he concludes that "when communities plan for their future in a rigorous and serious way, they often end up doing the 'right' thing."

The community visioning model he espouses emerged from his experiences with the city of Corvallis—"the trailblazer for visioning in Oregon's communities"—and other communities across Oregon. During the 1970s, Oregon developed a comprehensive planning system to manage rapid growth, safeguard natural resources (including farms and forests), and preserve the area's quality of life. The planning system required local communities to formulate land use plans in accordance with statewide goals. It was the only system of its kind in the United States at the time and today is still regarded as a "progressive model for the rest of the nation." The Corvallis vision process, called "Charting a Course for Corvallis," emerged just as Oregon was hit by serious recession.

Charting a Course for Corvallis (1988–89) laid the foundation for visioning in Oregon and led to many planning innovations. The process involved considerable community involvement, with the city leaving "no stone unturned in finding ways for people to engage in the process," including "informational presentations and community meetings, splashy public events with national speakers and children's visioning activities, a task force and special focus groups." The Corvallis vision and goals linked directly into city council activities, with a focus on the downtown and riverfront. Within ten years, officials concluded that most of the vision had been realized sooner than expected. The city then began a process to update its vision, achieving another first in Oregon.

Corvallis now has a new 2020 vision statement:

We envision that in 2020 Corvallis will be . . .

- a compact, medium-sized city (population range: 57,500 to 63,500) nestled in a beautiful natural setting;
- the historic, civic, cultural, and commercial heart of Benton County;
- an economically strong and well-integrated city, fostering local businesses, regional cooperation, and clean industry;
- a university town, a regional medical center, a riverfront city;
- an environmentally-aware community with distinctive open space and natural features, protected habitats, parks, and outdoor recreation;
- rich in the arts and recreational opportunities, celebrating the talents and culture of the people who live here;
- a community that values and supports quality education throughout the age continuum;
- known for its comprehensive health and human services, and for its services for the elderly and disabled;
- a hub in a regional transportation system that connects Linn and Benton counties and provides a link to the north-south high-speed rail system;
- a highly livable city which employs local benchmarks to measure its progress in areas such as housing, economic vitality, educational quality, environmental quality, and overall quality of life;
- blessed with an involved citizenry that actively participates in public policy and decision making;
- committed in its support for children and families;
- a community that honors diversity and is free of prejudice, bigotry, and hate;
- home . . . a good place for all kinds of people to live and to lead healthy, happy, productive lives.[2]

The Oregon Model for community visioning, described by Ames, includes a four-stage process, each based on a key question:

1. Where are we now?
2. Where are we going?
3. Where do we want to be?
4. How do we get there?

The first two stages need to identify the ecological and social assets of the community as well as the constraints. The Melbourne Principles can provide a framework for such an audit. For example ecological footprint calculations could be a useful part of this process (see chapter 4), as could many of the points elaborated in the sections on economy, sense of place, biodiversity, and governance.

"Where do we want to be?" is a core question for sustainability. It makes us think ahead and evaluate what matters to us. It enables a community to set its goals for each of the areas examined in the audit. The ten Melbourne Principles and the rest of this book provide food for thought for the third and fourth stages of the visioning process by highlighting issues to consider, along with possible solutions and case studies to guide and inspire positive change. When communities find out what is happening in other cities, they begin to imagine how they too can change.

Visioning, Ames argues, has numerous benefits. The process brings community members together and creates the space for imagining new opportunities and possibilities for the future. From this a "shared sense of purpose and direction" can emerge and coalesce into an action plan with tangible goals and strategies for realizing the vision. Yet there are other deeper, less tangible benefits, which include nurturing new generations of community leadership, enriching community engagement with government and civic life, fostering "new public/private partnerships for action," and strengthening "community cohesion, identity and livability."

Based on his experiences, Steven Ames identifies several important elements of an effective visioning process:

- Involve key institutions in the community, including government and private sector groups
- Attract the support of key opinion leaders
- Formulate clear goals and objectives for the process itself
- Allocate sufficient resources
- Engage people authentically.

He argues that the power of a vision lies in the degree to which it is shared by many people: "Whether the creation of a bold leader, a group of committed citizens, or dedicated planners, a vision must in time catch fire with the people of a place—or it will not succeed." To ensure this sense of ownership he recommends that people get involved early in the process and frequently. He highlights the importance of time and the need for "courage, hard work, persistence, flexibility, even a touch of obsession. . . ." Ames argues that visions never manifest entirely as expected: "be prepared for synchronicity and serendipity." Envisioning is a continuing process that involves honoring the past, being present, looking ahead, and keeping future generations in mind.

Conversely, the contributors to an ineffective visioning process include communities fragmented by conflict, resistant political leadership, "a poorly designed or managed process," insufficient resources, and the lack of an implementation plan or a commitment to carrying it out.

Between 2001 and 2006, all Australian cities developed strategic plans. All were based on sustainability principles, and all were participatory, vision-building processes. The most innovative in its participative processes was the plan for Perth, Western Australia, modeled on the visioning process developed for the rebuilding of the Ground Zero site in New York City. Dubbed "Dialogue with the City," this process provided an opportunity for people to be involved in planning Perth as it will be in the year 2030. Leading up to the Dialogue with the City forum, a community survey was conducted in July 2003 to find out people's views on issues that were to be considered in the forum. Over 1,700 people from randomly selected households across Perth were invited to share their views on transport, housing densities, residential development, and the environment.

The whole-day community forum had over a thousand participants. They were grouped into tables of about ten people, each with a volunteer facilitator and a volunteer scribe. Questions were posed, and responses recorded. Short speeches and video footage informed participants of the dilemmas of urban growth and the options for managing future growth. In the afternoon, participants were involved in a planning game to identify where and how to accommodate Perth's anticipated growth in population. All outcomes were recorded at the tables, and then collated and summarized by a team of volunteers using networked computers. The process provided participants with an opportunity to reflect, learn, and share ideas and deal with the complexities of planning. The ability to see the results of their deliberations immediately on big screens and see how their priorities were emerging created greater enthusiasm for the process.

The outcomes of the Dialogue forum, along with a combined workshop of community, industry, local, and state governments, contributed to the formulation of a vision that will guide Perth and the region of Peel for the coming decades: "By 2030, Perth people will have created a world-class sustainable city; vibrant, more compact and accessible, with a unique sense of place."[3] A set of priority areas developed by the attendees surprised all the public servants by how green they were:

- Strong local communities (city of villages)
- Clean, green city
- Urban growth boundary
- Connected, multicentered city
- Reduced car dependence and better public transport, especially more rail, better local biking/walking options, and integrated transport/land use
- Housing diversity (more options)
- Access to city services for all

The importance of the Perth vision process went beyond its content. When a newspaper campaign tried to denigrate the plan as an attempt to force the city into high-density flats and destroy all open space, the media became flooded with people who were able to refute the scare tactics and show what was really envisaged (Hartz-Karp and Newman 2006).

Vancouver, Canada, is another city with a history of visioning. The Greater Vancouver Regional District (a combination of twenty-one municipalities) had a series of planning exercises that led to their Livable Region Strategic Plan in 1999. This has guided urban development for the period since, leading Vancouver to become something of a model in sustainability (Newman and Kenworthy 2007). Another plan was produced to incorporate new factors and provide a greater vision for sustainability. "A Sustainable Urban System: The Long-Term Plan for Greater Vancouver" (2003) looks at the forces shaping cities, including climate change. It takes a systems view of the region and suggests alternative approaches to planning. Backcasting (as opposed to forecasting) is used to formulate water strategies: planners set targets and then work backward to determine how to get there. The impact of a "business-as-usual" approach is illuminated through the use of charts and graphs produced with software developed by Vancouver's Envision Sustainability Tools.

Another innovative visioning project is Imagine Chicago, a nonprofit organization founded by Chicago resident Bliss Browne in the early 1990s. The visioning work of the group rests on three core processes: dialogue, curriculum development, and network formation. Working in partnership with local institutions—schools, museums, churches, and businesses—Imagine Chicago "helps people develop their imagination as city creators." It has sponsored literacy development programs for parents, personal renewal programs for teachers, and an array of initiatives to educate and sustain Chicago's children. Its intergenerational and intercultural conversations have promoted understanding among diverse communities. Civic training has also been central to the group's mission in its efforts to cultivate grassroots activism, inspire at-risk youth, and empower neighborhood leaders. Imagine Chicago "offers everyone, especially young people, the opportunity to invest themselves in the city's future." It has become a model for cities worldwide who have begun to develop similar visioning projects.[4]

Effective visioning depends on people working well together. In her book *The Key to Sustainable Cities: Meeting Human Needs, Transforming Community Systems* (2005), Gwendolyn Hallsmith recommends that the planning process be based on "mutual respect, whole systems understanding, peaceful resolution of conflict, and openness to new mindsets and paradigms." The quality of communication, listening, and learning that occurs during the process will be reflected in the outcomes. The best place to start, she suggests, is with an inventory of all the positive qualities of a community, community assets, and the ways that needs are met. By starting with our assets, Hallsmith argues, it is "easier to create a collective vision of how we can meet needs with less impact. When we start with problems, often the vision is limited to having fewer problems, or solving an isolated problem; it does not necessarily encompass how we can satisfy our needs more effectively, or how we can live rich and meaningful lives" (10). This approach was applied in Burlington, Vermont, where they developed the Burlington Legacy Project.[5]

Strategies for Visioning

Developing vision statements calls us to ask deeper questions such as what progress means and what humans need to live healthy, happy lives. In the quest for sustainability we are invited to ask what sustains us and what do we want to sustain. In formulating a vision, the following questions could be considered:

1. What do we value? How do we define human progress?
2. What are human needs?
3. What are our ethics? How should we treat each other and the natural world?
4. What is the role of technology?
5. What is the role of place in sustainability?

Strategies for generating a vision will be related to each of these questions.

Strategy 1: Relate Vision to Ideas of Progress

In discussions about future visions for sustainability, clarifying the worldviews, values, and ethics of all participants helps to make discussions clearer and more fruitful. It allows genuine differences and common ground to be identified, particularly on what people value regarding future development and what would constitute progress.

Perceptions of progress and development differ according to people's worldviews. City communities need to reflect on their ideas of progress, considering what matters to them, their aspirations, and how they fit within the wider circle of life. Progress in the modernist world became focused on economic ends. Sustainability challenges this notion, asserting that unless environmental and social goals are incorporated with economic goals, progress is hollow. Sustainability helps us redefine progress to ensure that every generation can work to create a better future for the next generation.

As Kinnane (2002) points out in a paper contrasting indigenous and nonindigenous visions for the future in the East Kimberley region of Western Australia, indigenous communities "recognize that damage to spiritual and cultural values is as threatening to future generations as an economic slump or physical decline." In stark contrast to the modernist agenda, many indigenous perspectives provide a holistic view of progress, in which humans and the more-than-human world are seen as inseparable, and human progress is not viewed in isolation from the more-than-human world. As one indigenous voice explains,

> Sustainable development includes the maintenance and continuity of life, from generation to generation, in which human beings do not travel by themselves through time; we travel in community with the seas, rivers, mountains, trees, fish, animals, and our ancestral spirits. They accompany and drive us to the cosmos, the sun, the moon and the stars, which also constitute a whole. From our indigenous perspective, we cannot refer to sustainable development if it is not considered an integral, spiritual, cultural, economic, social, political, territorial, and philosophical process.[6]

Similar views are likewise discernable deeper in Western and Eastern spiritual traditions. By enabling people to consider environmental and social goals as well as economic goals, communities can be persuaded to believe that progress is possible and that development need not be negative.

Strategy 2: Relate Vision to Human Needs

Meeting human needs is a critical dimension of sustainability, as acknowledged in one of the first definitions of sustainable development, in *Our Common Future* (WCED 1987): "development that meets the needs of the present without compromising the ability of future generations to meet their own needs."

The subject of human needs has been explored from many perspectives, including philosophy, humanistic psychology (Maslow 1954, 1968), ecopsychology (Roszak 1992; Sewall 1999), environmental health, development practice (Max-Neef 1992; Nussbaum 2006; Gough 2003), and human evolutionary perspectives (Boyden 1992).

One of the most well-known models of human needs is Maslow's Hierarchy of Needs. Humanistic psychologist Abraham Maslow argues that human needs arise hierarchically, so that the most basic needs have to be met to a certain degree before higher-order ones can be attended to. The needs in ascending order are "physiological, safety, love, esteem, and self-actualization" (Maslow 1996, 173). Some have begun to apply the ideas of Maslow to how we look at development (Schumacher 1973; Sirolli 1999). Others in development practice view human needs as universal qualities or capabilities that form the basis for a program of justice for all (Nussbaum 2006; Gough 2003). Thus there is beginning to be some overlap in seeing human needs as a series of basic survival requirements of water, food, and shelter, above which are deeper issues of belonging, identity, and community.

The Chilean economist Manfred Max-Neef (1992) and biohistorian Stephen Boyden (1992) build on these models and examine how human needs relate to sustainability. Both authors argue that human needs are essential characteristics associated with human evolution and thus are constant across all cultures and historical time periods. Max-Neef suggests that while needs remain constant, satisfiers, which are the ways in which needs are met, can vary across cultures and over time. Another important distinction is that goods are seen as the means that people employ to facilitate satisfiers, to fulfill their needs. However, some satisfiers require goods, while others do not.

Max-Neef identifies the following needs: subsistence, protection, affection, understanding, participation, leisure, creation, identity, freedom, and transcendence. These needs intersect with four different aspects of activity—being, having, doing, and interacting—forming a forty-cell matrix that can be filled with examples of satisfiers for those needs. He also suggests that some satisfiers may appear to meet a need, but they actually prevent its true fulfillment (1992, 208). Box 1.1 outlines the different types of satisfiers, from violators to synergic satisfiers.

Sustainability is based on finding synergic satisfiers. Max-Neef's analysis makes clear the distinctions between needs, satisfiers, and goods, and highlights the way a society's

---

Box 1.1 **Types of Satisfiers to Meet Human Needs**

- **Violators and destructors** are claimed to satisfy a given need but actually make its fulfillment impossible while also destroying the fulfillment of other needs. These appear to be related especially to the need for protection (e.g., the arms race).
- **Pseudo-satisfiers** give a misleading sensation of meeting a particular need (e.g., mechanistic medicine that appears to satisfy the need for protection; chauvinistic nationalism that appears to meet the need for identity).
- **Inhibiting satisfiers** impair significantly the possibility of satisfying other needs (e.g., extreme economic competitiveness to meet the need for freedom impairs subsistence, protection, affection, leisure, and participation needs).
- **Singular satisfiers** meet only one need (e.g., welfare programs to provide housing meet the need for subsistence).
- **Synergic satisfiers** promote and assist in the simultaneous fulfillment of other needs by the manner in which they meet a particular need (e.g., participatory democracy satisfies the need for participation but also for protection, understanding, identity, and freedom).

Source: Max-Neef 1992

---

cultural ideas and worldview influence its choice of satisfiers. Reflections of this kind create the opportunity of finding other ways to meet our needs, ways that are more gentle on each other and the Earth. For city dwellers, Max-Neef's matrix can be used to consider how needs are met currently and how they might be met more sustainably. It becomes a useful tool for envisioning ways forward, to reduce a city's ecological footprint (chapter 4) and to achieve the other objectives outlined in the Melbourne Principles.

Boyden has devised a set of universal health needs using a biohistorical perspective. The principle of evodeviation proposes that when an animal is subject to conditions that deviate from those it is genetically adapted to, the animal is likely to show signs of maladjustment. Applying this principle of evodeviation to humans, Boyden presents "a list of postulated life conditions likely to be conducive to health in *Homo sapiens*, this list being, in fact, a summary of the conditions likely to have prevailed in the natural habitat of the species" (1992, 90; see box 1.2).

Nussbaum, coming from a development practice background, puts forward "ten capabilities as central requirements of a life with dignity" (2006, 76–77). These ten capabilities are universal statements expressing the necessary minimum entitlements for a fully just society:

1. Life. Being able to live to the end of a human life of normal length: not dying prematurely, or before one's life is so reduced as to be not worth living.
2. Bodily health. Being able to have good health, including reproductive health; to be adequately nourished; to have adequate shelter.

Box 1.2 **Boyden's Universal Health Needs of Humans**

Clean air (not contaminated with hydrocarbons, sulfur oxides, lead, etc.).
A natural diet (sufficient calorie intake; adequate nutrition; balanced; free of additives and con-
taminants; containing fiber).
Clean water (free of contamination with chemicals or pathogenic microorganisms).
Absence of harmful levels of electromagnetic radiation.
Minimal contact with microbial or metazoal parasites and pathogens.
Dwelling that provides adequate protection from extremes of climate.
An emotional support network, providing a framework for care-giving and care-receiving behav-
ior, and for exchange of information on matters of mutual interest and concern.
Opportunities and incentives for cooperative small-group interaction.
Levels of sensory stimulation which are neither much lower nor much higher than those of the
natural habitat.
A pattern of physical exercise which involves some short periods of vigorous muscular work, and
longer periods of medium (and varied) muscular work—but also frequent periods of rest.
Opportunities and incentives for creative behavior.
Opportunities and incentives for learning and practicing manual skills.
Opportunities and incentives for active involvement in recreational activities.
An environment which has interest value and in which changes of interest to the individual are
taking place (but at a rate that can easily be handled by the human psyche).
Opportunities for spontaneity in human behavior.
Variety in daily experience.
Satisfactory outlets for common behavioral tendencies.
Short goal-achievement cycles and aspirations of a kind likely to be fulfilled.
An environment and lifestyle conducive to a sense of personal involvement, or purpose, of
belonging, of responsibility, of challenge, of comradeship and love.
An environment and lifestyle which do not promote a sense of alienation, of anomie, of being
deprived, of boredom, of loneliness, of frustration.

Source: Boyden 1992, 91

3. Bodily integrity. Being able to move freely from place to place; to be secure
against violent assault . . . ; having opportunities for sexual satisfaction and for
choice in matters of reproduction.
4. Senses, imagination, and thought. Being able to use the senses, to imagine, think,
and reason . . . informed and cultivated by an adequate education. . . . Being able
to use one's mind in ways protected by guarantees of freedom of expression with
respect to both political and artistic speech, and freedom of religious exercise. . . .
5. Emotions. Being able to have attachments to things and people outside ourselves
. . . ; in general, to love, to grieve, to experience longing, gratitude, and justified
anger. Not having one's emotional development blighted by overwhelming fear
and anxiety, or by traumatic events of abuse or neglect. . . .

6. Practical reason. Being able to form a conception of the good and to engage in critical reflection about the planning of one's life. . . .
7. Affiliation. (A) Being able to live with and toward others, to recognize and show concern for other human beings, to engage in various forms of social interaction. . . . (B) Having the social bases of self-respect and nonhumiliation; being able to be treated as a dignified being whose worth is equal to that of others. This entails, at a minimum, protections against discrimination on the basis of race, sex, sexual orientation, religion, caste, ethnicity, or national origin.
8. Other species. Being able to live with concern for, and in relation to, animals, plants, and the world of nature.
9. Play. Being able to laugh, to play, to enjoy recreational activities.
10. Control over one's environment. (A) Political. Being able to participate effectively in political choices that govern one's life; having the right of political participation, protections of free speech, and association. (B) Material. Being able to hold property (both land and movable goods), not just formally but in terms of real opportunity . . . ; having the right to seek employment on an equal basis with others; having the freedom from unwarranted search and seizure. . . .

Nussbaum's approach focuses attention on the possibilities for human unfolding, the qualities that allow us to fully express our humanity—being able to love other people and other species as well as express ourselves emotionally, rationally, politically, and creatively.

Ecopsychologists argue that humans need contact and engagement with other humans and the more-than-human world. Depression and alienation, rather than reflecting personal pathology, may reflect sensitivity to environmental destruction and the loss of real engagement with the living world:

> Living in an era of ubiquitous environmental degradation is depressing to sensitive organic systems. Humans are no exception. . . . We no longer know what a depth of sensory awareness is. . . . The rhythms and patterns of the earth slip away. . . . We become lonely, hungering for a sense of belonging. . . . We lose the whole picture, and a sense of wholeness. We drink and drug in a mad search for satiation. It makes us sick, our souls so unsatisfied. Ultimately, we lose our health, our own wholeness. (Sewall 1999, 67, 71)

What is being lost in modern cities is not just natural resources and processes that support life, but experiences of the more-than-human world that are important to our spiritual, psychological, and physical health. For example, a team of Japanese researchers have shown that people in cities live longer, healthier lives if their streets are tree lined and they have a park within easy walking distance. Their findings, published by the British Medical Association, suggest that parks and gardens should not be treated as merely cosmetic and that green space should be given greater priority as planners prepare cities for an expanding population of elderly people. The researchers say that no matter what a person's social or economic status, half of the factors which will determine how long they live are associated with ready access to a green environment.

The research team, headed by Professor T. Takano of the Graduate School of Tokyo Medical and Dental University, used as their study sample 3,144 Tokyo residents born between 1903 and 1918. The study lasted five years, and by the end of the period, 897 of the elderly people had died. At the beginning of the study, each person had been asked to complete a questionnaire on such matters as his or her living environment, monthly expenses, proximity to urban green space, traffic noise, amount of sunlight entering the home, "neighborliness," and local crime levels.

Not unexpectedly, the oldest and poorest people died sooner. However, more hours of sunlight in the home and lower environmental noise levels were both associated with longer lives, while being able to walk to a nearby park or tree-lined streets—which made them feel positive about their community—was significantly associated with living longer (Takano, Nakamura, and Watanabe 2002).

Health researchers are finding evidence that interaction with the more-than-human world may provide many health benefits. Frumkin concludes:

> Perhaps this reflects ancient learning habits, preferences, and tastes, which may be echoes of our origins as creatures of the wild. Satisfying these preferences—taking seriously our affiliation with the natural world—may be an effective way to enhance health, not to mention cheaper and freer of side effects than medications. If so, then medicine and the other health professions will need to articulate a broad vision of environmental health, one that stretches from urban planning to landscape architecture, from interior design to forestry, from botany to veterinary medicine. (2001, 238)

Cities need to express these dimensions, providing rich and varied experiences, which nourish human well-being, otherwise they will foster the alienation that Boyden discusses. By considering more deeply the whole issue of human needs, city vision statements can provide a basis for finding creative and imaginative ways of meeting these needs sustainably in our cities and bioregions.

Strategy 3: Relate Vision to Ethics

Vision statements need to address ethical questions because they are central to sustainability:

> Achieving sustainability is largely a matter of asking ethical questions. Will this community project contribute to greater justice in our community? Will it harm the ecosystem? Will it harm communities elsewhere in the world? Are we living in such a way that our children's children will be able to live as well or better? Moving from such broad questions to daily action involves not only individuals asking themselves such questions about their own activities, but our community groups, associations and governments using tools to grasp what it might mean to live well, within the limits of nature. (Hawkins 2003)

Beatley and Manning (1997) argue that sustainability is essentially about taking on a new ethic of living that expands our circle of concern to future generations and the natural world, and promotes social equity and justice.

Anthropocentric ethics see the human as the locus of all value and the nonhuman world only as a resource. Indigenous ethics generally reflect a communal view of life, in which the lives of other beings also matter and the process of sustainable development encompasses all spheres of human existence, not merely the economic and technological. It celebrates the evolution of all species, not just human evolution. This view is echoed in various ancient and contemporary environmental ethics.

Deep ecology is a philosophical movement founded on the concept of self-realization and biocentric equality. The work of spiritual unfolding is seen as expanding the narrow ego-self to embrace the more-than-human world. Biocentric equality recognizes the intrinsic value of other life and all beings and ecosystems, and their right to unfold in their own way (Devall and Sessions 1985). This does not mean that humans should not harm anything, but rather that activities should be directed toward meeting vital needs.

The elements of a world ethic for living sustainably were presented in *Caring for the Earth: A Strategy for Sustainable Living* (1991), published jointly by the World Conservation Union (IUCN), United Nations Environment Program (UNEP), and World Wide Fund for Nature (WWF). This publication recognizes the rights of all humans, including the right to life, freedom, security, education, and expression, along with the intrinsic value of other life forms. It proclaims that "each generation should leave to the future a world that is at least as diverse and productive as the one it inherited" (14).

The opening principles of the Earth Charter, described above, are based on respect and care for the whole community of life. The charter's other basic values are ecological integrity, social and economic justice, and peace: "Let ours be a time remembered for the awakening of a new reverence for life, the firm resolve to achieve sustainability, the quickening of the struggle for justice and peace, and the joyful celebration of life."[7]

Newman and Kenworthy (1999) have developed ethics for sustainability in cities based on local ecology, human ecology, and urban ecology, drawing on the work of Gilbert White, Fritz Schumacher, and Jane Jacobs. They suggest that the elements of environmental spirituality associated with indigenous ethics can also be found in Western spiritual traditions. Similarly the UNEP Interfaith Partnership on the Environment has found common aspects of environmental ethics among the world religions (see box 1.3).

The process of developing vision statements provides an important opportunity for cities and urban dwellers to reflect on our ethical obligations to each other and other life, within our communities, cities, bioregions, and the biosphere as a whole.

Strategy 4: Relate Vision to Technology

In any considerations of sustainability, the role of technology is crucial. We use technologies to shape our world, and in turn technologies shape our perception of the world. Technology provides us with significant power, which challenges us to give careful con-

Box 1.3   **Ethics and Sustainability: The Religions of the World Are United**

The UNEP Interfaith Partnership on the Environment's 2000 publication *Earth and Faith: A Book of Reflection for Action* states, "The spiritual challenge of the ecological crisis draws us back to our religious traditions to reflect on and celebrate the natural world in its most profound sense of mystery as a manifestation and experience of the sacred." The publication presents a summary of points of agreement among the world religions on environmental ethics:

- The natural world has value in itself and does not exist solely to serve human needs.
- There is a significant continuity of being between human and nonhuman living beings, even though humans have a distinctive role. This continuity can be felt and experienced.
- Nonhuman living beings are morally significant, in the eyes of God and/or in the cosmic order.
- The dependence of human life on the natural world should be acknowledged in ritual and other expressions of appreciation and gratitude.
- Moral norms such as justice, compassion, and reciprocity apply (in appropriate ways) both to human beings and nonhuman beings. The well-being of humans and the well-being of nonhuman beings are inseparably connected.
- There are legitimate and illegitimate uses of nature.
- Greed and destructiveness are condemned. Restraint and protection are commended.
- Human beings are obliged to be aware and responsible in living in harmony with the natural world, and should follow the specific practices for this prescribed by their traditions.

Source: UNEP Interfaith Partnership on the Environment 2000

sideration to the choice and application of technologies and to take responsibility for them. This issue is raised in more detail in chapter 9, but it is also something that should be addressed as part of a city's vision.

The dilemma that the use of technology poses is pointed out by Davison:

> The fulfillment of the promise of liberation in everyday practice is problematic because we are simultaneously liberated from what burdens us and from what we care about. . . . Devices undermine our relationships to those things, places, and people we want to be free to be able to cherish. (2001, 111)

Thus, in gaining comfort and control, we lose engagement. Relationships with the nonhuman world can be severed or distorted, undermining a potential source of sustenance. Spretnak presents virtual reality as an example of this. People can become so caught up in the cyberworld that their relationships with the machine or distant disembodied people become "more real and meaningful than interactions with family, neighbors, and others in the bioregion" (1999, 126).

The current direction of modern technological development seeks to find escape from "the constraints of body, nature, and place" (Spretnak 1999, 128). Davison (2001) takes up this theme too, arguing that the technocratic agenda is driven by the desire for security but, in the process of creating a thoroughly technological world, undermines the possibility of a sustaining world, a world worth caring for. A way forward is to develop technologies that facilitate intimate engagement with the world. For cities as sustainable ecosystems, this will mean technology that facilitates bioregional and community connections.

Technology is also entangled with issues of power. It can enable some to have control, while others become dependent or marginalized. The development and use of new technologies need to be guided by community visions and aspirations to meet genuine human needs. Technologies should empower communities rather than reinforce or create dependence.

Thus, technologies provide means to meet our needs in cities, but their effectiveness in truly satisfying these needs has to be considered. As discussed earlier, there are many possible satisfiers to meet a certain need, and these may or may not require goods and technologies. Different technologies will have different impacts, and the choice of technology will affect where the satisfier lies on the continuum from destructive to synergic, applying Max-Neef's analysis.

The scale of technology is an important factor in determining whether it is meeting needs. For the past fifty years, technological development has been based on economies of scale that have often lost the bioregional or community context. Schumacher (1973) has stressed the need to choose technologies appropriate to a particular situation. This book argues that Cities as Sustainable Ecosystems need a scale of technology that matches bioregions and communities.

Strategy 5: Relate Vision to Place

Place is described by Susan Moore as "the intersection of people's physical, biological, social and economic worlds" (1997, 1). Sustainability, Moore suggests, depends on all four worlds and most significantly the integration of these worlds.

Berry argues for the need to bring the search for sustainability down to the local arena, rather than focusing on abstract global solutions. This brings us back to the places where we live, the arena where physical interactions occur, and joys and losses are experienced:

> When one works beyond the reach of one's love for the place one is working in, and for the things and creatures one is working with and among, then destruction inevitably results. An adequate local culture, among other things, keeps work within the reach of love. (Berry 1991)

Communities provide the most immediate expression of connections to place and people. Bioregions provide the broader ecological context. Bioregions are "life-places" defined by ecological characteristics, and indigenous and local communities. They offer a wider but still tangible context for our communities and the development of sustainable ways of living.

The importance of place in sustainability is highlighted by Van Der Ryn and Cowan in their book *Ecological Design* (1996). They argue that if imposed by outside forces sustainability will fail, as one solution cannot be replicated for every situation. Instead, they conclude there must be a diversity of solutions within the various communities in a bioregion, suited to the characteristics of place.

Susan Moore (1997, 6) cautions that even though the notion of place may be important to sustainability, a sense of place alone may not be sufficient for sustainable practices. Yet she also points out that the lack of sense of place may be related closely to unsustainable practices.

Beatley (2005) suggests that in modern global cities we are "Native to Nowhere"; we have become disconnected to our places. However he lists hundreds of small examples of communities beginning to reclaim their identities in their bioregions and in the heritage of their built environments. Such activities need to be grasped formally as part of the vision for the future in every city.

Charles Landry (2000) has developed a series of approaches to how a city can be more creative about its future through emphasizing its sense of place. In his 2006 book *The Art of City Making* he suggests some principles for cities to follow:

- A city should not try to be the most creative city in the world (or region or state) but the most creative for the world. This means that each place has something special to give.
- A city should emphasize local cultures and distinctiveness but be open to the outside world.
- A city should involve ordinary people in decisions as they can make extraordinary things happen.
- A city should learn about world best practice and not just copy it but create its own adaptation of it.
- A city should see its economic projects as adding value to its local community and environment or not pursue them.
- A city should use its imagination more if it is to rise to its potential.
- A city should foster as its ethos "civic creativity": imaginative problem solving applied to public-good objectives, which arises from the identity and environment of the place.

The unique characteristics of place and people's connection with their bioregions need to be reflected in city visions for sustainability. Thus, visions are placed within a context that is more tangible than the global arena but that provides a basis for global concerns. Moreover, the diversity of approaches enhances resilience (see chapter 5).

Examples of Vision Statements

A series of generic vision statements from the Earth Charter, Healthy Cities, and Child-Friendly Cities initiatives are included here as relevant examples. The Earth Charter is an attempt to create a vision for the global community. It provides an overarching framework, which is useful for identifying broad values and ethics (see box 1.4).

The Healthy Cities movement initiated by the World Health Organization (WHO) has formulated the following list of the qualities of a healthy city, which could form part of a vision statement for a sustainable city:

Box 1.4   **Earth Charter Extract**

We urgently need a shared vision of basic values to provide an ethical foundation for the emerging world community.

I. Respect and Care for the Community of Life
1. Respect Earth and life in all its diversity.
2. Care for the community of life with understanding, compassion, and love.
3. Build democratic societies that are just, participatory, sustainable, and peaceful.
4. Secure Earth's bounty and beauty for present and future generations.

II. Ecological Integrity
5. Protect and restore the integrity of Earth's ecological systems, with special concern for biological diversity and the natural processes that sustain life.
6. Prevent harm as the best method of environmental protection and, when knowledge is limited, apply a precautionary approach.
7. Adopt patterns of production, consumption, and reproduction that safeguard Earth's regenerative capacities, human rights, and community well-being.
8. Advance the study of ecological sustainability and promote the open exchange and wide application of the knowledge required.

III. Social and Economic Justice
9. Eradicate poverty as an ethical, social, and environmental imperative.
10. Ensure that economic activities and institutions at all levels promote human development in an equitable and sustainable manner.
11. Affirm gender equality and equity as prerequisites to sustainable development and ensure universal access to education, health care, and economic opportunity.
12. Uphold the right of all, without discrimination, to a natural and social environment supportive of human dignity, bodily health, and spiritual well-being, with special attention to the rights of indigenous peoples and minorities.

IV. Democracy, Nonviolence, and Peace
13. Strengthen democratic institutions at all levels, and provide transparency and accountability in governance, inclusive participation in decision making, and access to justice.
14. Integrate into formal education and life-long learning the knowledge, values, and skills needed for a sustainable way of life.
15. Treat all living beings with respect and consideration.
16. Promote a culture of tolerance, nonviolence, and peace.

Source: Earth Charter, http://www.earthcharter.org/files/charter/charter.pdf

- A clean, safe physical environment of a high quality (including housing quality)
- An ecosystem that is stable now and sustainable in the long term
- A strong mutually supportive and nonexploitative community
- A high degree of participation and control by the public over the decisions affecting their lives, health, and well-being

- The meeting of basic needs (food, water, shelter, income, safety, and work) for all the city's people
- Access to a wide variety of experiences and resources, with the chance for a wide variety of contact, interaction, and communication
- A diverse, vital, and innovative city economy
- The encouragement of connectedness with the past, with the cultural and biological heritage of city dwellers and with other groups and individuals
- A form that is compatible with and enhances the preceding characteristics
- An optimum level of appropriate public health and sickness care services accessible to all
- High health status (high levels of positive health and low levels of disease)[8]

The Child-Friendly Cities initiative presents a vision of cities in which the rights of children are paramount. The initiative was launched in 1996 as an outcome of the World Conference on Human Settlements (Habitat II) resolution to make cities livable places for all and, in UNICEF terms, for "children first." The Istanbul conference declared that the well-being of children is the ultimate indicator of a healthy habitat, a democratic society and good governance.

A Child-Friendly City guarantees the right of young citizens to:
- Influence decisions about their city
- Express their opinion on the city
- Participate in family, community, and social life
- Receive basic services such as health care, education, and shelter
- Drink safe water and have access to proper sanitation
- Be protected from exploitation, violence, and abuse
- Walk safely in the streets on their own
- Meet friends and play
- Have green spaces for plants and animals
- Live in an unpolluted environment
- Participate in cultural and social events
- Be an equal citizen of their city with access to every service, regardless of ethnic origin, religion, income, gender, or disability[9]

The formulation of more local visions provides the opportunity for greater community participation and engagement with issues at a practical level, which is likely to produce visions that are better matched to local ecological and social realities. The Western Australian State Sustainability Strategy has been developed around eleven sustainability principles, six vision statements, and six goals for government (see box 1.5). The strategy applies these principles to governance, global issues, natural resources, settlements, community, and business. The settlements section is based on the Extended Metabolism Model (see figure 1.1), which is an ecosystem-based model developed by Newman and Kenworthy (1999).

In the United States, a number of cities are now developing sustainability visions as a basis for future planning. The mayor of New York, Michael Bloomberg, announced on December 12, 2006, that the city would make a sustainability plan, not a land use plan, and set out the broad principles and goals in a document for public response. According to Bloomberg, the plan envisages:

- Creating enough housing for almost a million more people, and finding even more creative ways to make housing more affordable for more New Yorkers.
- Ensuring that even as land becomes more scarce, every New Yorker lives within a ten-minute walk of a park, so that every child has the chance to play and be active.
- Adding to the capacity of the regional mass transit system, so that travel times stay the same—or get better.
- Developing critical back-up systems for the water network, so every New Yorker is assured of a dependable source of water even into the next century.
- Reaching a full state of good repair for New York City's roads, subways, and rails for the first time in history.
- Providing cleaner, more reliable power for every New Yorker by upgrading the energy infrastructure.
- Reducing the city's global warming emissions by more than 30 percent by 2030, a target that is achievable even just using technology that exists today.
- Achieving the cleanest air quality of any big city in America.
- Cleaning up all of the contaminated land.
- And, finally, opening 90 percent of the rivers, harbors, and bays for recreation by reducing water pollution and preserving natural areas.

Mayor Bloomberg concluded by saying, "Now it is up to us to look ahead, as earlier generations did, and to begin planning for a better, stronger, and more sustainable future for our children, and for theirs. It is our city. It is our future. It is our choice."[10]

Cleveland, Ohio, provides another good example of a vision statement. EcoCity Cleveland is a nonprofit organization founded in 1992 to promote "the design of cities in balance with nature in Northeast Ohio." Through a two-year process of holding public meetings and engaging citizens and planning agencies, a Citizens' Bioregional Plan was developed which presents an alternative vision for the bioregion. It challenges the trends of increasing urban sprawl and loss of rural land and open space. The plan makes the following recommendations:

- Adopt a new vocabulary to describe the region. The old vocabulary describes an old urban core competing against new suburbs and outer counties. The

Box 1.5 Sustainability Strategy in Western Australia—Vision Statement

The Western Australian State Sustainability Strategy is the first comprehensive strategy at a state level to examine what sustainability can mean across forty-two areas of government responsibility. It is based on seven foundation principles and four process principles:

Foundation Principles

- **Long-term economic health.** Sustainability recognizes the needs of current and future generations for long-term economic health, diversity, innovation, and productivity of the earth.
- **Equity and human rights.** Sustainability recognizes that an environment needs to be created where all people can express their full potential and lead productive lives, and that significant gaps in sufficiency, safety, and opportunity endanger the earth.
- **Biodiversity and ecological integrity.** Sustainability recognizes that all life has intrinsic value and is interconnected, and that biodiversity and ecological integrity are part of the irreplaceable life support systems upon which the earth depends.
- **Settlement efficiency and quality of life.** Sustainability recognizes that settlements need to reduce their ecological footprint (i.e., less material and energy demands and reductions in waste), while they simultaneously improve their quality of life (health, housing, employment, community . . .).
- **Community, regions, "sense of place," and heritage.** Sustainability recognizes the reality and diversity of community and regions for the management of the earth, and the critical importance of "sense of place" and heritage (buildings, townscapes, landscapes, and culture) in any plans for the future.
- **Net benefit from development.** Sustainability means that all development, and particularly development involving extraction of non-renewable resources, should strive to provide net environmental, social, and economic benefit for future generations.
- **Common good.** Sustainability recognizes that planning for the common good requires equitable distribution of public resources (like air, water, and open space) so that ecosystem functions are maintained and a shared resource is available to all.

Process Principles

- **Integration.** Sustainability requires that economic, social, and environmental factors be integrated by simultaneous application of these principles, seeking mutually supportive benefits with minimal trade-offs.
- **Accountability, transparency, and engagement.** Sustainability recognizes that people should have access to information on sustainability issues, that institutions should have triple bottom-line accountability, that regular sustainability audits of programs and policies should be conducted, and that public engagement lies at the heart of all sustainability principles.
- **Precaution.** Sustainability requires caution, avoiding poorly understood risks of serious or irreversible damage to environmental, social, or economic capital, designing for surprise and managing for adaptation.
- **Hope, vision, symbolic, and iterative change.** Sustainability recognizes that applying these principles as part of a broad strategic vision for the earth can generate hope in the future, and thus it will involve symbolic change that is part of many successive steps over generations.

Source: Government of Western Australia, Department of the Premier and Cabinet, http://www.sustainability.dpc.wa.gov.au/index.cfm?fuseaction=sustainability_strategy.the_strategy

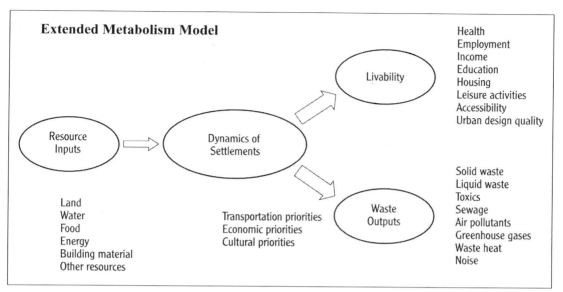

Extended Metabolism Model

Livability

Health
Employment
Income
Education
Housing
Leisure activities
Accessibility
Urban design quality

Resource
Inputs

Dynamics of
Settlements

Waste
Outputs

Land
Water
Food
Energy
Building material
Other resources

Transportation priorities
Economic priorities
Cultural priorities

Solid waste
Liquid waste
Toxics
Sewage
Air pollutants
Greenhouse gases
Waste heat
Noise

Figure 1.1

The Extended Metabolism Model suggests how cities can become more sustainable by reducing their resources and wastes while increasing their livability.

new vocabulary describes a network of high density centers—urban cores, edge cities, Western Reserve towns—existing in balance with open space and rural areas.

- Maintain and redevelop existing cities and towns. Much of the region's new housing construction could occur as infill redevelopment in existing urban areas or as conservation development subdivisions adjacent to town centers. Rural development programs should enhance the viability of family farms.

- Begin a major campaign to preserve open space. Now is the time to create an Outer Emerald Necklace for the next generation.

- Change transportation priorities. Transportation investments should promote quality of life in existing urban areas by creating great public spaces that are not dominated by cars. The urban centers of the region should be efficiently linked by alternative modes of transportation, such as light rail.

- Create new partnerships at the regional level. These partnerships should include not only citizens and organizations in Northeast Ohio, but also the State of Ohio, which must realign its policies to support urban redevelopment and open space protection.[11]

The Citizens' Bioregional Plan for Northeast Ohio includes bioregional maps and a composite map showing possible development and conservation zones.

Conclusions

The importance of vision to cities is emerging as a key element in achieving sustainability. Sustainability is about making choices and changing our current course. Cities in recent years have generated visions to stress their competitiveness; however, sustainability promotes other values that will gain greater recognition as the sustainability challenge is embedded and internalized. Visioning offers a chance for communities to reflect on what they want to sustain and how to achieve this. It gives them a chance to shift direction. The visioning process enables communities to express their fundamental values related to their long-term progress, needs, technology, ethics, and sense of place. It is an evolutionary process that ideally encourages participation and community building, and inspires shared action. Every city is constantly rebuilding and renewing itself—none can stay still and rest on their past. The community visioning process gives a city a chance to rebuild itself around sustainability. The visioning process also gives cities the opportunity to be inspired around new ideas. This book sets examples of new visions including the potential for cities to not just reduce their impact but to become a positive force for the ecological regeneration of their bioregion, how they can contribute to global resource constraints through going carbon neutral, how they can be more local and responsive to their bioregional places. Each step toward such visions will make our cities more sustainable ecosystems.

2 | *Economy and Society*

PRINCIPLE 2
Achieve long-term economic and social security.

Elaboration: Long-term economic and social security are prerequisites for beneficial change and are dependent upon environmentally sound, sustainable development.

To achieve triple bottom-line sustainability, economic strategies need to increase the value and vitality of human and natural systems, and conserve and renew human, financial, and natural resources. Through fair allocation of resources, economic strategies should seek to meet basic human needs in a just and equitable manner. In particular, economic strategies should guarantee the right to potable water, clean air, food security, shelter, and safe sanitation.

Cities are the locus of human diversity; their policies, structures, and institutions significantly contribute to fostering cohesive, stimulating, safe, and fulfilled communities.

Integrating Economy and Society

Cities emerged around commerce. They provide the opportunity for people to exchange goods and services in close proximity as well as allowing for a diversity of social and cultural exchanges. Cities have always represented more than their economies, reflecting cultural values through architecture, public spaces, religious symbols, festivals, and community services. Cosmopolitan cities provide a diversity of cultural expressions and exchanges. Cities can be places that inspire and nurture ideas and expressions of tolerance. Sustainability enables cities to reexamine their economic and cultural base.

Economies are systems for producing, distributing, and allocating goods and services according to supply and demand. Commentators such as Max-Neef suggest that Western society has fallen into the trap of making economies into ends rather than means to provide for our needs:

When the form of production and consumption of goods makes goods an end in themselves, then the alleged satisfaction of a need impairs its capacity to create potential. This creates the conditions for entrenching an alienated society engaged in a productivity race lacking any sense at all. Life, then, is placed at the service of artifacts, rather than artifacts at the service of life. (1992, 202)

Current economic processes represent one way to meet our needs, but it is not the only way, or necessarily the best way. For many people in developing countries basic needs are not being met, while in wealthy countries many people still feel unfulfilled. The Earth Charter declares that once basic needs have been met, human development is mainly "about being more, not having more."[1]

Cities that have failed to integrate their social values and economies into a sustainability framework have collapsed or declined (Jacobs 1961; Lawton 1989; Diamond 2005). Cities face a range of fundamental challenges—including climate change, water supply declines, oil supply disruptions due to global peaking in production, regional environmental damage, loss of biodiversity—that require a new kind of clean, green economy to emerge. Cities have been the basis of every new stage in economic development, and it will be innovative cities that forge this new economy.

In the last few decades, the trend toward globalization and the rise of transnational corporations have caused local and regional economies to become more entangled in the complex global economy. Nobel laureate and Columbia University economist Joseph Stiglitz, in his 2006 book *Making Globalization Work*, criticizes global financial institutions for being out of touch with what is happening in the cities and bioregions of the world. He believes that too much emphasis has been placed on global finance and not enough on how to make growth sustainable "economically, socially, politically, and environmentally."

Increasingly, economies of local sustenance have been replaced with economies driven by global money and scarcity (Korten 1999). Cities are more and more dependent on sources of sustenance outside their boundaries and bioregions:

The only thing that keeps our present large metropolitan areas going is that they can still exploit their region or other regions for their continued support. For example, Los Angeles gets water from the Colorado River and northern California. Its liquid natural gas is from Indonesia. A large percentage of its labor comes from Mexico. Its electrical energy is derived from coal that comes from the Four Corners area of the Southwest. (Berg 2001)

This dependency disconnects people from the impact of their consumption, disrupting vital feedback loops and undermining economic and social security.

Sustainability challenges this trend, and the Melbourne Principles provide the basis for cities to transform their economies to serve bioregional and community priorities as well as global demands related to greenhouse gases, oil, and biodiversity (which often cross national borders). This chapter will examine the economic and social processes driving cities, followed by the patterns and processes of life communities (ecosystems) as a basis for reshaping economic and social patterns. The bioregional and local community scales are emphasized through urban ecovillages in bioregional economies—in any city, whether large or small.

City Economies and Communities: Trends and Processes

Cities have existed for around eight thousand years based on the benefits that can be found by networks of people sharing a common outcome through a division of labor. Such social outcomes include enhanced opportunities for trading products and services, innovation in technology and culture, and agglomeration efficiencies (the advantages of scale and density). Cities have embedded these opportunities, innovations, and efficiencies in their physical capital (buildings and infrastructure) and in their social capital (institutions and social networks).

Cities today are critical to national economies. They are the drivers of economic growth. Bangkok for example produces 41 percent of the economic wealth of Thailand but accounts for only 9 percent of its population. A developed city like Prague produces 20 percent of the wealth from 10 percent of the economy. So, cities are critical to the future economy of most places.

Cities have grown through the migration of people from surrounding rural areas and from other cities in search of new opportunities, particularly employment. As the Organization for Economic Cooperation and Development notes, "Innovations flowed from urban workshops and were diffused through trade routes. The phenomenon of novelty—the expectation of something new—has endured as a distinctive feature of the consumer economy in cities since the Renaissance" (OECD 2003, 36).

The opportunities and innovations created by cities have included some of the most important aspects of the common good now considered critical to sustainability:

- Law and market regulations were created for the orderly processes of commerce in cities, well before nation-states.
- Educational institutions, libraries, theaters, and hospitals were city institutions created to further city development goals.
- Pluralism and the virtues of social and cultural diversity were developed as part of city democracies to cope with the challenge (and the need) for immigrant labor in cities.

Cities continue to attract people because of the opportunities they provide. This has accelerated in the twentieth century as economies become increasingly urban. World urban population has multiplied twentyfold since 1900 compared to a fourfold increase in total world population. Currently the world's urban population is expanding at 1.78 percent per year, while rural population growth is about to zero out and go negative (O'Meara Sheehan 2007). Between 1990 to 2025, if current trends continue, the number of urban dwellers will double to constitute almost two-thirds of the world's population. Developing countries are expected to contribute about 90 percent of this increase. Rapid urbanization is occurring in Asia and Africa. Most of this population increase is occurring in cities of less than half a million (53 percent of the world urban population) and cities between 1 and 5 million (22 percent) (UN-Habitat 2006). Although only 9 percent of the world urban population live in cities over 10 million—so-called megacities—these are the cities that are growing the fastest. (Only 4 percent of the world urban population lived in megacities in 1975.) Today the world has 22 megacities and a new phenomenon called metacities—cities over 20 million. Tokyo, the world's first metacity, is now at 35 million, while Mumbai, Delhi, Mexico City, São Paulo, New York, Dhaka, Jakarta and Lagos are all expected to be over 20 million by 2020 (UN-Habitat 2006).

Along with opportunities, there are numerous impacts and externalities in the urban economy, particularly in the rapidly growing cities of the developing world. Air and water quality is being diminished severely within and beyond city boundaries as urban processes convert energy and materials, acquired regionally and internationally, into products and services for global markets. Social disparities grow as the rural poor join the ranks of the urban poor. In cities where urbanization has created sprawl and car dependence, a sense of community has been eroded and social alienation has increased. Loss of contact with local ecosystems and the broader bioregional context has left urban dwellers disconnected from this source of sustenance. Increasing violence in many cities provides evidence of a breakdown in community and social relations.

Awareness is growing of two critical energy-related issues, climate change and oil depletion, that will be key forces shaping the future of cities. As one leading oil producer puts it, "Energy will be one of the defining issues of this century. One thing is clear: the era of easy oil is over. What we do now will determine how well we meet the energy needs of the entire world in this century and beyond."[2] The responses presented in this book offer a way forward, and in this chapter a key response is developing stronger local and bioregional economies. Local needs can be met with much less travel if a city and its bioregion provide most local goods and services. Local food movements that enable cities to consume more locally produced food not only create thriving bioregional and local economies but also provide better, fresher food and substantially reduce transportation energy requirements—considering the average US plate of food has taken 1,500 to 2,500 miles of transport energy to get it on the table (Beatley, 2005). Vibrant communities offering diverse local economic, social, and cultural opportunities will enable people to live with less need for transport energy. In an oil-constrained future, the structural issues associated with public transport, cycling, and walking (outlined in chapter 5) will also become a higher priority.

Climate Change

A series of reports from the UN's Intergovernmental Panel on Climate Change, which have emphasized the science of climate change, has elicited a number of responses from business, insurance, and national governments on the implications for cities. Perhaps the most strident in its portrayal of serious implications ar. action was Britain's Stern Report (H.M. Treasury 2006).

Climate change poses an increasing threat to urban governa. particularly in lower-income populations, predominantly within tro. tries as sea level rises and low-lying infrastructure like water system. ...imate change is increasing the rate at which natural hazards impact citie. ... intensity of storms is increasing; the devastation of New Orleans by Hurricane Katrina has come to symbolize the climate-induced urban problems that face the world's cities. Heat waves in western Europe have doubled in duration since 1880. UN estimates suggest $60 billion in costs due to these kinds of freak weather events in 2003 alone (UNEP 2003). Many cities are losing their wetlands which protect them from storms and flooding. New Orleans, for example, is losing coastal wetlands at a rate of one and a half football fields an hour due to local and bioregional land use and water management (Young 2006).

Greenhouse gas forcing in the twenty-first century could set in motion large-scale, high-impact, nonlinear, and potentially abrupt changes in physical and biological systems over the coming decades, with a wide range of associated likelihoods. Cities are causing most of this climate change, as they account for 75 percent of the world's fossil fuel consumption, and cities will be the most impacted if they do not change (World Council on Renewable Energy 2005). Yet it is in cities where economic change can bring about the most reductions in greenhouse gases. New York is the first megacity to develop a plan for reducing greenhouse emissions by 30 percent before 2030.[3] The Clinton Foundation is funding forty megacities to become leaders in demonstrating how to respond to climate change.[4]

Oil Depletion

The Oil Depletion Analysis Center (ODAC) is an independent, UK-based charity formed to enhance international public awareness and foster improved understanding of the issue of global oil depletion. It presents the following conclusions:

- Oil is the world's premier source of energy and is fundamental to almost every important function of modern life. It fuels 95 percent of land, sea, and air transport, so the efficient movement of raw materials and goods, as well as personal mobility, is almost entirely oil-dependent. . . .
- Global demand for oil has increased seven fold over the past half-century due to rapid population growth and industrial expansion. . . .
- Oil industry leaders acknowledge that new sources of oil are becoming increasingly difficult to find and more costly to exploit. . . .
- The world has now consumed almost half the total amount of conventional oil most experts estimate will ever be available for recovery. . . .
- A growing number of experts now foresee a permanent downturn in global oil production rates within a matter of years and perhaps even decline rates of 5 percent could set in. . . .

- As growing demand exceeds available supplies, oil prices will rise substantially and the effects will be felt throughout the global economy. . . .
- The world will become increasingly dependent on oil from the Middle East as supplies from elsewhere decline. Already over 50 oil-producing countries have passed their peak production, including the United States, once the world's largest producer, which now relies on imported oil for over 60 percent of its domestic needs. . . .
- The productive capacity of Middle East oilfields is uncertain and the risks of supply disruptions are heightened by continuing political instability in the region. . . .
- The era of cheap, plentiful supplies of oil is coming to an end, requiring fundamental restructuring of the world's urban energy systems. . . .[5]

Clearly, the trends and processes in global cities are not sustainable considering these two great developments of our era, climate change and oil depletion. The two problems are clearly linked—if cities try to move from oil to "dirty fuels" like oil shale, tar sands, or coal to liquids (CTL), this will be much worse in greenhouse terms. Saving oil on the other hand will be a major contributor to reducing greenhouse. In ecological terms, cities are taking the resources of the Earth and creating economic activities that are taxing regional and global ecosystems. The new challenge for cities is sustainability-based economies: how to realize the aspirations stated in the Melbourne Principles and enable future generations to live well but with a fraction of today's oil usage and greenhouse emissions.

This book suggests that the global economic forces shaping cities need to be modified by awareness of bioregional- and community-scale ecosystem dynamics and social dynamics. Although such change has to be seen in a long-term context, some hints are emerging about how to take the first steps. Case studies of more sustainable initiatives are presented throughout the book such as the UK Transition Towns Initiative, which engages small towns across the UK in peak oil and climate change awareness, planning, and action.[6]

City Economies and Ecosystems

Economic and social security arise from creating human communities and institutions that are equitable, resilient, psychologically fulfilling, flexible, and ecologically minded. Our economies need to be consistent with our social goals. True triple bottom-line accounting requires meeting ecological, social, and economic goals simultaneously. We must match our economies and social institutions to the community of life by learning from the strategies that we can observe in ecosystems and the ways of more ecologically oriented cultures. This approach has been adopted by various authors and movements, including biomimicry, permaculture, bioregionalism, and ecological design (see chapters 5 and 9).

Life communities and economies observable in ecosystems are place based, cooperative, diverse, self-regulating through feedback loops, decentralized, conserving, and solar based. The economies of more ecologically oriented human communities are local and bioregional, matching the patterns and processes of the life economies of which they are a part. Economic activities are usually focused on meeting human needs equitably.

Many indigenous and traditional communities have their economies and resource management practices embedded in life-affirming worldviews and ethics, which recognize the land as something that nourishes humans and needs to be nourished in turn (see more in chapter 5). Natural, social, and economic capital are protected simultaneously, providing a genuine basis for social and economic security. However, many cities have lost this connection among the three kinds of capital.

With the increased capacity of cities to capture extrasomatic energy, what Boyden refers to as "technometabolism" (1992, 72), over time the urban form of cities has gone from compact, mixed-use, relatively small, walking cities to large sprawling segregated megalopolises. Similarly, their economies draw in resources from ecosystems across the globe. Thus, the trend has been away from small, place-based economies to much more distant global economies. The challenge for cities will be to create more locally oriented economies within this broader global economy. Many big cities like Tokyo and New York are filled with small distinct places that can provide the basis for cities to reclaim their "localness" in more ways than just having a local culture.

Increasingly, urban ecosystems are heterotrophic (unlike most ecosystems that are autotrophic; see box 2.1)—that is, they are unable to support total ecosystem metabolism solely from internal production, as their overall consumption of organic matter (ecosystem respiration incorporating the burning of fossil carbon) outstrips the production of new organic matter by photosynthesis (Luck et al. 2001). They import energy from outside the system in the form of food and fossil fuel use for domestic, commercial, municipal, and industrial purposes. Alberti states:

Box 2.1 **Autotrophic and Heterotrophic Ecosystems**

While ecosystems are part of a global ecosystem with inputs of solar energy and global biogeochemical cycles, the capture of energy for ecosystems occurs on a more local and bioregional level. Most ecosystems are **autotrophic**—they capture sufficient energy for their needs. Green plants, through the process of photosynthesis, convert solar energy to glucose, which is used for plant growth and functioning. These producers provide energy to the rest of the living system, through complex food webs. Energy flows through the system, from producers to consumers, with some being lost at each stage as waste heat. Some ecosystems are **heterotrophic**—that is, they do not produce sufficient energy to meet their needs. However, they usually receive their additional energy requirements from adjacent ecosystems so that they can be regarded as autotrophic on a bioregional level (e.g., rivers and their watersheds). McDonough and Braungart (2002) suggest that cities can become autotrophic by tapping solar energy through every building, becoming "photosynthetic."

> Compared to a "natural" ecosystem with a typical energy budget ranging between 1,000 and 10,000 Kcal per square meters per year, cities consume a vastly larger amount of energy. The budget of an urban ecosystem in an industrialized country can range between 100,000 and 300,000 Kcal per square meter per year. (Alberti 2002; Odum 1997)

These economies are beyond the reach of our natural capacity to care and register impacts from the production and consumption of goods, thereby disrupting feedback loops. However it is possible to imagine a different kind of city economy that is far more local and autotrophic (see more in chapter 5).

Lessons from Sustainable Communities

Ecotrust, a North American nongovernmental organization, was formed to create a "conservation economy" in the temperate rainforest region of the Pacific Northwest, dubbed the "Salmon Nation" bioregion. A conservation economy is an economy in which economic arrangements are transformed to restore rather than degrade natural and social capital. Fundamental human needs and the ecosystem services that sustain them are seen as "the starting point for a different kind of economic prosperity that can endure generation after generation."[7] Box 2.2 outlines more of the work of Ecotrust.

According to Ecotrust, a conservation economy functions on a global scale, but it should "be imagined as a healthy mosaic of bioregional economies forged within coherent biological and cultural units." The group argues that bioregional economies, which are better able to meet their own needs, will be "more competitive and less vulnerable" even within the context of a globalizing economy. It offers the following description of bioregional economies:

> Bioregional economies reflect the capacities and limitations of their particular ecosystems, honor the diversity and history of local cultures, and meet human needs as locally as possible. Bioregional economies are diverse, resilient, and decentralized. They minimize dependence on imports while focusing on high-value-added exports. Paradoxically, this gives them an important competitive advantage in a global economy, allowing them to trade on favorable terms without sacrificing their economic sovereignty in the process.
>
> Bioregional economies recognize the need for fair trade, refraining from importing or exporting goods produced unfairly or in an ecologically destructive manner. They make a transition to true cost pricing, building actual social and environmental costs into market prices. In order to provide independent certification of product attributes (e.g., sustainably harvested, fair trade, organic, shade grown, green power, Indigenous justice), they promote product labeling.
>
> Bioregional economies do not deplete their own social capital, natural

Box 2.2 **Ecotrust and the Conservation Economy**

Ecotrust was created in 1991 by a small group of people from diverse backgrounds with the aim of bringing together some of the emerging ideas in sustainability to enrich the Pacific Northwest region of North America. They set out to define their bioregion—which they call "Salmon Nation"—and develop strategies for achieving a conservation economy. Five integrated program areas have defined and guided their efforts: native programs, fisheries, forestry, foods and farms, and citizenship.

Ecotrust works in urban and rural areas to support entrepreneurs whose activities improve environmental, economic, and social conditions. In a decade of working for a conservation economy, the organization has:

- Cofounded an environmental bank, ShoreBank Pacific, helping small businesses profit while improving social and environmental performance
- Cofounded Ecotrust Canada, a Canadian charity supporting the emergence of a conservation economy in British Columbia
- Cofounded ShoreBank Enterprise Pacific, a nonprofit business support organization offering capital and information to rural businesses that benefit community and landscape
- Redeveloped the Natural Capital Center, a historic 1895 warehouse in Portland, Oregon, as a landmark green building and incubator for businesses and nonprofits
- Cultivated local leadership and nurtured institutional capacity in communities throughout the bioregion
- Mapped and analyzed the bioregion in fresh ways.

Source: Ecotrust, http://www.ecotrust.org; ConservationEconomy.net, http://www.conservationeconomy.net

capital, or economic capital. They export only their sustainable surplus, most often taking the form of intellectual property or high-value products and services rather than bulk commodities. Their sense of place becomes the key component of their brand identity. In the coastal temperate rainforest, products evocative of place include Copper River salmon, Tillamook cheese, Willamette Valley wine, and Walla Walla onions.

Bioregional economies are physically constrained by the network of connected wildlands, and the availability of productive rural areas. This allows them to substitute ecosystem services for more expensive imported alternatives. It also makes them attractive destinations for ecotourism.

Bioregional economies can have vastly different mixes of local foods, energy sources, building materials, land-uses—all responding to the possibilities of place. However, their underlying design principles are remarkably consistent. Together they form an interdependent, mutually beneficial conservation economy at the global scale.

Bioregions need to reclaim a strong measure of economic sovereignty by becoming more self-sufficient and trading on their own terms. They can create economies that celebrate and mirror local ecosystems and cultures.[8]

Strategies for Economic and Social Security

Cities need to revive their social, economic, and environmental capital through local communities and economies, which encourage urban ecovillages and bioregional economic and social processes. Cities need to build social and economic security at the local and bioregional level, focusing on trying to meet more of their needs locally and bioregionally. In box 2.3 a Community Sustainability Assessment enables a local or bioregional community to assess how well they are doing on building their local economy in a more sustainable way. This assessment tool is part of a series of checklists developed by the Global Ecovillage Network.

Numerous strategies are available to transform economic and social relations at either the local or bioregional scale. Nine strategies are outlined below that could assist urban economies to become more community and bioregionally focused:

1. Local enterprise facilitation
2. Local/bioregional infrastructure for cities
3. Urban ecovillages
4. Community spaces, pedestrianization, and overcoming car dependence
5. Urban agriculture and community gardens
6. Complementary currencies and "sustainable development rights"
7. True-costing initiatives
8. "Buy Local" campaigns and ecolabeling
9. Community arts

Strategy 1: Local Enterprise Facilitation

Local economic development is often difficult in the real world of local government politics. In North America many cities have lost their local businesses in their traditional centers to multinational chains in big-box shopping centers and office parks. Michael Shuman in *Going Local* (2000) and *The Small-Mart Revolution* (2006) has provided the rationale and a manual of actions for how to retain and facilitate a town's local enterprises. The most significant thing to do is for the government to stop paying huge subsidies to the big out-of-town firms that undermine local economies. In a chapter called "Wreckonomics" he outlines how Wal-Mart in the United States was given over $1 billion in state and local government subsidies in over 244 separate deals in the past ten years. Most states and local governments pay from $10,000 to $30,000 a job to retain or attract large corporations to their areas. In this no-win war of competition, the solutions—in terms of local businesses—are usually better and without subsidy. Local businesses multiply local economic advantages as the money stays local and creates much more employment. Moreover local businesses build up the local social capital and sense of place through emphasizing local products. Shuman works through the Business Alliance for Local Living Economies, which has over two hundred networked groups working to make local economies more successful.[9]

Ernesto Sirolli has spent a lifetime showing communities how to create local

Box 2.3 **Community Sustainability Assessment**

Sustainable Economics—Healthy Local Economy

For each item in this questionnaire, check the box(es) that you believe most closely describes the truth for your community. After each answer that you select, there is a number in parentheses—that is your score for that item. At the end there is a space to add up your total score.

A. There is explicit encouragement for community members creating businesses that:
  enhance the local economy: ❑ yes (4) ❑ no (0)
  do NOT generate pollution: ❑ yes (4) ❑ no (0)
  do NOT exploit human resources: ❑ yes (4) ❑ no (0)
  do NOT exploit natural resources: ❑ yes (4) ❑ no (0)

B. Local banks lend in support of sustainability projects: ❑ yes (4) ❑ no (0)

C. An estimate of how many youth leave the community for a livelihood:
  ❑ majority (-5) ❑ some (0) ❑ minority (3) ❑ few or none (5)

D. The extent to which community members experience unemployment or lack of work for which they receive funds or other exchange is:
  ❑ rarely (2) ❑ occasionally (1) ❑ often (-1) ❑ frequently (-2)

E. An estimate of how many community members have difficulty providing for their basic needs (food, shelter, clothing, etc.):
  ❑ most (-6) ❑ some (-1) ❑ few (3) ❑ none (6)
    If there are economic inequalities among community members, is there a system for dealing with this: ❑ yes (3) ❑ no (0)

F. Economic systems active in the community. Check as many as apply:
  ❑ self-sufficiency for basic needs (5) ❑ ecologically friendly cottage industry (2)
  ❑ sustainable small businesses (2) ❑ barter and exchange systems (2)
  ❑ education/programs (2) ❑ telecommunications or other work at home (2)
  ❑ volunteerism/work contribution (2) ❑ local market days (2)
  ❑ fund-raising for modeling sustainable practices (2) ❑ voluntary levies within the community for sustainability project development (2) ❑ exchange with other eco-villages and sustainable communities (2) ❑ fund-raising for community operations (0)
  ❑ leaving the community for paid work (-2) ❑ Other (1 point for each)
  Specify: _____

enterprises through facilitation of local ideas and local entrepreneurs (many of whom are hidden until communities go looking). His best-selling book *Ripples from the Zambezi: Passion, Entrepreneurship, and the Rebirth of Local Economies* traces his story from a series of failed development projects in Africa (which were too top-down) to discovering how the ideas of economist E. F. Schumacher and psychologist Carl Rogers could be forged into a powerful new approach to local business. The book outlines how he began applying this approach in Esperance, a remote country town in Western Australia, before the idea took off. He now works on every continent.

Box 2.3   *(continued)*

G. Community members actively engage in economic cooperation:
   in their bioregion: ❏ yes (2) ❏ no (-2)
   in their country/state: ❏ yes (1) ❏ no (-1)
   with other parts of the world: ❏ yes (1) ❏ no (0)

H. An estimate of how many community members would describe their work as meaningful and fulfilling:
   ❏ all–very few exceptions (4) ❏ most (3) ❏ some (1) ❏ few/none (-2)

I. An estimate of how many community members would say they experience non-monetary abundance/prosperity in their life:
   ❏ all– very few exceptions (4) ❏ most (3) ❏ some (1) ❏ few/none (-2)

Add up the numbers in parentheses for each item above that you checked.

Sustainable Economics—Healthy Local Economy Total:_____
   50+   Indicates excellent progress toward sustainability
   25–49 Indicates a good start toward sustainability
   0–24   Indicates actions are needed to undertake sustainability

Source: Global Ecovillage Network, http://ecovillage.org/gen/activities/csa/pdf/CSA-English.pdf

When invited into a town, Sirolli and his team of Enterprise Facilitators help organize a community-based group containing a mix of local entrepreneurs, marketing and finance people, as well as community-minded citizens. This group then sets out to instill a renewed sense of community pride and civic spirit, and to provide a base of support for new businesses. The nonprofit Sirolli Institute, which Sirolli founded in 1985, operates on the belief that "the future of every community lies in the dreams and aspirations of its people." The institute's mission is "to promote economic and community revitalization by capturing the passion, intelligence, imagination, and resources of local entrepreneurs." Its secret appears to be in the re-creation of social networks that enable entrepreneurs to locate financing, accounting, and marketing assistance. Thus the community becomes the true basis of the local economy.[10]

Local economies can be built up anywhere. Roseland (2007) outlines best-practice examples of building local economies around the globe, including the developing world.

Strategy 2: Local/Bioregional Infrastructure for Cities

If we were to take a page from nature's book, we would try to adapt our appetites to where we live, getting our resources from as close by as possible. (Benyus 1997, 276)

Figure 2.1

Not-so-big box: the UK ban on big-box super- markets has led to small local markets that enhance traditional centers.

Photo Peter Newman

It is time to bring our economies back to more of a human scale, restoring feedback loops locally and bioregionally, and making cities more autotrophic. Cities are part of a global ecosystem, and as such they need to be responsible in terms of their impact on greenhouse gases, oil depletion, and biodiversity (all global issues). Cities also can help create new green technology and local products that are the basis of the new economy. Bioregional and global ecosystem goals often overlap; for example, bringing production and consumption closer together reduces the need for transport energy and hence greenhouse gases too.

The Cities as Sustainable Ecosystems (CASE) approach means seeing cities as part of the biosphere and as part of the bioregions in which they aim to achieve ecological balance. Bioregional economies can restore feedback loops to encourage cities into balance with the carrying capacity of their bioregions rather than yielding to the increasingly remote pull of the global economy. This means focusing on local and bioregional production of food, water, and energy and recycling of wastes. Furthermore, this approach promotes diverse solutions suited to the unique patterns of place. In supporting a more regional and local focus, CASE does not advocate isolation but rather a celebration of diversity and a greater emphasis on flows of information and cultural exchanges than on natural resources. Governance policies at the national and interregional scales need to be formulated to support bioregional infrastructure to match carrying capacity (Korten 1999).

Bioregional and local economies conserve energy and other resources, drawing on renewable sources, particularly those that are solar based. The dominant ecosystems on Earth are solar economies, drawing on the most abundant and ubiquitous energy source on the planet. The communities of life have thrived by the amazing ability of green plants to capture solar energy and make it available to other life-forms. Indigenous soci- eties relied on this energy from plants for food and fuel. By contrast, modern cities are dependent upon vast inputs of both plant-based and fossil fuel energy. Their energy metabolism has risen significantly in the past fifty years. Ultimately, cities' reliance on fossil fuel energy is unsustainable, as reserves are finite and the cost of supply increases as easily accessible sources are depleted.

The transition to a solar economy will require us to develop the necessary infrastructure so cities can produce their own photosynthetic power. This renewable energy is likely to be produced locally and bioregionally from various resources. It can trap the sun through technologies like photovoltaics and solar water or air heaters. It can generate fuels through wood and through new systems that grow algae in rooftop tubes, which can then be converted to biofuels. However it can only replace fossil fuels if significant reductions in use are instituted through energy-efficiency improvements in buildings, transport, and industry. This process of building new infrastructure can take decades; thus the shift needs to be planned and initiated now. Conserver lifestyles can be encouraged by ensuring that satisfiers for genuine needs are met in ways that conserve resources. Sustainable consumption patterns will be further discussed in chapter 9.

One of the most significant ways to start building sustainably is to stop spending money on highways and instead prioritize sustainable transport. The highway-to-transit transition is what unleashed so much of Portland's sustainability juices in the 1980s. And now we better understand why. Highways undermine urban economies. They create car dependence, which is very expensive, as shown by Newman and Kenworthy (2007):

- Cities that are car dependent spend between 15 and 20 percent of their wealth just on getting around, whereas transit-oriented cities spend only 5 to 8 percent of their wealth on transport.
- Out of a sample of one hundred global cities, those with strong rail systems were 43 percent more wealthy than weak rail cities.
- The key reason why car dependence wastes money is because cars waste space; cars take 2,500 people per hour down one lane, but trains can take 50,000—that's twenty times the space efficiency. Asphalt for roads and parking can cover over a third of a city.
- At a household level, people who live in car-dependent cities use over 20 percent of their income on transport with some more than 40 percent. Affordable housing on the fringe is leading to a transport poverty trap which will worsen as oil prices go up and carbon is taxed.
- Those who live near a rail station are found to own fewer cars (0.7 fewer per household in the United States), thus freeing up 20 percent of their income which they can then spend locally—hence transit-oriented developments will bring much more money into the local economy.

Ideally a future city's infrastructure would look like this: Quality transit would determine how the city is structured, with walking and cycling paths lacing through the city. Urban ecovillages would have autotrophic energy systems providing much of the energy. Water systems would be local and distributed, as well as being part of a grid. Most waste systems would be turned around so that little is lost in the process of producing materials, and most products would be recycled (Newman and Kenworthy 1999; McDonough and Braungart 2002).

No physical infrastructure can work unless it is part of a social infrastructure committed to the ideas of local and bioregional economies. New understanding about the importance of community and bioregional networks for the economies of cities and their regions has been developed by Robert Putnam (1993). Studying city regions in Italy, Putnam found that their wealth depended mostly on their social capital—their networks of trust, mutual interest, and support—that is, the strength of their communities' social connections. In view of this insight, economic planners are recognizing the importance of building social capital through social infrastructure. For cities this gives an even greater rationale for focusing on the bioregional and community scale—the scale at which social capital works most effectively.

Being part of a bioregion and a local community provides a context for belonging and for responsibility. Restoring bioregional and local economies offers the opportunity to combine the best of indigenous, traditional, and modern ingenuity. Cities can create symbiotic relationships with their wider bioregions, providing mutual sustenance, recognizing that life is a collective enterprise and that our survival is based on cooperative interactions. Cities also need to develop community-scale, local economies, in which an even greater sense of belonging emerges, transport energy savings become even more marked, and feedback loops become most visible.

Strategy 3: Urban Ecovillages

The Global Ecovillage Network offers the following definition of ecovillages:

> Ecovillages are urban or rural communities of people, who strive to integrate a supportive social environment with a low-impact way of life. Ecovillages are communities in which people feel supported by and responsible to those around them. They provide a deep sense of belonging to a group. They are small enough that everyone feels safe, empowered, seen, and heard. People are then able to participate in making decisions that affect their own lives and that of the community on a transparent basis.[11]

Ecovillages seek to nurture social and economic security through creating cooperative, empowered communities, and local production and livelihoods. Jackson and Svensson (2002) suggest there are a range of characteristics of ecovillages (see box 2.4). Ecovillages will be discussed further in upcoming chapters.

Although urban ecovillages are less common than rural ecovillages, they are becoming important models for the future. Ithaca Ecovillage was founded in 1991 with thirty group homes and a community building; it has expanded to sixty homes and has a range of ecological and social innovations with some attempts at developing more of a local economy (Walker 2005).

Several other ecovillages have sprung from Ithaca Ecovillage. Across America there are now 93 "intentional communities," with 107 being built.[12] Not all of these

Box 2.4 **Ecovillage Characteristics**

Ecological Dimension

- Growing organic food as much as possible within the community bioregion
- Creating "living" homes out of natural, locally available materials, and using local (architectural) traditions
- Using village-based integrated renewable energy systems
- Ecological business principles (local green businesses)
- Assessing the life cycle of products used in the ecovillage from a social/spiritual and ecological point of view
- Preserving clean soil, air, and water through proper energy and waste management
- Protecting and encouraging biodiversity and safeguarding wilderness areas

Social Dimension

- Recognizing and relating to others
- Sharing common resources and providing mutual aid
- Learning to make good decisions and solve conflicts
- Emphasizing holistic and preventive health practices
- Providing meaningful work and sustenance to all members
- Allowing for a whole life for children, the elderly, and marginal groups

- Promoting lifelong education
- Encouraging unity through respect for differences
- Fostering cultural expression
- Green economics

Economic Dimension

- Complementary currencies (LETS systems, Friendly Favors, ecovillage currency)
- Alternative banks
- Voluntary simplicity
- Local income-generating (green businesses, consulting)
- Expanded formal economy (communal meals, services)

Cultural/Spiritual Dimension

- Fostering a sense of joy and belonging through rituals and celebrations following natural cycles
- Emphasizing creativity and the arts as an expression of unity and interrelationship to our universe
- Expressing a spiritual worldview of global interconnectedness
- Respecting that spirituality manifests in many ways
- Respecting the expression of different cultures
- Facilitating personal growth and integral spiritual practices

Source: Jackson and Svensson 2002, 10–12

communities have attempted to create a strong economic base for their residents, though all emphasize their local bioregional economy. The SomerVille Ecovillage in Chidlow, Western Australia, with over one hundred households, has a strong economic base, including its own construction company, bank, school, shops, and offices.[13]

The Los Angeles Ecovillage provides a good example of what ecovillages can mean in a city. Located three miles west of downtown Los Angeles in a two-block, multiethnic, working-class neighborhood, it is home to about five hundred persons. The area is close to public transit (including the Metro Red Line subway), schools, churches, stores, commercial services, and light industry. These are the characteristics that can reshape urban economies.

Figure 2.2

Ithaca Ecovillage

Photo Peter Newman

Some neighborhood achievements of the LA Ecovillage include:

- Purchasing a forty-unit apartment building in 1996 and an eight-unit building in 1999 with monies raised through an ecological revolving loan fund
- Creating an environmental educational program for K-2 children
- Planting nearly a dozen small gardens and more than one hundred fruit trees
- Composting approximately one hundred cubic yards of green wastes
- Diverting twenty tons of red clay brick from the 1994 earthquake from the landfill for ecovillage beautification projects
- Hosting weekly community potluck brunches or dinners to build a sense of community among neighbors
- Conducting tours throughout the year to acquaint the general public with the processes of creating a sustainable community[14]

Some of the LA Ecovillage's immediate goals include:

Housing and Land
- Converting its two apartment buildings to permanently affordable co-op ownership
- Participating in the development of a community land trust[15]
- Planning for the development of seven live/work ecological loft spaces

Transportation and Streetscape
- Reducing the number of cars owned by ecovillagers by 50 percent of their number in 2000
- Enhancing pedestrian- and bicycle-friendly streets
- Eliminating diesel trucks and buses on one of the neighborhood's two thoroughfares

Energy and Water
- Retrofitting buildings for substantial reductions in energy and water consumption
- Installing a solar hot-water system in the forty-unit apartment building, and a "solar tent" in one parking lane to charge electric vehicles
- Installing a demonstration graywater system

Waste
- Installing a demonstration biological wastewater treatment system
- Reducing ecovillagers' landfill waste by 75 percent of its 1995 volume

Food
- Increasing neighborhood organic food production to provide 20 percent of the diet for 20 people, and obtaining another 40 percent from an organic food-buying co-op

Livelihood
- Establishing new neighborhood-based ecobusinesses sufficient to be a significant means of support for twelve persons

Education
- Further developing the Institute for Urban Ecovillages, which offers educational programs on all aspects of sustainable urban community living
- Establishing a public charter school or homeschooling program for up to twenty children.[16]

The LA Ecovillage is on a journey that has only just begun. Over the coming decades, it will demonstrate how cities can be vastly different from what they are today. It is showing already that much can be done if people work together at a neighborhood scale, rather than staying in isolated family units in which neighborhood means little.

All ecovillages are like ecosystems: they are very diverse but work together to provide lots of activities and opportunities. Residents and friends seek to establish good relationships with one another with a high level of trust. They try to figure out how the problems in their neighborhood are related to the problems in the bioregion and its political jurisdiction. They are especially interested in how these problems relate to their ability to have healthy air, water, and soil, a decent standard of living, a high quality of life, a good transit system, a walkable safe neighborhood, a nonpolluting livelihood, and a strong sense of community. Working together with their own skills and resources, they begin to create changes in their neighborhood. The processes for effecting change are always open and participatory, and they happen in many ways: informal dinner gatherings, meetings, work parties, sidewalk encounters, workshops, conferences, forums, special events, and electronic communications. They are a small sample of how every good city has always worked and what cities will need to rediscover for the future.

Strategy 4: Community Spaces, Pedestrianization, and Overcoming Car Dependence
Sustainable transportation is crucial to economic and social security. Our heavy reliance on food and material inputs transported over long distances, and increasing car dependence in cities and elsewhere, leave us vulnerable in the face of future oil shortages. Bioregional and local community economies go part of the way to addressing this. Developing a more compact form for cities encourages walking and public transport systems, thereby promoting greater energy independence, fairer access to transportation, and a greater sense of community as outlined above. Thus, cities could be renewed as a network of compact ecovillages, connected to each other by effective public transport systems, and surrounded by integrated food, water, and energy systems, and biodiversity reserves. This urban form that gives substance to bioregional and community economies will be discussed further in chapter 5. It is an image that motivates the eco-city social movements outlined through this book.

As Beatley and Manning have noted, "The physical characteristics of a sustainable community help to create a sense of community—a sense of ownership, commitment, and a feeling of belonging to a larger whole. Walking spaces, civic buildings, plazas and parks, and other public places have the potential to nurture commitment and attachment to the larger collective" (1997, 37). The provision of attractive, safe community spaces, good public transport, and abundant walking/cycling facilities creates the opportunity for convivial human interactions—compared to car-based communities, in which incidental meetings are minimized. Car dependence can be overcome through the implementation of traffic calming, quality transit, cycling and walking facilities, urban villages, growth management strategies such as urban growth boundaries, and transportation taxes to cover external costs (Newman and Kenworthy 1999, chap. 4). Many older cities, such as those in Europe, were built for walking (see figure 2.1), while other cities, such as Portland, Curitiba, and Bogotá, are reversing their car dependence (see Newman and Kenworthy 2007). The move toward sustainable transport systems is underway in the United States, where transit has grown 25 percent in ten years. Over one hundred US cities are building new rail projects, and in the past three years communities across the country have voted in $110 billion of new transit initiatives. Similar trends can be seen in Australia, Canada, and Europe, and many Third World countries are starting to realize that the days of building cities around cars are over (Newman and Kenworthy 2007).

Strategy 5: Urban Agriculture and Community Gardens

> Chickens on housetops, Swiss chard sprouting out of abandoned tires on high-rise rooftops, grape vines cascading down apartment balconies, corn stalks lining a tiny city lot. This is farming in the city—a.k.a. urban agriculture. An estimated 800 million people harvest 15 percent of the world's food supply by growing vegetables and raising livestock in cities. In the process, they are continuing a tradition that is probably as old as cities themselves (Halweil 2002).

High-intensity farming was a defining characteristic of early civilizations on Java and in the Indus Valley. The Aztecs created artificial farmland in today's Mexico City by dredging mud from the bottom of Lake Texcoco and piling it along the shores. These artificial fields, called *chinampas*, or "floating gardens," produced more than 45,000 tons a year of maize alone. And one-sixth of nineteenth-century Paris was devoted to urban gardens that were fertilized by urban-produced horse manure.[17]

Figure 2.3a

False Creek urban village, Vancouver, Canada

Photo Jeff Kenworthy

Figure 2.3b

Urban villages along Vancouver's SkyTrain

Photo Jeff Kenworthy

Urban agriculture in the form of city farming and individual, communal, and community-assisted agriculture provides examples of meeting food requirements locally and bioregionally, thereby facilitating greater economic and social security. Closing nutrient cycles through urban agriculture is a key way to foster more sustainable urban ecosystems.

City farming is a significant contributor to world food production, and this trend is expected to increase. City farming also plays a big part in addressing poverty and hunger, especially in the developing world. This is a traditional role for cities, which throughout urban history have been closely linked to food production. For example, Paris growers exported produce to outlying regions based on intensive agriculture made possible by composting the city's horse manure and "nightsoil" and applying it to urban gardens. Throughout Asia the city model known as Desakota is based on intense urban development and pockets of agriculture in close cooperation. Community gardens also provide a chance for meaningful social interaction and contact with natural cycles, both of which enhance communities.

The use of permaculture in cities has become widely accepted as a good basis for intensive urban agriculture since Bill Mollison first proposed the system in the 1970s. Because permaculture has not often been adopted in the developing world, its use in helping to preserve biodiversity and build up a local economy in suburban Bogor, on the outskirts of Jakarta in Indonesia, is of special interest. Harry Harsono Amir, former

Box 2.5 **The Development of Permaculture in Sukabumi, Indonesiary**

By Harry Harsono Amir

In the 1970s, during the first Five Year Development Plan, the Indonesian government undertook a thorough reform of the agricultural sector in order to attain self-sufficiency in food production, particularly rice. The green revolution in agriculture began with initiatives to raise production by encouraging farmers to increase the use of chemical fertilizer and pesticides, and new varieties of paddy.

The introduction of green revolution technologies undoubtedly brought Indonesia close to self-sufficiency in food production by 1984. However, a few years later the production of rice leveled off, and Indonesia was forced to import grain once again. The fall in production was mainly the result of an outbreak of insects known as brown plant hoppers (*Nilaparvata* sp.) which had become resistant to pesticides. The government acted to ban certain pesticides and implement integrated pest management, but there is no question that the environment was already badly affected. Despite regreening and reforestation programs implemented by the government, there has been widespread poisoning of the land by chemical fertilizers, a reduction in genetic diversity through the loss of local paddy varieties, and pollution of soil and groundwater by pesticides. In upland areas, soil degradation has resulted from inappropriate farming techniques. An alternative approach must be sought which is beneficial to the environment, and also takes into consideration the socioeconomic and cultural aspects of the local people.

The English term for this alternative approach is "permaculture," or permanent agriculture, as set out by Mollison (1988). This agriculture is intensive, uses a mixture of species and layers of activity similar to a forest, it recycles all waste, uses organic principles of pest-management, and builds up the soil with compost and earthworms. To Sundanese people (from West Java) this approach is well known as *kebon talun*. In different parts of Indonesia it may have different names; however, the principles are the same: to achieve maximum productivity from a piece of land with minimum inputs of energy and effort. Kebon talun (or talun) is regarded as a transition stage between shifting cultivation and permanent agriculture. As the Indonesian way of life became more settled than nomadic, species of hardwood, softwood, and bamboo were preserved in their gardens. Seeds discarded from fruits such as avocado (*Persea americana*), mango (*Mangifera indica*), rambutan (*Nephelium lappaceum*), durian (*Durio zibethinus*), salak (*Salacca edulis*), sawo (*Achras zapota*), and kedondong (*Spondias dulcis*) germinated beneath the hardwoods. And cassava, corn, taro, vegetables, ornamental, and medicinal plants were grown in the lower strata.

The garden is rich in biodiversity and mimics the stratification which naturally occurs in tropical rain forests. The stratification of plant species is efficient in capturing energy from sunlight and is more productive than a monoculture farming system with a high input of chemical fertilizers and pesticides. The talun system was also able to maintain pest species populations in balance with their predators in a similar way to that achieved in natural ecosystems. Consequently, they do not require the use of pesticides. The soil in a talun system is continually enriched by fallen leaves and tree trunks. Natural fertilizers consisting of chicken, goat, cow, and buffalo manure are sometimes added to the soil by farmers.

Source: Harry Harsono Amir, "Community Participation in the Development of Permaculture in Sukabumi, Indonesia" (2000), Institute for Sustainability and Technology Policy, Case Studies, http://www.sustainability.murdoch.edu.au /casestudies/Case_Studies_Asia/sukabumi/sukabumi.htm

Through the integration of ecological components in the talun system, the well-being of the farmers is maintained. Produce can be harvested year-round, and they can sell the surplus to the local market. Hardwood and bamboo is available for furniture and building materials. Cassava (*Manihot esculenta*), corn (*Zea mays*), sweet potato (*Ipomoea batatas*) and taro provide carbohydrates. Tropical fruits and vegetables supply vitamins and minerals. Various herbs, such as ganda rusa (*Justicia gandarussa*), cabe jawa (*Retrofracti fructus*), kapulaga (*Amomum kepulaga*), asem jawa (*Talinum paniculata*), tapak dara (*Vinca rosea*), and temulawak (*Curcuma xanthorrhiza*) are used as traditional medicines. It can be concluded, then, that the principles of talun are economically viable, environmentally sustainable, and culturally acceptable for most Indonesian farmers. Unfortunately, this eco-sustainable agricultural practice is slowly disappearing, replaced by highly inefficient monoculture farming.

An Eco-Friend Project (run by the author) was started in Sukabumi in 1990 to demonstrate the value of talun principles. The demonstration project includes at least ten local varieties of chicken, forty-five species of medicinal herbs, several types of bamboo (*Dendrocalamus asper, Gigantochloa apus, G. verticillata, Bambusa vulgaris*), softwoods, and hardwoods. Vermiculture has also recently been introduced.

Various initiatives have been undertaken to encourage farmers to implement the talun principles, including instruction in talun methods. Informal meetings were held to air the problems, aspirations, and hopes of the local farmers. They were informed of the benefits of conserving genetic biodiversity, particularly of local chicken species and medicinal plants. Some practical training in raising a local variety of chicken and in the use of Effective Microorganism 4 (EM4) to speed the compost process was also provided. Farmers interested in growing medicinal plants were provided with the species they required from the author, who grew the plants and bred the chickens in his suburban home. In one initiative, 452 local chickens were distributed amongst 115 households with varying levels of income. The chickens belonged to different varieties, each with its own characteristics but all with a higher economic return than other chickens. They included kedu hitam, kedu putih, pelung, nunukan, cemani, sentul, and lamongan. Farmers successful in raising the chickens must, after one year, give a chicken of the same variety to their neighbor.

The first stages of rebuilding talon agriculture in the village of Sukabumi is under way. The provision of species of plants and animals (many quite rare and endangered) from the author's permaculture plot at home in suburban Bogor has shown that the city can provide ecological assistance to its surrounding bioregion. More resources for the poor farmers are required. Cooperatives could play a more significant role in providing credit for farmers. Other income-generating activities, such as ecotourism packages and small-scale home industries, could work to lessen the pressure on the land. Business partnerships need to be developed for the marketing of talun and home industry products, and the promotion of ecotourism.

adviser to the Indonesian Minister for the Environment Elim Salim (who was the first Third World environment minister), developed permaculture to raise a variety of rare Javanese chickens, fish, medicinal plants, and food plants in his yard and on his rooftop. He then took some of the produce to a village that had been substantially degraded environmentally and helped them to develop traditional *talun* agriculture to supplement their incomes (see box 2.5). The result has been an improved economy as well as an improved environment in the bioregion.

The links between urban agriculture and a city's economy are much more obvious in cities that are poor and where residents need to grow food for subsistence and to make some money. In Rosario, Argentina, an economic meltdown plunged 800,000 of the 1.2 million residents into poverty and unemployment. The city turned to urban agriculture and opened up its public spaces and reserves for use; within weeks, 800 community gardens were started. Seven farmers' markets began so people could trade and make money. After the economy improved many left these gardens, but they have continued to be productive, with over 3,000 urban farmers. The UN has estimated that there are 800 million urban farmers globally, including 2.7 million in Shanghai (of which a high proportion work in peri-urban locations). Many creative ways of using urban land for agriculture have been developed in Cuba (Holmgren 2002).

In South Africa the Food Gardens Foundation (FGF) has demonstrated considerable assistance to the urban poor.[18] Started in 1977 in Soweto, this organization was formed to help people overcome malnutrition, famine, and hunger by growing food using sustainable organic methods. FGF's motto is "Maximum nutrition in minimum space with limited water and resources." The foundation has gone on to work with numerous urban and rural communities in southern Africa, focusing on the poor and hungry. FGF provides training for community leaders and community development workers to assist them in promoting and teaching food gardening in their communities. The FGF method of vegetable growing is a low-cost, land- and water-efficient method that basically involves digging a trench that is half filled with organic matter and topped with the dugout soil, into which seeds and seedlings are planted.

Erica Jacobs, the group's project development coordinator, sums up the achievements of the Food Gardens Foundation:

> The 25 years of Food Garden Foundation's existence have been among the most momentous in the history of this country and, not only has the work of the Foundation been profoundly affected by those changes, it has itself been an important agent for change in the fields of helping people to help themselves by growing food, and [it] has had a significant impact on education and environmental awareness. So unique is our concept that like-minded organizations have also recognized the need for food gardening. . . . Our roots have been established far and wide throughout South Africa and other African countries.[19]

In more wealthy cities the growing of food is less critical to the local economy, but urban agriculture remains important as it is used for rebuilding derelict communities, greening areas that are bereft of nature, and providing an outlet for many who enjoy gardening. Montreal has eight thousand community gardens, and Toronto has more than one hundred in one network alone (Butler 2006). Even in places without community gardens or urban agriculture, it is still important to make links between urban residents and the bioregion in which their food is being produced. Community-supported agriculture is an approach that links consumers with farmers in the bioregion, providing economic security to farmers and nurturing more sustainable farming practices (see chapter 8 on partnerships).

Some cities have established food policy councils to develop comprehensive, coordinated programs to provide healthy, sustainable food for all and where possible to promote local food systems. The first food policy council was formed in Knoxville, Tennessee, in 1982 some five years after Robert Wilson, a professor of urban planning at the University of Tennessee, raised the question of why city governments do not create departments to plan for food security as they do for transportation and other vital services. Since then, numerous cities across North America have developed food policy councils. They may be grassroots initiatives or officially sanctioned by city councils. Some North American examples are given in box 2.6.

Canada's McGill University and the International Development Research Center (IDRC) embarked on an international research initiative called Making the Edible Landscape to study the importance of planning for urban agriculture. The findings from this initiative, led by architecture professor Vikram Bhatt, were presented at the 2006 UN-Habitat's World Urban Forum in Vancouver (Butler 2006). Soon after the project's launch, the *McGill Reporter* offered this description of its focus and objectives:

> By the year 2030, the urban population is expected to be 5 billion (of a projected 8 billion), and almost all the population increase until then will occur in urban areas of less developed regions.
>
> To fight the shortfall of resources that are inevitable with this surge in urban living, people are turning to urban agriculture. This includes growing plants, medicinal, and aromatic herbs, and fruit trees, and raising livestock, either for household use or to sell to neighbors.
>
> Some governments encourage and support urban farms and gardens, like in Havana, Cuba, where roughly 30 percent of available land is under cultivation. Others, such as those in sub-Saharan Africa, aren't supportive, even though urban agriculture helps poor people meet nutrition requirements in the face of economic crises.
>
> Montreal's own city-sponsored community gardens are an example of urban agriculture, but they aren't crucial to the well-being of Montrealers. In the overcrowded slums of developing-world cities, initiatives such as urban agriculture can make a huge difference to the quality of life.

The challenge is to view lettuce and chard on equal footing with bricks and mortar. Urban planners and architects first think of housing, parking, and commercial development when they design cities, but they should consider the benefits—social, visual, and physical—of producing food on urban land. City farming, no matter how small in scale, contributes to food security and energy conservation, and a sense of community. People can glean satisfaction and pleasure from making fertile use of roadside patches of land and abandoned lots, as well as save money.

Three partner cities from different continents were chosen for the Edible Landscape project: Colombo, Sri Lanka; Kampala, Uganda; and Rosario, Argentina. By collaborating with local researchers, architects, and community leaders, the group will test the potential of urban agriculture in meeting the UN Millennium Development Goals, which include squatter settlement upgrading, poverty alleviation, food security, and gender equity.[20]

Strategy 6: Complementary Currencies and "Sustainable Development Rights"

City economies in the past had their own currencies. Jane Jacobs (1984) argues that national currencies often fail to express the true value of a city and its bioregion. Some places have been able to move their economies toward a bioregional focus by adopting complementary currencies as an alternative to national currencies and by establishing local financial institutions. Korten (1999) points out that a common currency not only facilitates change but also creates a community with a reciprocal interest in productive exchange among its members in the bioregion. In this way, a community affirms its identity and creates a natural preference for its own products. Over a thousand communities around the world have issued their own local currencies to encourage local commerce, including the following examples:

- **LETS initiatives:** Local Exchange Trading Systems (LETS) are trading networks supported by their own internal currencies. The systems are self-regulating and allow users to manage and issue their own "money supply" within the boundaries of the network.[21] Numerous communities have adopted such an approach, including the Crystal Waters Permaculture Village near Maleny in Australia, where a LETS scheme was adopted along with the creation of a credit union and various cooperatives to establish local businesses.[22]
- **Minneapolis HeroDollars:** This experimental system uses dual smart cards to allow simultaneous payment in both US dollars and complementary currency. The HeroDollars system is presently in the trial phase in Minnesota. It allows the generation of funds to foster socially responsible development.[23]
- **Curitiba, Brazil:** In this city of over two million inhabitants, complementary currencies have been used over the past twenty-five years to spur economic growth and improve living standards.[24]

Box 2.6 Food Policy Councils (FPCs)

Portland Food Policy Council, Oregon, USA

The City of Portland and Multnomah County formed a food policy council in 2002 to "nourish the heart, the soul, the soil, and the pocketbook." The Portland FPC has worked with farmers, planners, hunger advocates, chefs, environmentalists, government agencies, and citizen groups on a range of collaborative projects. One of its initiatives is the development of a network of small urban farms, which would provide sites for teaching and learning and connect people to the "heritage of food and the future of sustainable agriculture." The FPC envisions "a community where healthy food is available to everyone, grown with respect for land, air and water, produced and consumed by our neighbors, and eaten with joy."

Source: City of Portland, Office of Sustainable Development, Food policy: At the core of a healthy community (2004), http://www.portlandonline.com/shared/cfm/image.cfm?id=116845

Toronto Food Policy Council, Ontario, Canada

Toronto was one of the first world cities to sign onto the WHO Healthy Cities initiative, and in 1991 the city established a food policy council. The Toronto FPC works with business and community groups to develop policies and programs promoting food security. Its goal is "a food system that fosters equitable food access, nutrition, community development, and environmental health."

Source: City of Toronto, Board of Health, http://www.toronto.ca/health/tfpc_index.htm

Vancouver Food Policy Council, British Columbia, Canada

The Vancouver FPC, created in 2004, supports the development of a "just and sustainable food system for the city of Vancouver that fosters sustainable equitable food production, distribution, and consumption; nutrition; community development; and environmental health."

Source: City of Vancouver, Social Planning Department, http://vancouver.ca/commsvcs/socialplanning/initiatives/foodpolicy/policy/council.htm

Berkeley Food Policy Council, California, USA

The Berkeley FPC grew out of the Edible Schoolyard program initiated by a local chef (see chapter 10). Since its inception in 1999, the FPC has placed a strong emphasis on local schools. Its goal is "to build a local food system based on sustainable regional agriculture that fosters the local economy and assures all people of Berkeley have access to healthy, affordable and culturally appropriate food from non-emergency sources."

Source: Berkeley Food Policy Council, http://www.berkeleyfood.org/archive/index.html

Like other Brazilian cities, Curitiba grew dramatically in the last decades of the twentieth century, and a majority of its newcomers lived in *favelas*, shanty towns made of cardboard and corrugated metal. Garbage collection in the favelas was a problem because there were no streets suitable for the trash trucks. As a result, the garbage piled up, attracting rodents and prompting outbreaks of disease. Because the city did not have the money to apply "normal" solutions, Curitiba created new currencies to encourage citizens to bring their garbage to authorized dumping stations: sorted recyclables could be exchanged for bus tokens; biodegradable garbage could be exchanged for tokens good for parcels of fresh produce; and a school-based program allowed students to swap garbage for notebooks. Curitiba neighborhoods were soon garbage free. Moreover, favela residents used the bus tokens to travel downtown, where the jobs were, thus becoming integrated in the formal economy (Lietaer and Warmoth 1999).

The bus, food, and notebook tokens were all forms of complementary currency. The garbage program was a huge success: by the late 1990s, 70 percent of all Curitiba households were participating in this process. Curitiba also has another complementary currency system commonly used by many city planning departments, though not usually thought of as a complementary currency. Their system is called *sol criado* (literally "created surface"), and it is similar to the bonuses given to developers when they do something that a local government wants but cannot always require, such as heritage restoration, conservation of green spaces, affordable housing, or social infrastructure.

To illustrate Curitiba's sol criado system, Lietaer and Warmoth (1999) offer the example of the Garibaldi House, a historic landmark building that needed a serious restoration job that the owners could not afford. Because the property is located in a zoning area that would allow up to 2 floors of new construction to be built, the owners "sold" 50,000 square meters (2 floors x 25,000 square meters) to the highest bidder—in this case, the developer of a new hotel, who wanted to build 5 more floors (at 10,000 square meters each) than the city normally allowed. According to the sol criado rules, the proceeds of this transaction belonged to the Garibaldi House owners to administer, but had to be used to restore the property. Thus the hotel developer ended up paying for the restoration of a historic building in order to obtain the right to add extra floors to a new construction.

Curitiba has used this system to finance public parks and other projects. Most developed cities have created similar development bonuses that are part of the nonmonetary economy of the city. For example in Vancouver the city requires that 5 percent of the value of a development be directed into what they call social infrastructure. This is worked out by the developer and council in discussion with the local community, who may want better streetscapes, more pedestrianized areas, or a community meeting space, even an art-house cinema. Social housing is worked out on the basis of receiving a density bonus for more development rights. The more that Vancouver exercises these complementary currency requests, the more the development process works to create better public spaces to go with the private spaces that the market is for. Thus sustainability can be made to mean something at a very local level through the planning system.

All cities have the opportunity through their planning systems to create their own currencies that work in a parallel way with normal money. These sustainability credits are not owned by the developer or by the city, but they are real—they are in fact owned by the community, as it is their values that are being expressed in the development bonuses granted. Thus cities can create community banks of sustainability credit. Most cities in the Third World don't have much to invest in their public spaces, hence the whole city economy suffers. Curitiba showed how it could break that mold. Through their planning systems, cities can create their own currencies for what they most need, as determined by local citizens—they just need to define them as development rights. These new "sustainable development rights" could be related to biodiversity credits, greenhouse reduction credits, salinity reduction credits, affordable housing credits, or anything else that a community can create a "market" for in their city and bioregion. Experiments in these new forms of city currency need to be undertaken by innovative city councils wanting to develop their economies around sustainability.

Strategy 7: True-Costing Initiatives

Market-based instruments are available to internalize social and environmental costs not accounted for in markets (see Pearce and Barbier's book *Blueprint for a Sustainable Economy*, 2000). These could be applied at the national, regional, or city scale:

- Taxes
- Subsidies
- Tradeable or marketable quotas
- Compensatory incentives
- Enforcement incentives

By focusing the benefits from such mechanisms on bioregional economies and local economies in cities, it is possible to internalize some of the social and environmental costs of the global economy. This could facilitate better operation of these parallel and more sustainable aspects of city economies.

The problem with these mechanisms is that they are not going to provide long-term change toward sustainability in cities unless they are part of a coherent visionary process.

Figure 2.4

Curitiba, Brazil: the city that left the Third World through urban planning

Photo Jeff Kenworthy

The most effective way to change the economy of cities so that they promote sustainability is to recognize that redistribution of wealth from some of these economic mechanisms should support bioregional and local economies. Shuman's analysis of the subsidies given to transnational companies by local and state governments, discussed earlier in the chapter, demonstrates that the playing field is not level when it comes to local and bioregional economies. More effort should be made to explain these areas of finance to the public when decisions are made and to open up the decision-making process.

Strategy 8: "Buy Local" Campaigns and Ecolabeling

Two mechanisms developed by cities to foster more local economic development and consequently reduce a city's ecological footprint are "Buy Local" policies and ecolabeling. "Buy Local" campaigns are adopted by urban governments that want more local content in their procurement of goods and services. Firms can be encouraged to show their social responsibility by following the same policy.

Ecolabeling is an extension of this process. It encourages consumers to recognize and purchase products and services that are not only local but also ecoconscious. Ecolabeled

Figure 2.5

Village of Arts and Humanities, Philadelphia:
Angels and the Tree of Life

Photos Peter Newman

goods and services are accredited as meeting specified ecological standards and criteria. Cities and bioregions need to encourage their local and bioregional economies to produce and consume in an environmentally and socially responsible way. Governments can facilitate technological change by implementing the procurement of ecolabeled products. The development of ecologically sound technologies and processes needs to be supported and can form an important part of future economies. Sustainable consumption patterns and technologies for sustainable production are discussed in more detail in chapter 9.

Strategy 9: Community Arts

The arts have a significant role to play in fostering a sense of community and place and in building social capital. Providing an outlet for creativity is important to human psychological health, and community arts programs can help people gain a sense of belonging and connection to their community and place. Although this sense of place is critical in itself (see chapter 6), it contributes to diversity of economies as well.

The Village of Arts and Humanities in Philadelphia is a powerful example of the use of the arts to promote community renewal and build social capital. Established in 1986 as a summer park-building project, the Village has grown to become a wide-ranging arts program that has revitalized a blighted urban landscape and reinvigorated community pride (see figure 2.6).

The Village's mission is "to build community through innovative arts-based programs in education, land transformation, construction, and economic development."[25] Located in inner-city North Philadelphia, the organization has helped residents reclaim garbage-strewn vacant lots and transform derelict buildings with sculpture parks, vegetable gardens, and murals. In the process, it has rebuilt "a sense of hope and possibility" in the community. Besides its many visual and performing arts programs and events, the Village has renovated abandoned properties, sponsored community health events, and provided job training.

In 1993 the Village's founder, Lily Yeh, spent three months in Kenya working with residents of the Korogocho slum near Nairobi, transforming a barren courtyard into a place of beauty. The success of this project led to an ongoing exchange between Korogocho and the Village. Since then, the Philadelphia organization has expanded its work globally, assisting communities in the Republic of Georgia, Ecuador, China, and Italy in implementing arts-based education and revitalization programs.

Conclusions

Cities are formed because of the economics of opportunity, innovation, and agglomeration efficiencies. There is little likelihood that these forces are going to change; hence the world is becoming rapidly more urban. However, there is growing recognition that the economic and social patterns of cities must change to reflect sustainability concerns. Focusing on reviving local and bioregional economies and communities brings power and thus economic and social security back to communities and cities. This scale allows for matching ecological realities, making the most of local and bioregional characteristics and enhancing the resilience of cities and their regions. The local and bioregional levels provide a scale at which people can care for each other in practical ways. Innovative and creative strategies can be applied from the local through bioregional scales. This approach is heightened in priority by the looming problems of climate change and peak oil, which require reductions in transport fuel that will inevitably favor the growth of local and bioregional economies linked to cities.

One of the great success stories in Latin America is Curitiba, Brazil, as it has developed considerably through a series of sustainability innovations. Most people know the city for its innovative transit system, but it is also an example of a city that has developed its economy around many local and bioregional innovations, discussed in this chapter. A series of social, cultural, and ecological initiatives led to Curitiba's receiving the award for "the most ecological city in the world" from the United Nations in 1992. These sustainability innovations have helped the Curitiba economy generate an economic growth rate 40 percent higher than any other city in the country. Cities should not fear moving toward a sustainability-based economy.

Biodiversity

PRINCIPLE 3
Recognize the intrinsic value of biodiversity and natural
ecosystems, and protect and restore them.

*Elaboration: Nature is more than a commodity for the benefit of humans. We
share the Earth with many other life-forms that have their own intrinsic value.
They warrant our respect, whether or not they are of immediate benefit to us.*

*It is through direct experience with nature that people come to understand
its value and gain a better appreciation of the importance of healthy habitats
and ecosystems. This connection provides them with an appreciation of the
need to manage their interactions with nature empathetically.*

*Just as humans have the ability to alter habitat and even to extinguish other
species, we can also protect and restore biodiversity. Therefore, we have a
responsibility to act as custodians for nature.*

Defining Biodiversity

Life on Earth is estimated to have arisen almost four billion years ago. The pattern of evolution since then can be represented by a tree structure expanding vertically to create greater complexity, and horizontally to create greater diversity (de Duve 1995). Throughout Earth's history, major catastrophes caused by such events as tectonic movements, volcanic eruptions, climatic changes, and asteroid impacts have destroyed many of the existing life-forms. Each time, over the millions of years following these massive disturbances, life has not just regenerated but developed "decisive innovations" (de Duve 1995, 221).

The biosphere, the relatively thin layer of Earth where all life occurs, is a mosaic of living communities of species interacting with their environment—in other words, a mosaic of ecosystems. The complexity of ecosystems and the biosphere is highlighted by de Duve:

> Even the simplest fields or ponds are multifactorial systems stitched together
> into intricate networks by dynamic interactions among the plants, animals,

fungi, and microorganisms they contain. Such systems, in turn, join to create larger, more complex fabrics, eventually closing into a single, gigantic web of formidable complexity that envelops the entire Earth: the biosphere. (1995, 217)

Biological diversity—or biodiversity—is the term given to the variety of life on Earth and the natural patterns it forms, encompassing the full range of species, genetic variation, and ecosystems in a given place. Living communities form patterns of complex interactions and relationships with each other and their life-places. These ecosystems occur over a broad range of scales. The biosphere can be divided into biomes: large-scale ecosystems characterized by vegetation type and climatic characteristics, including deserts, different types of forests, mountains, and grasslands. Tropical forests, coral reefs, and Mediterranean heathlands are the most species-rich ecosystems (UNEP 2002). While about 1.75 million species have been identified to date, mostly small invertebrates, estimates suggest that there may be as many as 14 million species (UNEP 2002).[1]

The Value of Biodiversity

Biodiversity—the variability within and among living organisms and the systems they inhabit—is the foundation upon which human civilization has been built. In addition to its intrinsic value, biodiversity provides goods and services that underpin sustainable development in many important ways, thus contributing to poverty alleviation. First, it supports the ecosystem functions essential for life on Earth, such as the provision of fresh water, soil conservation, and climate stability. Second, it provides products such as food, medicines, and materials for industry. Finally, biodiversity is at the heart of many cultural values.[2]

Biodiversity forms the web of life of which humans are an integral part, and forms the basis for healthy ecosystems that provide a large number of goods and services that sustain our lives physically, psychologically, and spiritually (see Table 3.1). All urban activities ultimately depend on healthy ecosystems and a healthy biosphere. The importance of ecosystem services to city functions has been recognized for many years, but the link between biodiversity and these services for water, air, waste dispersion, and recycling often goes unrecognized. The networks of biodiversity in ecosystems are only beginning to be understood, and their significance for cities requires urban planning to build in a new awareness of biodiversity.

Apart from the value that biodiversity has to humans, many people now recognize the intrinsic value of this diversity—that is, its value for its own sake:

Values of diversity—biological, cultural, and linguistic—are intrinsic to life itself and celebrated by myriad cultures and societies that have coevolved with the natural and metaphysical worlds that surround them. Indeed, human beings are an integral part of biodiversity, not merely observers and users of the "components of biological diversity." (Posey 1999, xvii).

The Earth Charter echoes this view in its first principle: "Respect Earth and life in all its diversity—recognize that all beings are interdependent and every form of life has value regardless of its worth to human beings."

Loss of Biodiversity: The Current Situation

From the dawn of agriculture, some ten thousand years ago, through the Industrial Revolution of the past three centuries, humans have transformed landscapes on an ever-larger and lasting scale. Urbanization involves the most significant modification of the landscape through the wholesale replacement of vegetation with human structures such as buildings, roads, and other infrastructure. Introduced species and changed disturbance cycles place pressure on the remaining fragments.

While loss of species has always been a natural phenomenon, the rate of extinction has accelerated dramatically due to human activity, as expressed in the Strategic Plan for the Convention on Biological Diversity, adopted in 2002:

> The rate of biodiversity loss is increasing at an unprecedented rate, threatening the very existence of life as it is currently understood. The maintenance of biodiversity is a necessary condition for sustainable development, and as such constitutes one of the great challenges of the modern era.

The first comprehensive global assessment of biodiversity, initiated by the United Nations Environment Program (UNEP), was released in 1995; a further assessment was made in 2005. The report concluded that between 5 and 20 percent of some groups of animal and plant species could be threatened with extinction in the foreseeable future.

Posey points out that "human cultural diversity too is threatened on an unprecedented scale" (1999, 3). There is growing recognition of an inextricable link between biological and cultural diversity, with many areas of megabiodiversity being sites of high cultural diversity too. With the loss of cultural diversity, important knowledge on sustainable ways of living in particular places is being lost. Thus, we need to approach the preservation of biological and cultural diversity as an integrated process (Maffi 1999).

Global Initiatives for Biodiversity Protection

At the 1992 Earth Summit in Rio de Janeiro, one of the key agreements adopted by world leaders was the Convention on Biological Diversity. The Convention establishes three main goals: the conservation of biological diversity, the sustainable use of its components, and the fair and equitable sharing of the benefits from the use of genetic

Table 3.1   **Ecosystem Services and Health Needs**

Ecosystem Services

Provisioning	**Regulating**	**Cultural**
Goods provided by or produced by ecosystems:	Benefits obtained from regulation of ecosystem processes:	Nonmaterial benefits obtained from ecosystems:
• Food	• Climate regulation	• Spiritual
• Freshwater	• Disease control	• Recreational
• Fuelwood	• Flood control	• Aesthetic
• Fiber	• Detoxification	• Inspirational
• Biochemicals		• Educational
• Genetic resources		• Communal
		• Symbolic

Supporting

Services that maintain the conditions for life on earth:
- Soil formation
- Nutrient cycling
- Pollination
- Maintenance of biological diversity

Ecosystem Health Needs

- No net soil loss
- Intact nutrient cycles
- Absence of polluting gases or particles in the atmosphere
- Absence of harmful concentrations of chemical compounds in water bodies and soil
- Absence of harmful levels of ionizing radiation

Source: Adapted from Reid et al. 2002; Boyden 1992

resources. Significantly, the Convention is legally binding; countries that join it are obliged to carry out its provisions.[3]

Besides its estimates of future species losses, UNEP's 1995 global biodiversity assessment also covered strategies to protect biodiversity. According to the World Resources Institute, scientific opinion on this topic has changed over the years:

> The traditional approach to protecting biodiversity emphasized the separation of ecosystems, species, and genetic resources from human activity through the creation of protected areas, prohibitions on harvesting endan-

gered species, and the preservation of germ plasm in seed banks or cryogenic storage facilities. Scientists now think that it is impossible to shield all genes, species, and ecosystems from human influence. Instead, preservation efforts must include a blend of strategies, including programs to save species by creating controlled environments and policies to manage natural environments in ways that minimize adverse impacts on biodiversity.[4]

This new approach brings cities into the biodiversity ambit.

Since then, the Millennium Ecosystem Assessment (MA) has provided a detailed overview of the state of global biodiversity. It suggests a bleak future unless we introduce significant changes in how we interact with the natural world. Based on a global cooperative effort from the world's scientific community, the MA shows how ecosystem services, such as those outlined above, are related to biodiversity (MEA 2005). It suggests that approximately 60 percent (15 of 24) of the world's ecosystem services are being degraded or used unsustainably. The degradation of ecosystem services often causes significant harm to human well-being and represents a loss of a natural asset or wealth of a country. The MA also finds that:

- Ecosystem services, as well as resources such as mineral deposits, soil nutrients, and fossil fuels, are capital assets
- Traditional national accounts do not include measures of resource depletion or the degradation of these resources
- A country could cut its forests and deplete its fisheries, and this would show only as a positive gain in GDP without registering the corresponding decline in assets (wealth)
- A number of countries that appeared to have positive growth in net savings in 2001 actually experienced a loss in wealth when degradation of natural resources was factored into the accounts.[5]

Strategies for Biodiversity Protection and Enhancement by Cities

Cities place heavy burdens on the ecosystems that they occupy, and these burdens increase with the tendency to spread out through low-density suburban development. Furthermore, urban consumption and production patterns take their toll on ecosystems across the planet through their consumption of energy and other products from well beyond their bioregions. However, cities can be transformed to reverse this situation. By seeing cities as networked ecovillages embedded in their bioregions, we can develop strategies and initiatives to protect biodiversity in the city and its bioregion, along with broad-scale landscape and bioregional processes.

The city and its bioregion need to be viewed as linked rather than as separate. Cities can contribute to biodiversity at community and bioregional scales in two main ways. First, on the cultural level, nurturing biodiversity is about rebuilding real connections between city dwellers and the living world so as to foster attitudes of respect and care. This may be achieved by encouraging cultural practices and stories that sustain connections, and by creating the opportunity for daily interaction with the more-than-human world through parks, city farms, and green architecture. Urban ecovillages encourage this interaction at a community scale. Practically, this assists in encouraging more sustainable urban lifestyles, reducing the impact on biodiversity outside the city. Once basic needs for food, water, and shelter are met, the focus is more on living graciously and abundantly with less, as an expression of love for the exuberance of life and the rich possibilities of a compassionate, creative, and relational life. Secondly, on a physical level, a system of nature reserves from the city into the bioregion, as well as the ecological design of city infrastructure, provides places for biodiversity to flourish and evolve.

Strategies for biodiversity protection by cities are set out below. They are arranged from the broad bioregional scale through city scale to household scale.

1. Restoring or maintaining healthy bioregions through connected and representative systems of static and dynamic reserves within the city itself and its bioregion
2. Conducting bioregional celebrations and education
3. Reducing the ecological footprints of cities
4. Re-creating cities as biodiversity arks
5. Designing ecological architecture and infrastructure.

Strategy 1: Healthy Bioregions through Dynamic and Static Reserves

To protect ecological diversity, a linked network of representative reserves in the city and throughout the bioregion should be created, as well as an enhancement of biodiversity in gardens and in support ecosystems in the bioregion. Bengtsson et al. (2002) argue for a system of static and dynamic reserves to support ecosystem reorganization after large-scale natural and human-driven disturbances. Current static reserves are likely to be inadequate to deal with large-scale and long-term ecosystem dynamics. These would be complemented by spatially and temporally dynamic reserves in managed landscapes and more intact ecosystems. These dynamic reserves promote landscape-level resilience through the creation of ecological memory. The authors recommend three types of reserves:

- **Ecological fallows**: Areas put aside for natural regeneration following a disturbance
- **Ephemeral reserves**: Areas for protecting species in the early exploitation phase of succession
- **Mid-succession reserves**: Areas where management may cease or change, if there are other areas close by that will provide landscape continuity (Bengtsson et al. 2002, 17).

This approach integrates existing reserves and national parks with managed landscapes, recognizing their interdependence. The biosphere reserve concept follows this notion.

Biosphere Reserves

Biosphere reserves are regions of terrestrial and coastal/marine ecosystems that are recognized within the framework of UNESCO's Man and the Biosphere Program as being of international significance in demonstrating three complementary functions: nature conservation; environmental education, research, and monitoring; and sustainable development. The program aims to create a worldwide network of biosphere reserves. This concept could be usefully applied to cities, as Douglas and Box suggest:

> Urban development should incorporate the maintenance of natural areas and the protection of biodiversity. Planning of new housing and industrial areas, extensions to existing cities, and the regeneration of old urban areas should respect areas of wildlife significance, provide opportunities for people to have contact with nature close to their homes, allow for the creation of many diverse habitats, and link the historic heritage with nature conservation. Wherever possible areas of high biological interest and specific conservation value, whether within the city or on its periphery, should be seen as potential core areas of Biosphere Reserves. (2000, 25)

The core, transition, and buffer zones of the biosphere reserve provide an aid in untangling diverse community interests, ensuring that core areas keep their essential character and ecological values and that other activities can happen in the buffer and transition zones. A system of multinodal core areas and buffer zones can be developed with linkages and integration with the built environment.

Europe has strategies for integrating cities into this biosphere concept as explained by Douglas and Box:

> The strategy for urban Biosphere Reserves in Europe over the next 50 years is . . . a marriage of natural areas around towns and cities with the urban "green." . . . The reclamation and re-use of old industrial land, the opening up of urban floodplains as green corridors, and the retention of hills within the city as greenspaces all make use of the legacies of past industrialization in a positive way. They challenge both the growing cities of southern Europe and the old industrial areas of central and northern Europe to take a view of sustainable development and strategic planning which recognizes that urban planning and countryside management cannot be separated. (2000)

The notion of biosphere reserves allows cities to plan green spaces that are not just public open space for urban people to enjoy but areas critical to the survival of ecosystems and biodiversity. Box 3.1 shows how the Dutch are creating wildlands within their most intensively developed urban areas.

The concept of biosphere reserves could be integrated with the concept of connected wildlands (below), providing a broad pattern of zoning between areas of high human use to those with minimal or no human interaction.

Connected Wildlands

The preservation of large blocks of wildland is essential to the survival of many species. Unfortunately, as human populations increase, the pressure to develop and exploit these areas often overrides any perceived benefits of keeping the land wild. Yet a study of ecosystem services provided by wild nature (such as those enumerated in table 3.1) found that their value topped $30 trillion annually. This figure does not include the intangible services we derive from maintaining a diversity of ecosystems and species. This diversity provides humanity with environmental resilience in the face of global climate change, the convenience of having a varied storehouse of foodstuffs and pharmaceuticals, and creatures we can appreciate for their aesthetic merit or even for their intrinsic right to exist.[6]

Box 3.1   **The Green-Blue Meander, South Holland**

In the southern part of the Randstad, the Netherlands' most densely populated region, a major project has been initiated to retain a strong ecological and recreational zone between Rotterdam in the south and The Hague to the north.

The Green-Blue Meander covers more than 200 square kilometers and winds through an S-shaped open area between the cities in the South Wing. The Green-Blue Meander will connect existing but currently fragmented bodies of water and green areas, thus unifying the landscape.

Supporters hope that this ecological and recreational buffer will resist future urbanization pressures. Water is the key design element reinforcing the existing identity of the landscape. Sixteen hundred hectares of land will be converted to new natural conservation and recreational areas, along with 125 kilometers of new connections. The Meander will function as a boundary to future urban expansion, as well as offer an important ecological and recreational space, and play a crucial role in sustainable water management.

Planning and elaborating the Green-Blue Meander occurred from 1995 to 2000. The next stage has focused on acquiring land, developing implementation plans, and implementing the first rural projects. The aim is to finish the entire project by 2013.

The Green-Blue Meander is a complex undertaking. The Province of South Holland, in the lead coordinating role, is working closely with no less than two urban agglomerations, sixteen local authorities, four water boards, three reconstruction programs for the rural areas, and many nature conservation and special-interest groups.

Source: The Green-blue meander: City and countryside in balance (2002), Projectbureau Groenblauwe Slinger, http://www.zuid-holland.nl/3/groenblauweslinger#5145 (click on "English Brochure" under Documenten)

According to Ecotrust, biodiversity can be maintained only through a three-pronged network of core reserves, wildlife corridors, and buffer zones:

> Core reserves should be large enough to provide functional habitat for the creatures that inhabit them. Where necessary, they should be re-wilded, with top predators and critical "keystone" species reintroduced. They should receive the highest possible wilderness designation (e.g., national parks, wilderness areas), with minimal-impact forms of recreation. A network of core reserves should include representation from all levels of biodiversity, including populations, species, and landscapes. It should include terrestrial, freshwater, and marine ecosystems.
>
> However, even the largest core reserves cannot provide for ongoing evolutionary processes unless they are connected by wildlife corridors. For instance, grizzly bears require up to 100 square miles of habitat, and a genetically viable population consists of at least 500 animals. Such corridors allow species to search for food, disperse into new territory after natural disturbances, and breed. Finally, the core reserves and wildlife corridors should be surrounded by buffer zones that contain uses compatible with wildlife, including subsistence gathering, cultural activities, and certain forms of sustainable agriculture or sustainable forestry.[7]

Current attempts to maintain systems of connected wildlands include the Yellowstone to Yukon Conservation Initiative, a joint US-Canadian project attempting to protect a continuous network from Wyoming to the Yukon-Alaska border; and the Rainforest to Rockies Conservation Initiative, seeking to connect the Coast and Cascades ranges of the northwestern United States with the interior Rocky Mountains. A similar initiative in Western Australia is Gondwana Links (see box 3.2), which is forging a link between several major national parks and reserves by turning strategic farmland back into natural bush. Through purchases and help from farmers, the natural link will eventually reach over two thousand kilometers, from the coastal forests to the outback woodlands.[8]

Complex issues regarding the size of reserves and connectivity need to be considered and adjusted to suit the characteristics of place. Biodiversity hot spots are likely to require a more complex reserve system and a broader range of strategies. There is evidence that private block size for households does little for biodiversity as only urban-adapted species use suburban lots no matter what their size. Biodiversity can only be increased to include non-urban-adapted species by linking remnant open space and regenerated bush (including green roofs) into the bioregion (Moroney and Jones 2006). City reserves need to be seen in their wider context, connecting with reserves in their bioregion and beyond. These connections may serve to facilitate ecological processes such as the movement of animal and bird populations and seed dispersal, as well as providing trails for humans to walk or cycle from the city into the bioregion.

Cities need to work together, and wealthier cities may need to provide funds or other protection strategies to safeguard biodiversity in their neighboring bioregions or further afield. The work of groups such as the Nature Conservancy provides some ideas for different approaches to funding and securing biodiversity protection. They provide a model for biodiversity protection and partnerships with the private sector, which could be adapted to include city communities (as in the Gondwana Link project described in box 3.2).

Strategy 2: Bioregional Education and Celebrations

Bioregions are the places within which our lives unfold. Bioregional celebrations honor the biodiversity of the bioregion along with indigenous and local wisdom. These events

---

Box 3.2 **The Nature Conservancy and the Gondwana Link**

Australia has some of the oldest rocks in the world. Hence most of its soil dates back hundreds of millions of years to the time when the supercontinent Gondwanaland split into the continents of the Southern Hemisphere. Western Australia's vegetation evolved with the soil, in distinct and localized "soil islands," helping to create the world's most diverse area for vascular plants. Now, protecting this patchwork of vegetation has brought together six Australian NGOs (nongovernment organizations) as diverse as the ecology itself. Their ambitious goal is to create a wildlife corridor across one-third of the continent—from Western Australia to South Australia—connecting fragments of wetlands, woodlands, mallee, and heath.

The Gondwana Link project, coordinated by Keith Bradby from the Wilderness Society, aims to reverse decades of habitat fragmentation. Since the 1950s, Western Australia's native vegetation has yielded to agriculture, leaving patches of native growth isolated from each other—a recipe for extinction. For example, thousands of emus have died because farmland and fences block their migration from the dry inland to wetlands. "The only real chance for stopping this is restoring the corridor," Bradby says.

The Gondwana Link project will use numerous conservation measures, including acquisitions, easements, and native plant restoration, to link two large national parks (one of which is surrounded by a larger biosphere reserve) with smaller reserves, bushland, and farms. So far, the project has secured individual parcels of private land, created small wildlife corridors, and encouraged farmers to join the project by setting aside bush and by planting more compatible crops. "But there is a limit on what you can do on a property-by-property basis," explains Bradby.

For help in working on a large landscape, the group looked to the American NGO the Nature Conservancy. The Conservancy has been able to provide technical assistance in such areas as ecoregional planning, organizational development and fundraising. In addition, "The support of a large, international group like the Conservancy has opened the eyes of Australians to this corner of the continent," says Bradby. "The vision we're projecting and the on-the-ground stuff is the single biggest restoration project in Australia. Nothing on this scale has been attempted before, but the climate is ripe." Small towns and settlements along the path are being drawn into the vision of how their reserves and tree planting can be integrated into the functions of the bioregional corridor, and the city of Perth is helping to fund the project through a series of carbon neutral commitments from large corporations.

Source: Gondwana Link, www.gondwanalink.org

may follow the seasons and involve storytelling, dancing, music, and other community gatherings. For nonindigenous cultures, this celebration is a process of coming home to a place and learning to love and respect the other life and ecosystems of one's bioregion. Awareness of biodiversity and its value should be part of ecoliteracy programs in schools. In the community this awareness can be cultivated more broadly through the development of a sense of place, which necessarily should include indigenous and other cultural stories of the land and biodiversity (this point is expanded in chapter 6).

Strategy 3: Reducing Ecological Footprints of Cities

By transforming cities to be more like ecosystems, resource use can be reduced and waste production virtually eliminated. Through this transformation, along with conserver lifestyles, the footprint of the city can be reduced to match the bioregion, thus removing the pressure to clear more land (see more in chapters 4 and 5).

Strategy 4: Cities as Biodiversity Arks

Cities are often seen as threats to biodiversity, but they also provide unique opportunities for biodiversity conservation and regeneration due to the possibilities of intensive land use and labor not found in rural areas. If city dwellers change their focus and vision to embrace biodiversity, they can take the key step forward.

Cities can provide labor, land, and resources for restoration work in the urban area and bioregion, thus acting as biodiversity arks. They can nurture biodiversity through community gardens, restored public spaces, school gardens, backyards, and roadside plantings. Plants can also be integrated into buildings (see the next section on ecological architecture and infrastructure).

Figure 3.1

Lady Bird Johnson Wildflower Center in Austin, Texas, demonstrates the value of biodiversity and a sense of place through native plants.

Photo Peter Newman

Cities can assist in the growing and breeding of plants and animals, including rare and endangered species for restoration projects in the city or in the rural areas of their bioregions. These programs may take place in zoos, botanical parks, or small wildlife sanctuaries within the city boundaries or on the urban fringe (see box 3.3). Furthermore, urban agriculture can be used to revive breeds of animals and varieties of plants that are dying out, thus enhancing agricultural diversity. Harry Harsono Amir's attempt to revive Indonesia's *talun* agricultural system, described in chapter 2, was part of an economic project for restor-

---

Box 3.3 **Perth and the Southwest Australia Ecoregion: Safeguarding Local Plants and Animals**

Perth, in southwest Western Australia, is in the center of one of the world's top twenty-five biodiversity hot spots due to the high number of species it supports, the high degree of endemism of these species, and the degree of threats to these biodiversity values. Recent studies conducted by Dr. Steve Hopper concluded that "Perth is probably the most biodiverse city in the world." A number of biodiversity initiatives or projects exist.

Perth has a long tradition of retaining native vegetation. A large central city park, Kings Park, was set aside as bushland in the late nineteenth century. Between 1961 and 2006 the state government purchased some 22,000 hectares of bushland, foreshore, and river frontage as public open space through a land tax imposed on all undeveloped land holdings (it has cost around A\$1.2 billion and although hugely successful in terms of the open space dividend it has been a largely unnoticed tax). A program called Bush Forever has identified additional land that should be protected for conservation in the city metropolitan area. The involvement of local communities in their management is critical to retaining biodiversity values. Since the city potentially has sufficient labor to weed and rehabilitate many degraded bush areas, bush regeneration has become a feature of urban parks rather than large rural parks.

The Australian Orchid Council works to save the many species of native orchids found in southwest Western Australia. In a recent exercise they were awarded a grant from a local utility to propagate six rare types of orchids and the associated, very specific fungi which each orchid needs to extract nutrients from the harsh sandy soil. Apart from storing genetic material, the project was able to take the six propagated species (together with their fungi) and scatter them around a number of Perth bush sites to ensure that they had sufficient range for survival. Perth's bush is thus acting as an urban ark (Heath 1999).

Perth has also played a role in protecting the region's native fauna. The world's first mammal species to be removed from the World Conservation Union (IUCN) list of threatened species—the woylie, a small marsupial—was brought back from the edge of extinction due to the work of scientists in Perth and its bioregion. Karakamia Wildlife Sanctuary on the outskirts of Perth is a private bush sanctuary run by the Australian Wildlife Conservancy. It has removed ferals through fencing and baiting, resulting in a return of native marsupials similar to their populations before settlement.

Finally, the World Wide Fund for Nature (WWF) has targeted the bioregion around Perth—dubbed the Southwest Australia Ecoregion—for a cooperative program of creating biodiversity partnerships between the city and its region.

Source: *World Wide Fund for Nature, www.worldwildlife.org/wildworld/profiles/terrestrial; www.wwf.org.au/publications /southwest-australia-ecoregion-jewel-booklet/*

Figure 3.2

Before (a) and after (b) rehabilitation of Clear Paddock Creek,
Sydney, Australia

Photos Peter Dixon

ing village agriculture, but it was simultaneously a project to protect genetic diversity. This approach could be applied in intensive urban agricultural programs anywhere.

Restoration work such as that done by land-care groups or friends of wildlife should be encouraged for its contribution to biodiversity conservation, and also for the education it provides and its community-building aspects. The Lady Bird Johnson Wildflower Center in Austin, Texas (see figure 3.1), serves all these functions. It restores native landscapes, demonstrates how to garden using native plants, and offers courses for the local community. Through its buildings (designed in the style of indigenous settlements), programs, and shop (which sells local products that celebrate the region's biodiversity), the Wildflower Center provides a strong sense of place and local identity.[9]

Strategy 5: Ecological Architecture and Infrastructure

The separation between the organic and inorganic has been very stark in most cities, with buildings and structures kept separate from greenery. Interest is now growing in how to integrate plants into the fabric of urban structures, as they are in natural ecosystems—plants growing on roofs and walls, for example, as well as inside. This greening of architecture can considerably ameliorate the heat-island effect, provide cooling to individual buildings, help in water recycling, and enhance air quality both inside and out. Making structures organic opens up the prospect of creating habitats to nurture urban biodiversity. Plants can include native and food-producing varieties. New South Wales government planner Chris Johnson (2003) outlines a range of approaches to greening the urban environment in his book *Greening Sydney*. Other texts that deal with this topic include *Ecological Design* by Van der Ryn and Cowan (1996), *Designer's Atlas of Sustainability* by

Figure 3.3

Green roof on Ford plant,
Dearborn, Michigan

© *Ford Photographic, Courtesy
William McDonough + Partners*

Ann Thorpe (2007), and *Resilience Thinking* by Brian Walker and David Salt (2006).

Infrastructure corridors, whether they be pipelines for gas and water or power lines for electricity, require space in a city. By careful design it is possible to turn such corridors into wildlife corridors through linkages into open space. Stormwater management has often taken urban creeks and turned them into concrete channels for managing flooding. New techniques of water-sensitive design that can slow down water as it crosses urban surfaces have allowed these channels to be rebuilt into aquatic ecosystems. The urban creek can become an important corridor for bird life in a city and a vehicle for bringing back aquatic species. *Restoring Streams in Cities* by Ann Riley (1998) outlines how to do this. Photos of a restored Clear Paddock Creek in Sydney, Australia, are shown in figure 3.2.

Integrating plants with tall buildings to create bioclimatically controlled structures has been pioneered by Malaysian architect Ken Yeang and by US architect William McDonough, who invented the modern "green roof." Green roofs are built ecosystems created on an impervious surface so that rainfall seeps slowly through the system rather than rushing off the hard surface. They are able to mitigate climate, and (of most relevance to this section) they can fit into the bioregional ecosystem, especially assisting bird life. Green roofs are now on over two hundred buildings in Chicago and on several large industrial complexes like The Gap in San Francisco and Ford Motors in Dearborn near Detroit, where birds are now laying eggs. Figure 3.3 shows the green roof on the Ford Motor plant.

Conclusions

Cities occupy only a small percentage of Earth's surface, but their impact on biodiversity extends to their bioregions and beyond (see the next chapter on ecological footprints). Biodiversity can be reclaimed and restored in a city's bioregion through new strategies involving cities in the preservation and linking of remnant reserves. Cities can lead in the development of new techniques that involve the urban population in creating reserve networks, greenways, trails, and "arks" to maintain regional biodiversity. Urban architecture and infrastructure, too, can be designed to support and enhance biodiversity. It is possible to begin to imagine ecological architecture emerging where the city is able to give back more to the natural ecosystem, in terms of biodiversity, than it takes.

4 | *Ecological Footprints*

PRINCIPLE 4
Enable communities to minimize their ecological footprints.

Elaboration: Cities consume significant quantities of resources and have a major impact on the environment, well beyond their borders. These unsustainable trends need to be substantially curbed and eventually reversed. One way of describing the impact of a city is to measure its ecological footprint. The ecological footprint of a city is a measure of the "load" on nature imposed by meeting the needs of its population. The footprint represents the land area necessary to sustain current levels of resource consumption and waste discharged by that population. Reducing the ecological footprint of a city is a positive contribution toward sustainability.

Like any living system, a community consumes material, water, and energy, processes them into usable forms, and generates wastes. This is the "metabolism" of the city, and making this metabolism more efficient is essential to reducing the city's ecological footprint. In reducing the footprint, problems should be solved locally where possible, rather than shifting them to other geographic locations or future generations.

Ecological Footprints and Biocapacity

Human health and survival depend on the goods and services provided by ecosystems. However, human activities are eroding the capacity of the land and sea to sustain us. The Living Planet Index, which indicates the state of the world's natural ecosystems, shows an overall decline since the 1970s. Indeed, some scientists argue that since the 1980s human demands on the biosphere have exceeded its regenerative capacity. Canadian researcher William Rees originated the concept of ecological footprint (Rees 1992), which he further developed with Mathis Wackernagel in their 1996 book *Our Ecological Footprint: Reducing Human Impact on the Earth*, to provide an indication of the human load on the biosphere.

Since then, the concept has attracted considerable interest, with many countries, cities, regions, and organizations undertaking ecological footprint analyses.

Chambers, Simmons, and Wackernagel define ecological footprint as "the land and water area that is required to support indefinitely the material standard of living of a given human population, using prevailing technology" (2000, 17). The Global Development Research Center defines the ecological footprint of a city as "the amount of land required to sustain its metabolism; that is, to provide the raw materials on which it feeds, and process the waste products it excretes."[1] Visually, it could be conceived of as the area that a glass dome over the city would have to cover in order to maintain the population at their current standard of living. As ecological footprints are calculated on year-specific data, they provide a snapshot of current impacts. Thus they are likely to vary over time, with changes in technology and variations in material flows (Best Foot Forward 2002).

To decide how sustainable a population is, human demand is compared with what is available—an area's biocapacity. Biocapacity refers to the amount of "nature" or biologically productive resources available to supply human demand. Original estimates of global biocapacity by Wackernagel and Rees (1996) excluded areas of low biological productivity such as deserts, ice caps, and open ocean. The remaining area is adjusted for biodiversity protection purposes and then divided by the global population of that year to estimate a per capita supply figure, sometimes called the average "earthshare" (Best Foot Forward 2002).

If all the biologically productive land and sea on Earth is divided by the global human population, the average amount available is 1.8 hectares per person (Wackernagel et al. 2002). However, this calculation does not take into account areas to be left for biodiversity protection, which is necessary to maintain other important ecological services and to allow life to evolve and unfold free from human control. The Brundtland Report (WCED 1987) called on the global community to protect 12 percent of biologically productive areas for the protection of the ten million other species with whom we share Earth. Employing this conservative figure, this leaves only 1.6 hectares per person (Wackernagel et al. 2002).

Wackernagel et al. (2002) have compared humanity's demand for natural capital with the Earth's biological productivity (biocapacity) since the 1960s. The results give evidence that human activities have been exceeding biocapacity since the 1980s—that is, we have been in a phase of "ecological overshoot" from the 1980s onward. According to Wackernagel et al. (2002), humanity's load has risen from 70 percent of biocapacity in 1961 to 120 percent by 1999.

The Living Planet Report 2006, prepared by the World Wide Fund for Nature (WWF), the Zoological Society of London (ZSL), and the Global Footprint Network, shows that the global ecological footprint was 14.1 billion global hectares in 2003 or 2.2 global hectares per capita. The biocapacity was 11.2 billion global hectares or 1.8 global hectares per capita, thus there is an overshoot of 2.9 billion hectares or 0.4 hectares per person. There are great disparities in ecological footprints across the globe.

Economically richer countries like the United Arab Emirates, the United States, Australia, and many western European countries have per capita ecofootprints of double the global average, or greater. Countries such as Costa Rica, Paraguay, Uzbekistan, Syria, and China had per capita footprints below the global average.

Calculating Footprints

Two main methods of calculating ecological footprints have emerged (Chambers, Simmons, and Wackernagel 2000):

- **Compound method**: This method is the original approach that was developed by Mathis Wackernagel and William Rees (1996) to measure the ecological footprints of nations (see box 4.1);
- **Component method**: This method was developed by Best Foot Forward[2] to measure the ecological footprint of regions.

Lewan and Simmons (2001) point out that the main distinction between the two methods is that they use different data sources. The compound method draws on national trade figures and energy budgets while the component method uses local data and life cycle studies. Otherwise the methods resemble each other.

WWF–UK has developed a guide for local governments—"Taking the First Step: A 'How To' Guide for Local Authorities" (2006)—that explains the concept of ecological footprint (how it can be calculated, how it links to the wider local government agenda) and provides some UK case studies.

Many online ecofootprint calculators have emerged for calculating individual, household, or organizational footprints, such as Redefining Progress's Ecological Footprint Quiz at http://www.earthday.net/footprint/index.asp.

In a partnership between the Royal Melbourne Institute of Technology, Redefining Progress, and EPA Victoria, calculators were formulated for personal, home, school, office, and events. These calculators apply life cycle data of individual consumption items along with Australian Bureau of Statistics data on national consumption patterns (http://www.epa.vic.gov.au/ecologicalfootprint/calculators/default.asp).

The basic steps involved in conducting an ecological footprint analysis for an organization or a city include the following:

1. Define objectives: consider the reasons for conducting an ecological footprint analysis.
2. Define system boundaries: define the scope of the analysis, deciding what to include and what to omit.
3. Identify available resources: as extensive data will need to be collected, sufficient funds are required for staff time.
4. Identify inputs and outputs for the defined system.

Box 4.1 **The Compound Methodology for Calculating Ecological Footprints**

The compound methodology was developed by Mathis Wackernagel. The first stage of this methodology involves analyzing the consumption levels of over fifty biotic resources including fruit, vegetables, pulses, meat, and dairy produce. Consumption is calculated by combining imports and production figures and subtracting exports. Consumption figures are translated into appropriated ecologically productive areas by dividing each consumption amount by its corresponding world average bioproductivity figure, which gives the amount of arable, pasture, or forest land and productive sea areas required to sustain this consumption. FAO estimates of global average yields are used.

The second stage calculates the energy balance, taking into account both locally generated energy and that embodied in over one hundred categories of traded goods. The amount of land required to sequester (absorb) carbon dioxide emissions is calculated to estimate the energy footprint. Alternatively, the land required to produce sufficient biofuels to replace fossil fuels can be used.

Finally, the figures for each category of land or sea—growing crops, grazing animals, harvesting timber, accommodating infrastructure, fishing, and carbon dioxide absorption—are per capita figures and these are multiplied by the nation's population to give the total ecological footprint for the category. Land category figures are also multiplied by "equivalence factors," which scale the area categories in proportion to their productivities.

The ecological footprint (the demand or load on nature) is compared with the biocapacity of the nation. This is calculated by adjusting the actual land use area by using a "yield factor" to link local productivity for each land category to the global average, thereby scaling the national areas in proportion to their actual productivities. The total area of bioproductive land is then decreased by 12 percent to allow for biodiversity protection.

Source: Chambers, Simmons, and Wackernagel 2000, 67

---

5. Identify major areas of leverage.
6. Develop dissemination strategies for results.
7. Set realistic targets.[3]

Ecological Footprint Studies

Ecological footprint analyses have been applied globally (Wackernagel et al. 2002)[4]; nationally in WWF's biennial Living Planet reports; to a growing number of cities such as Toronto, London (see box 4.2), and Santiago; and to individuals, households, and organizations.

The Living Planet Report 2002 shows that the total ecological footprint for high-income countries was 6.48 global hectares per person, compared with a figure of 0.83 for low-income countries. This highlights the significant gap between the demand placed on nature by wealthy citizens compared to the poor.

Box 4.2   **London's Ecological Footprint**

The City Limits project was undertaken to document London's resource flow in 2000, complete an ecological footprint analysis for the city, evaluate the ecological sustainability of a range of improvement scenarios, and make recommendations to improve data collection where necessary. The ecological footprint of Londoners was calculated to be 49 million global hectares (gha), which is 42 times the city's biocapacity and 293 times its geographical area—that is, twice the size of the United Kingdom. The ecological footprint per London resident was 6.63 gha, which compares with the UK average of 6.3 gha and the global "earthshare" of 2.18 gha.

Components of London's ecological footprint and a breakdown of its biocapacity are shown in the tables below.

Table 4.1   **Ecological Footprint (EF) of Londoners by Component (2000)**

Component	Total EF (gha)	EF per capita (gha)
Direct energy	5,073,000	0.69
Materials & waste	22,465,000	3.05
Food	20,685,000	2.8
Transport	2,503,000	0.34
Water	160,000	0.02
Built land	348,000	0.05
Subtotal	51,234,000	6.95
Tourism's EF	-2,367,000	-0.32
Total	**48,868,000**	**6.63**

Table 4.2   **Biocapacity of London (2000)**

Land type	Total biocapacity (gha)	Biocapacity per capita (gha)
Arable farmland	87,000	0.012
Managed grasslands	114,000	0.016
Forestry & woodlands	15,000	0.002
Urban	983,000	0.133
Seminatural vegetation	10,000	0.001
Inland water	100	0.00002
Sea	60	0.00001
Total	**1,210,000**	**0.16**

Source: Best Foot Forward 2002

Strengths and Weaknesses of the Ecological Footprint

The ecological footprint, like any measure, has its strengths and weaknesses. Inevitably, data are not always available and their accuracy varies, impacting on the footprint figures. In the compound method for national accounting, due to a lack of data, only embodied energy related to the use of nonrenewable resources is included, neglecting the impacts associated with mining, processing, and consumption of those resources (Wackernagel et al. 2002). Similarly, lack of data has meant that other factors such as the impacts of freshwater use, the use of biodiversity services, and the loss of biocapacity from the release of wastes other than carbon dioxide have been omitted. Thus, footprint results probably underestimate human demands on the biosphere.

For city calculations, the use of average productivity in ecofootprint calculations has been criticized as an unrealistic assumption about the homogeneity of the production of ecosystem services (Luck et al. 2001). Luck et al. completed an alternative analysis for twenty US cities. Spatial heterogeneity of resources was incorporated along with consideration of the interactions between ecosystem services such as water and food supply, and also of transportation. Dubbed the "Urban Funnel" method, this method produced very different results from the nonspatial calculations. Luck et al. argue that their model offers a "promising first step toward the design of conceptual and analytical models that incorporate the appropriation of external resources."

Newman (2006) criticized "ecological footprint" as being too broad in its concept to enable any policy responses. Lewan and Simmons (2001) in their review of European Union footprint studies show that few cities or regions even undertake biocapacity studies to see if there is "overshoot" in their footprint.

Despite these weaknesses, the ecological footprint is a useful measure, its power lying in "its ability to convey an easily understood message about the interaction between an urban system and its environment" (Luck et al. 2001, 792). Rees sums up the appeal of the ecological footprint concept:

> It is not just the "environment" that needs to be fixed, but humans ourselves—the environmental crisis is the product of gross human ecological dysfunction (or, if you prefer, of humanity's spectacular evolutionary success).
>
> One concept that seems to be effective in bringing this reality home is "ecological footprint" analysis . . . . It grabs attention because it focuses on personal consumption and translates it into a corresponding land area—something else that ordinary citizens can understand. (2003, 898)

Strategies for Reducing Ecological Footprints

Cities need to reduce their ecological footprints to match their bioregions. This is a powerful reality, whether cities do this through the formalized methods of ecological footprint or the detailed assessments of how each bioregional ecosystem can manage waste loads locally.

Strategy 1: Reducing Local Ecological Footprint through Ecosystem Assessments

Local ecological footprint analysis can show cities how they need to come into balance with the capacity of their bioregions to provide essential resources such as food, water, materials, energy, and other ecosystem services. This restores negative feedback loops—that is, the flow of information about impacts and the corresponding response to check the growth or patterns of consumption. Bioregional economies were discussed in chapter 2. Feedback loops are discussed further in the next chapter.

Detailed ecosystem assessments are the requisite first step in determining ecological footprints locally. These assessments can determine the biocapacity of rivers, groundwater, soils, and airsheds. Once the environmental science is completed, the process needs to shift to instituting management regimes that can accommodate human activity in a bioregion.

Such processes are best done in a collaborative way by involving people in the bioregion who use the ecosystem services (e.g., sailors and fishermen on rivers and estuaries). By including the values of these people in the assessment, it is possible to develop regulations that can minimize the flow of nutrients or wastes into the ecosystem. Environmental management regimes can then be implemented through inspection and monitoring of regulations. Catchment management processes involving voluntary landcare and water-care groups build on this approach.

This approach to ecosystem management by the use of regulation is valuable but limited. The opportunities for creating more market-oriented approaches have only recently begun to be examined. The first examples were in the management of sulfur emissions in urban catchments. By setting a cap to these emissions, industries could then trade their ability to reduce sulfur and make money from their improved environmental performance. The same approach is now being taken to carbon emissions through a cap-and-trade approach for global greenhouse emissions.

It is now time for cities to demonstrate how they can be carbon neutral or even carbon positive by reducing their fossil fuel use, adding renewables (e.g., by requiring them to be part of each new development), and by capturing CO_2 in carbon forests in their bioregion or a sister city bioregion. Malmo is the first city to declare itself carbon neutral and the UK has announced that all new land development from 2016 must be zero carbon.

Bioregional cap-and-trade markets can also be started for a range of potential pollutants such as nitrates, phosphates, or even salt, which is released from certain land uses. These management techniques are still in their early days of development but can be developed to enable cities to provide reduced impact or even positive benefit to their bioregion.

Strategy 2: Managing Population Growth

The global ecological footprint appears to increase with each new additional person to a city. One might therefore conclude that cities should be smaller in population. However, a range of studies have shown that bigger cities have less per capita resource use than smaller ones of the same density (Newman and Kenworthy 1999). This is probably due to the economies of scale involved in better public transport, better recycling, etc. Bigger cities also tend to be denser, and evidence strongly suggests that density enables cities to be more efficient with resources (Newman and Kenworthy 1999). The spread of cities out into rural areas is thus likely to leave a bigger ecological footprint.

At the same time, many cities are not able to cope with increased population loads due to the sheer pace of their growth. Many Third World megacities may exceed their bioregional capacities due to their size and their inability to put management systems in place (see the final chapter on governance). Thus growth-management techniques are being developed that can enable a city to control their rate of growth. For example, the city of Boulder, Colorado, allows only a certain number of development applications each year.

Globally, population control has been shown to relate to grassroots economic development and access of women to greater educational and employment opportunities. Cities are found to accelerate this process and to provide the kind of social change precursors for reduced family sizes (Newman 2006).

Furthermore, some cities have gone into population decline without seeing a reduction in ecological footprint from either a local or global perspective. The remaining residents continue to follow the same unsustainable patterns, and the corresponding economic decline hinders their ability to change. No new technology, no new transit systems, or new recycling/waste management systems can be implemented as budgets tighten and the whole mentality of the city deteriorates. Thus population decline by itself is no guarantee of greater sustainability. Using growth to decouple ecological footprints from economic consumption is the new agenda for cities. Managing population growth so that a city can cope and use the growth to bring about new sustainable infrastructure and innovation is likely to reduce ecological footprints.

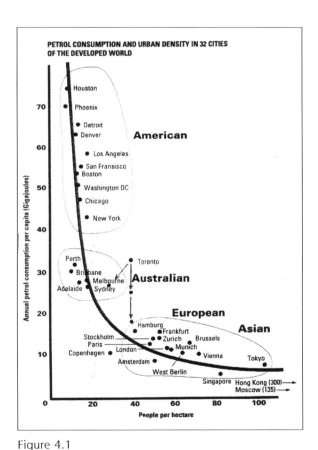

Figure 4.1

Gasoline consumption (footprint) gets bigger with the size of the urban area (the shoe).

Source: Newman and Kenworthy 1999.

Box 4.3 **Ecological Footprints: Making Tracks toward Sustainable Cities**

By Bill Rees

Have you ever asked yourself, "Just how much of the Earth is dedicated to sustaining just me?" Not many of us have—people today simply do not think of themselves as ecological entities. Urbanization, trade, and technology have alienated modern urbanites from the land.

The fact is, however, that the ecological ties that bind have never been stronger. High-income urban societies require a constant input of material and energy from nature not only to feed their citizens, but also to build and maintain their consumer and capital goods, the factories, buildings, machinery, service infrastructure—all the accoutrements of modern life.

The waste burden has, of course, increased proportionately. In fact, since the beginning of the industrial revolution, our industrial metabolism has grown so that it now far exceeds human biological demands on the ecosphere. As a result, popular illusions notwithstanding, people today make greater demands on nature's services than at any previous time in history.

Thirty years ago, American ecologist Eugene Odum wrote, "Great cities are planned and grow without any regard for the fact they are parasites on the countryside which must somehow supply food, water, air and degrade huge quantities of wastes." Indeed, with globalism and expanding trade, the material flows necessary to sustain our consumer lifestyles make direct and indirect claims on land and ecosystems all over the Earth.

Ecofootprint analysis enables us to estimate the extent of this global urban "parasitism."

Toward Urban Sustainability

For deep structural and ideological reasons, continued GDP growth in both the North and South remains virtually unchallenged as a goal of global sustainable development. Meanwhile, various studies suggest that even the present level of aggregate consumption exceeds the long-term human carrying capacity of the Earth.

Let's assume a near-doubling of population and a quadrupling of world output over the next fifty years (only 2–3 percent growth per year). Scientists agree that in these circumstances, resource use

Strategy 3: Managing City Sprawl

The size of a city's global (and local) ecological footprint will reflect demographic patterns and trends, consumption levels per capita, and the choice of technologies. In cities these patterns are shaped by urban form and function.

Any city, regardless of size, can reduce its ecological footprint in various ways by reducing sprawl through emphasizing redevelopment, a strategy that will reduce transport energy as well as other ecological footprint factors.

One clear example of cities' impact on the Earth is the relationship between their density and transport energy, a major factor in ecological footprint. This relationship is illustrated in figure 4.1. Besides higher gasoline consumption, low urban densities are associated with higher per capita water consumption, higher domestic energy use for heat-

Box 4.3 *(continued)*

and environmental impact per unit consumption in high-income countries must be reduced by up to 90 percent if we are to achieve sustainability fairly within the planet's ecological means.

Cities present both unique problems and opportunities in closing this sustainability gap. Perhaps the most significant problem is that cities typically disrupt the biogeochemical cycles of vital nutrients and other chemical resources. Removing people and livestock far from the land that supports them prevents the economic recycling of phosphorus, nitrogen, other nutrients, and organic matter back onto farm- and forest land. As a consequence, local, cyclically integrated ecological production systems have become global, horizontally disintegrated, throughput systems.

For example, instead of being returned to the land, Vancouver's daily appropriation of Saskatchewan mineral nutrients goes straight out to sea. Agricultural soils are therefore degraded (half the natural nutrients and organic matter from much of North America's once-rich prairie soils have been lost in a century of mechanized export agriculture), and we are forced to substitute non-renewable artificial fertilizer for the once renewable real thing. This further damages the soil and contaminates water supplies.

All this calls for much improved accounting for the hidden ecological costs of urbanization and a redefinition of economic efficiency. On the plus side, the sheer concentration of population and consumption gives cities considerable leverage in reducing their ecological footprints. Properly planned, urbanization can mean lower costs per capita of providing piped treated water, sewer systems, waste collection, and most other forms of infrastructure and public amenities; greater possibilities, and a greater range of options, for material recycling, re-use, remanufacturing, and the specialized skills and enterprises needed to make these things happen; high population densities which reduce the direct per capita demand for land; more opportunities through economies of scale, co-generation, and the use of waste process heat from industry or power plants, to reduce the per capita use of fossil fuel for space heating; great potential to reduce (mostly fossil) energy consumption by motor vehicles through walking, cycling, and public transit.

Source: Rees 2001

ing and cooling, and higher waste production due to the metabolism of the city's resource use. By taking out the population factor in both parameters in figure 4.1, you can see how a city's transport energy relates to its area: the bigger the shoe (city sprawl), the bigger the footprint.

Urban form and function need to be transformed to reduce the need for transportation and to restore sustainable patterns and processes. This idea of modeling the patterns and processes of cities on sustainable ecosystems will be taken up in the following chapter.

Strategy 4: Reducing Consumption Patterns

Consumption of resources is at the heart of the ecological footprint. Each unit of electricity or gas, each liter of fuel, each meal, each household appliance or piece of furniture is extracted or processed through the urban ecosystem and then must pass once again through the urban ecosystem as waste after its consumption. After basic needs are met, the reduction in things consumed needs to be on the agenda for each household in each city (Princen 2005).

Incorporating the cost of ecosystem services and impacts such as global warming in the price of goods and services is a first step toward reducing consumption in sensible ways. (Sustainable production and consumption will be discussed further in chapter 9.) But this step is not easy politically, so populations need to begin reducing their consumption voluntarily. The will and capacity to undertake changes in consumption and behavior to reduce ecological footprints depend on a number of factors that drive deeper into human motivations. These factors are functions of the dominant cultural worldview, community values and priorities, institutions, and flows of information. Issues of worldview were discussed in chapter 1 on developing a vision for sustainability. Institutional and educational issues will be taken up in chapters 6 to 8 and 10, covering sense of place, empowerment, partnerships, and governance.

In box 4.3, the originator of the ecological footprint concept, William Rees, presents his views on the forces driving the increase in urban ecological footprints and some of the ways in which we can begin to turn the situation around.

Conclusions

Cities need to reduce their ecological footprints. This is a fundamental part of sustainability. Whereas many of the other chapters focus on ways to accomplish this, the main recommendation of this chapter is that the ecological footprint or some equivalent way of auditing a city's consumption needs to be regularly calculated and used as an indicator of progress toward sustainability. The ecological footprint is mainly useful as a tool for seeing global impacts from resource consumption; thus, having a commitment to reduce a city's footprint is very useful. However local ecological footprints or impacts need to be managed through painstaking ecosystem assessments that can determine the biocapacity of rivers, groundwater, soils, and airsheds and through instituting management regimes to accommodate human activity in a bioregion. In the future it should be possible to significantly reduce ecological footprints through cities becoming the focus of ecologically regenerating architecture and infrastructure.

Modeling Cities on Ecosystems

PRINCIPLE 5

Build on the characteristics of ecosystems in the development and nurturing of healthy and sustainable cities.

Elaboration: Cities can become more sustainable by modeling urban processes on ecological principles of form and function, by which natural ecosystems operate.

The characteristics of ecosystems include diversity, adaptiveness, interconnectedness, resilience, regenerative capacity, and symbiosis. These characteristics can be incorporated in the development of strategies to make them more productive and regenerative, resulting in ecological, social, and economic benefits.

Applying a Systems Perspective

A systems perspective sees the world in a holistic way, looking at the relationships and interactions between parts, seeking to devise solutions that are integrative rather than merely reductionist. Reductionist solutions are powerful but often have unintended and unexpected impacts as they are focused on one part of the system only. Modernism, the dominant approach to professional life in this age of globalization, relies essentially on a reductionist approach to issues like energy, water, traffic, and housing. Many modernist solutions in these areas of urban life are now found to be unsustainable. A systems perspective may offer a better chance of finding ways to live sustainably.

As noted in chapter 3, the biosphere can be seen as a mosaic of ecosystems—or in de Duve's words, "multifactorial systems stitched together into intricate networks by dynamic interactions" among the species they contain. Ecosystems may be defined over a broad range of scales, from the community to the bioregional to the global, all "eventually closing into a single, gigantic web of formidable complexity" (de Duve 1995, 217).

Using a systems lens focuses our attention on relationships and processes (Capra

2005). Living systems are seen as nonlinear and as having emergent properties. Nonlinear processes may lead to a system suddenly shifting from one state into another. Emergent properties are properties that emerge through the interactions of the parts of a system, beyond the properties of individual components.

The strengths of the systems and ecosystem lens are thus:

- By focusing on relationships and processes, we gain a better understanding of emergent properties and the complexity of living systems.
- Context is recognized as important, as parts cannot be studied in isolation from the other parts of the system and from the wider systems within which they are embedded. Ecosystems are nested, as we are nested within ecosystems—systems within systems, wholes within wholes.

Cities as Ecosystems

In this chapter, the notion of cities as ecosystems will be discussed as a way to examine the dynamics of cities and the scope of urban challenges. The Cities as Sustainable Ecosystems (CASE) perspective takes this a step further, looking at the patterns and processes of sustainable ecosystems as the basis for a way forward. These patterns and processes are ones that cities need to emulate and/or restore to move toward sustainability, as Capra explains:

> To build a sustainable society for our children and future generations—the great challenge of our time—we need to fundamentally redesign many of our technologies and social institutions so as to bridge the wide gap between human design and the ecologically sustainable systems of nature. (2002)

Looking to living organisms and systems for sustainability strategies is the core theme of this chapter.

Cities are places where humans live, interacting with each other and with other living organisms as well as abiotic elements. Cities can be regarded as ecosystems like any other, as they are made up of interacting abiotic (nonliving) and biotic (living) components. There are new components such as buildings, transport, and sewerage infrastructure, formal parks and sporting grounds, and introduced plants and animals, but these components still fall within the biotic and abiotic categories that interact in a system.

Examining the city as an ecosystem enables flows of energy, materials, and information to be studied together, along with the interactions between human and nonhuman parts of the system (see Grimm et al. 2000). Furthermore, the dynamics and drivers of change in the system can be studied. The CASE approach is attracting increasing interest as an area of research. The Long-Term Ecological Research program in the United States has adopted two urban sites, Phoenix and Baltimore[1]; and the United Nations University/Institute of Advanced Studies has published several reports as part of its Urban Program, including "Defining an Ecosystem Approach to Urban Management and Policy Development."[2]

The CASE approach puts us humans firmly within the ecosystem, not apart from it as much modernist thinking does. Humans and our institutions are part of the system and interact with other parts. Every ecosystem on Earth includes humans or is impacted by human actions; in turn humans and our institutions are influenced by the ecological systems within which we function. Often research has focused on social problems or environmental problems separately. A systems perspective brings these concerns together.

The wisdom of people who use ecosystems as their model can provide guidance in transforming human processes in cities, as well as in changing urban form (the design of our food, water, and energy systems) and in restoring the capacity of urban bioregions to function sustainably. In this chapter, three models for how ecosystems can guide cities will be outlined:

1. The work of Bossel (1998) will be adapted and explored as a basis for understanding how sustainable ecosystems and sustainable socioecological systems work and how cities might be transformed into sustainable ecosystems. Bossel's work is based on a systems approach and provides high-level strategies for cities.
2. Ecosystem succession patterns are presented as a guide to how living systems change through time in their form and structure to optimize their use of energy, materials, and information. These patterns can then suggest how cities could similarly optimize their urban form and structure.
3. The way that cities throughout history have been shaped by the human ecology of travel-time budgets is used to show how cities work as a system of land uses dependent on different transport modes. City-shaping patterns can therefore be related to transportation priorities to give more specific planning direction on how sustainability can be achieved.

These three models are a nested set that moves from principles to practice. They are all based on an ecosystem perspective of how cities could work. The majority of the chapter will focus on the first model, as its discussion of the patterns and processes of sustainable ecosystems and indigenous cultures lays the foundation for more targeted approaches to achieving sustainability.

This chapter is presented in the spirit of Meadows, who offers these words of wisdom:

> The future cannot be predicted, but it can be envisioned and brought lovingly into being. . . . We can't surge forward with certainty into a world of no surprises, but we can expect surprises and learn from them and even profit from them. We can't impose our will upon a system. We can listen to what the system tells us and discover how its properties and our values can work together to bring forth something better than could be produced by our will alone. We can't control systems or figure them out. But we can dance with them! (2005, 195)

Model 1: Bossel's Systems Model of Sustainability

Bossel (1998) puts forward a definition of sustainability based on systems thinking. He defines any self-organizing system as sustainable or viable if all the system characteristics (or "orientors" as he calls them) are in a satisfactory state. Bossel states, "Obviously, the system equipped for securing better overall orientor satisfaction will have better fitness, and will therefore have a better chance for long-term survival or sustainability" (1998, 80). Drawing on Bossel's work, sustainable ecosystems can be characterized as ecosystems that are:

1. Healthy (effective)
2. Zero waste
3. Self-regulating
4. Resilient and self-renewing
5. Flexible

Bossel adds to these basic ecosystem characteristics some further human characteristics derived from the anthropology of traditional cultures and settlements. These will be added later to the model. The patterns and processes (strategies) of ecosystems that support these characteristics will be investigated below.

Sustainable ecosystems maintain their structure and function under conditions of normal variability. In the face of external or internal disturbance, the structure of the ecosystem may change and functioning may be disrupted, but the ecosystem will be able to restore healthy functioning to a level at which the new state of the system is as productive as before. However, as all ecosystems are nested within wider ecosystems (bioregions) up to the biosphere scale, the sustainability of an ecosystem is a function not only of its internal capacity, but the capacity of wider systems to sustain it. Systems are interdependent. For instance, a wetland cannot be sustained apart from the sustainability of its watershed. Sustainability operates at multiple spatial scales. Thus, sustainability refers to the capacity of a system to increase its likelihood of survival in the long term, but sustainability cannot ensure survival, especially if disturbances are completely outside the realm of a system's experience.

Characteristic 1: Healthy (Effective)

Ecosystems sustain themselves effectively and remain healthy by capturing and storing sufficient energy and matter to fulfill the needs of all the biotic participants. This is achieved in various ways: through meeting energy and matter needs in times of normal environmental fluctuations, and enhancing this capacity over time through biodiversity and coevolution.

Meeting Energy Needs

Ecosystems are either autotrophic or heterotrophic. Autotrophic ecosystems produce enough energy internally to meet ecosystem respiration needs through the actions of autotrophs (self-feeders). In most systems this is accomplished through green plants acting as solar energy collectors, converting sunlight to plant biomass. In a few systems, such as caves, the autotrophs capture energy through chemical processes. Food webs, whereby consumers or heterotrophs (other-feeders) consume autotrophs or other heterotrophs, provide the structure for the flow of energy through the system. Wind, water, and moving animals act as agents for the distribution of organic matter and thus energy through ecosystems (Lyle 1994, 26).

At each trophic level, energy losses occur through the production of waste heat during respiration, in line with the second law of thermodynamics. However, through the evolution of green plants to harness solar energy, ecosystems have tapped a regular, reliable, and ubiquitous energy source to sustain themselves and evolve, thus greatly enhancing their chances of sustainability. Additionally, ecosystems conserve energy requirements for movement by producers, consumers, and detritivores, along with other functional groups, being relatively close to each other ("proximity and functional matching") (Husar 1994, para. 10).

Heterotrophic systems do not capture sufficient energy through the work of internal autotrophs and so rely on inputs from other autotrophic systems. Lakes and rivers are seen as heterotrophic systems because they do not have sufficient plant biomass to match ecosystem respiration. However, fringing vegetation provides the necessary inputs. Thus, a heterotrophic system is more or less autotrophic when viewed as part of a wider system (an ecoregion or bioregion).

Meeting Matter Needs
All plants and animals need nutrients, which are the chemical elements or compounds needed to live, grow, and reproduce. Nutrients include carbon, oxygen, water, nitrogen, phosphorus, sulfur, and various trace elements—in total about thirty elements (Smil 1997, 8). These nutrients are available from the atmosphere, water bodies, or rocks and soil. Before the arrival of life, these elements cycled over vast time scales through geomorphic and geotectonic processes. In view of these slow cycles and the fact that the biosphere is a closed system, nutrients are in finite supply. Also relevant is the law of conservation of matter, which says that matter is neither created nor destroyed. Thus through respiration processes, organisms produce waste. Life has responded to this finite supply of accessible matter and the need to handle wastes with an innovative strategy: these nutrients are cycled continuously between living organisms and the air, water, and soil in what are termed biogeochemical cycles. Therefore, ecosystems, unlike organisms that are characterized by linear metabolism, are characterized by circular metabolism.

Biogeochemical cycles operate at different spatial and temporal scales, driven by the movement of water, wind, and animals. Global cycles involve the exchange of the gaseous elements of carbon, nitrogen, oxygen, and hydrogen between the air and biological organisms. As these elements are gaseous, transfers often occur over long distances. The hydrogen, oxygen, carbon, nitrogen, and sulfur cycles all operate relatively rapidly as they are mobile in their gaseous form. On the other hand, solid elements such as phosphorus, potassium, calcium, magnesium, copper, zinc, boron, chlorine, molybdenum, manganese, and iron cannot be transferred naturally over long distances, so they circulate in local and regional cycles (Krebs 1988).

Incoming solar energy and gravity drive these biogeochemical cycles either directly or indirectly. In some, such as the carbon cycle, living organisms are crucial, while in others, such as silicon, they are less critical. These cycles are shown in the Appendixes.

While nutrient cycling helps to maintain nutrients in ecosystems, they are still open systems, so nutrient losses through erosion by rain and wind and movement of animals need to be balanced by gains from rain, dust, litter, and soil and rock weathering, if ecosystem productivity is to be maintained (Krebs 1988; Boyden 1992). Vegetation plays a crucial role in maintaining stocks of nutrients in the system by inhibiting erosion processes.

Through integrative interactions, from predation on the one extreme to symbiosis on the other, living organisms gain their nutrient needs and provide food for others, so participating in nutrient cycling. Additionally, species or groups of species carry out various different roles in the system besides matter cycling and energy transfers, which support its overall functioning. These functional roles include pollination, seed distribution, opening of patches for reorganization, colonizing of patches, and altering water flows (Folke et al. 2002). Thus, at the ecosystem level, interactions between organisms tend to operate synergistically and therefore in symbiotic patterns (Peacock 1999).

Biodiversity and Coevolution

Some evidence suggests that biodiversity may enhance the long-term productivity of an ecosystem. Loreau (2000, 1), in a review of major theoretical advances in the area of biodiversity and ecosystem functioning, presents two types of biodiversity effects on ecosystem productivity in a fluctuating environment:

- A buffering effect: the variation in ecosystem productivity over time is reduced.
- A performance-enhancing effect: the mean of ecosystem productivity over time is enhanced.

Network coevolution, a new perspective based on recent theoretical advances in ecology (Yamamura, Yachi, and Higashi 2001), provides some evidence that diversity and coevolutionary processes may facilitate improvements in ecosystem productivity. According to Yamamura, this provides a basis for the role of species diversity at a trophic level as "*fuel* for ecosystem development" (981).

Characteristic 2: Zero Waste

Biogeochemical cycles are crucial in not only making nutrients available to living organisms but also processing wastes. In nature, waste materials are produced by living organisms (plants, animals, and people). These wastes include fecal materials, leaf litter, food wastes, and dead biomass. Detritivores have an important role in this process as the organisms that eat "waste" biological material, such as fallen leaves and trees, animal corpses, and feces, and thus make nutrients available again to producers and consumers. Thus, species depend on each other for food and for cleansing the system. In this way, organisms work together to make their environment hospitable for each other.

Plants and soil act as biological and physical filters to purify water and air. For example, in a forest ecosystem, the surface runoff has a low peak and extends over a longer period; hence solids are filtered from the water, and nutrients have a higher likelihood of being absorbed by plants. The soil in a forest ecosystem can provide additional purification processes. Soil bacteria will consume organic carbon and reduce biological oxygen demand (BOD). Soil minerals (particularly clay minerals) can absorb metals and phosphates. Plant roots take up nutrients released by bacterial decomposition from water percolating through the soil.

Characteristic 3: Self-Regulation

Feedback loops allow ecosystems to regulate themselves and maintain normal functioning, to reorganize themselves following a disturbance, and to facilitate evolutionary processes. A feedback loop is created when an organism acts in some way that generates an effect on its environment. The information that flows to the organism then discourages similar actions (negative feedback) or encourages similar actions (positive feedback) (Marten 2001). Close proximity and functional matching of organisms in ecosystems facilitates the flow of information to enable feedback loops to function (Husar 1994).

Negative feedback generates stability by keeping significant parts of the system within the limits needed for healthy functioning. It tends to organize and maintain the system around a particular state, an "attractor," even in the face of environmental change (Kay and Regier 2000, para. 1). Positive feedback, on the other hand, stimulates change when required (Marten 2001).

Negative feedback loops are crucial for keeping populations in check. Populations cannot keep growing indefinitely, as one or more factors will limit the number of organisms to a level called the "carrying capacity"—the size of the population that can be supported in the long term by the ecosystem. A negative feedback loop arises when population growth slows down as food supply (or some other requirement like nesting holes, light for photosynthesis, etc.) becomes exhausted or unavailable, waste builds up, or predator numbers rise. The population size of the species may fluctuate temporarily around the carrying-capacity level, which can vary temporally. A population can sometimes increase so quickly that it overshoots carrying capacity before negative feedback arrests the growth and brings the population size to below carrying capacity once more (Marten 2001).

Characteristic 4: Resilience and Self-Renewal

Stability and change in ecosystems is the subject of much ongoing debate in ecology. Wallington, Hobbes, and Moore (2005, 7) argue that "developments in ecological concepts and theories over the past few decades . . . indicate a radical shift in the way ecosystems and their components are viewed." The emerging view is that ecosystems are "complex and dynamic" and that structural change, including composition, tends to happen over time. This may include both slow change, as succession unfolds, and faster change, resulting from disturbance or episodic events. Thus, in any particular place, the structure and dynamics of an ecosystem depend on its history, including past disturbance and species arrivals and losses.

Sustainable ecosystems maintain their structure and function under conditions of normal variability. In the face of external or internal disturbance, the structure of the ecosystem may change and functioning may be disrupted, but the ecosystem will be able to restore functionality (Walker et al. 2002). Ecological resilience has emerged as an important term in the study of ecosystem change. Ecosystems may be able to exist in alternative "states" (Holling 1973, 1977 in Wallington, Hobbes, and Moore 2005, 4). Ecological resilience can be defined as "the capacity of a system to undergo disturbance and maintain its functions and controls, and may be measured by the magnitude of disturbance the system can tolerate and still persist" (Wallington, Hobbes, and Moore 2005, 4) Ecosystems need to respond effectively to disturbance, yet for many ecosystems, disturbance may be an integral and self-renewing process.

Resilience is enhanced through panarchy (patterns of nested adaptive cycles) and through diversity and ecological memory.

Panarchy

Since the 1960s, ecological theory has started to recognize that many ecosystems have evolved to undergo periodical disturbance in order to maintain "overall dynamic stability" (Holmgren 2002, 249). The disturbance may be an external pulse such as fire or a storm, or an internal one such as an insect outbreak. At the ecosystem level this disturbance may actually be beneficial. Typically, the system accumulates biomass slowly over a long period of time and then when the system is disturbed, biomass drops quickly, releasing nutrients for recycling.

Holling and Gunderson (2002, 101) have introduced the idea of the panarchy to describe this pattern of nested adaptive cycles:

> Sustainability is maintained by relationships among a nested set of adaptive cycles arranged as a dynamic hierarchy in space and time—the panarchy. The panarchy represents the dynamic interplay between processes and structures that sustains relationships on the one hand and accumulates potential on the other.

C. S. Holling first described the adaptive cycle as a process involving four stages, which incorporates the two stages of the classical succession cycle (see figure 5.1):

1. **Exploitation**: In the "birth" phase, pioneer and opportunist species proliferate, building up biomass and greater connectedness.
2. **Conservation**: In this climax phase, biological capital is stored and connectedness reaches its peak.
3. **Release**: This is the disturbance phase, which is usually short, causing the release of stored carbon and nutrients.

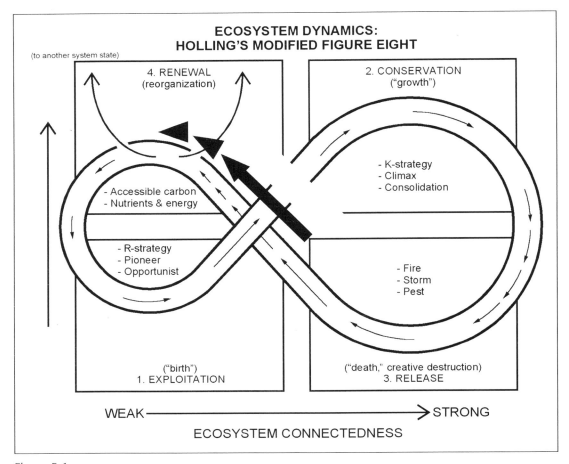

Figure 5.1

Ecosystem dynamics: Holling's modifed figure eight

4. **Renewal**: This is the phase of reorganization in which the system renews itself or flips to another state, which may be more or less productive and organized than the previous state. (Lister and Kay 1999; Holmgren 2002; Holling 1998)

Holling and Gunderson (2002) define connectedness as the level of internal control that a system can exercise over external variability. More connected systems are relatively resistant to external variability. Their internal processes exert a high degree of control, giving them a degree of "equilibrium stability" (50).

Holling (1998) points out that, during this four-phase figure-eight cycle, the flow of biological time is uneven. While the exploitation to conservation sequence is slow, the release stage is very rapid, and the system moves quickly through reorganization to the exploitation phase again. Connectedness and stability rise along with the slow accumulation of biomass and stored nutrients. Nutrient capital becomes bound more and more tightly, stopping other organisms from using the accumulated capital until, eventually, the system becomes so "overconnected that rapid change is triggered." The disturbance precipitates the release of stored capital and the breakdown of tight organization, allowing the system to reorganize and begin the cycle again. It is a process whereby "chaos emerges from order, and order emerges from chaos" (Holling 1998, para. 14).

During the reorganization phase, the system is characterized by weak connections, weak organization, and weak regulation. Consequently, this is the phase when the system is the most unpredictable. It is most vulnerable to erosion and the loss of accumulated nutrients and, consequently, to the possibility of shifting to a less productive state. It may also shift to a different, but possibly more productive, state if negative processes such as erosion are avoided. Positive feedback loops are crucial at this time.

Panarchy describes a pattern of adaptive cycles nested in space and time. The theory essentially says that the processes that build greater connectedness go hand in hand with the processes that disturb the system and stimulate it to release potential and to reorganize. These two opposing cycles exist as part of a whole, helping to build system resilience by creating ecological memory (see next section) and renewing the system through the release of stored nutrients. Strategies for building stability go hand in hand with strategies for breakdown and renewal, just as biosynthesis and biodegradation are part of organisms and the basis of everyday interactions between organisms. This dynamic pattern of renewal contributes to the overall resilience of ecosystems. The application of the concept of resilience to cities has attracted some controversy, which will be outlined later.

Diversity and Ecological Memory

In a major report titled "Resilience and Sustainable Development," Folke et al. (2002, 25) state, "Diversity plays a significant role in sustaining resilience in ecosystems." Functional redundancy and response diversity appear to be crucial. Functional redundancy refers to the presence of a number of species performing the same function. It provides "'biological insurance' against the disruptive effects of environmental fluctuations on ecosystem functioning" (Loreau 2000, 13). Within these functional groups, response diversity, whereby certain species will respond better to a disturbance and be able to sustain or restore a function, is also important (Folke et al. 2002).

Lister and Kay argue that directly following a disturbance is when biodiversity at various scales is crucial: "the abundance, distribution, and diversity of an ecosystem's structures (e.g., species) and functions (e.g., nutrient cycling) determine its ability to regenerate and reorganize itself, and its future pathway." Diversity provides the capacity for the ecosystem to regenerate to the same state or reorganize to a different state. They describe the role of biodiversity as:

analogous to a library of information (some recorded long ago, and some only now being written), that provides not only a wide range of possible pathways for the future development of life, but the library of learned repertoires for responding to environmental change and disturbance. (Lister and Kay 1999, 5)

Bengtsson et al. (2002) point out that the capacity for an ecosystem to reorganize after large-scale disturbances depends on its spatial resilience in the form of ecosystem memory. This ecosystem memory comprises the species, interactions, and structures that enable ecosystems to reorganize. These components may be found "within the disturbed patches as well as the surrounding landscape" (2002, 1). Following disturbance or alteration of environmental conditions in local systems, biodiversity in the surrounding landscape enables the suitable key species for ecosystem functioning to be recruited (Folke et al. 2002). In this way, ecological memory provides resilience across scales.

Different landscapes have different histories and, thus, different amounts of available ecological memory. Bengtsson et al. (2002, 7) argue that most ecosystems experience disturbance regimes at varying temporal and spatial scales, with natural disturbances usually being "pulse disturbances with a characteristic magnitude and frequency." In landscapes subject to minimal human impact, "the dynamics of the renewal cycles in different patches will usually be partly unsynchronized in time and space, leading to a mosaic of patches and successional stages" (Bengtsson et al. 2002, 9). Thus, panarchy leads to greater ecological memory in the landscape.

Characteristic 5: Flexibility

The network structure of ecosystems is decentralized, facilitating the flow of information necessary for the operation of positive feedback and flexible responses. According to Holling's adaptive cycle theory, connectedness can enhance stability, but overconnectedness (too many connections) can make a system rigid and prone to disturbance. Thus, periodic disturbance may also restore flexibility.

Clearly, nutrient cycles and energy flows through ecosystems, and the supporting functions, along with responses to disturbances, depend on living organisms "working together" through complex networks of relationships. Cooperation is being recognized as more important than competition in the self-organization of ecosystems. Capra (1996, 8) argues that partnership is a key feature of life and that self-organization is "a collective enterprise." Symbiotic patterns emerge at the ecosystem level.

Summary of Characteristics of Sustainable Ecosystems

Thus, the key structural and functional strategies that ecosystems use for sustaining themselves are:

- Harnessing a renewable, widely available energy source—the sun
- Being autotrophic (or regionally autotrophic)—capturing energy mostly internally through the photosynthetic processes of green plants

- Storing energy and materials through nutrient cycling, biomass accumulation, and erosion control
- Conserving energy through integration and adaptation to place
- Integrating functions
- Cycling matter to remove waste from the system and store nutrients and energy in the system
- Using feedback loops for self-regulation
- Building functional diversity
- Operating as panarchies (in nested adaptive cycles)
- Operating as networks
- Enhancing the system through cooperation and coevolution.

Table 5.1 shows a summary of these key strategies, grouped by the key characteristics of ecosystem sustainability to which they contribute. Most of these strategies operate at local scales. However, the cycling of matter, especially water and the flow of energy from autotrophs (producers) to heterotrophs (consumers), generally occurs over bioregional (ecoregional) scales, which link into global cycles.

Table 5.1 Characteristics and Strategies of Sustainable Ecosystems

Characteristics	Strategies
1. Healthy (Effective)	• Use of solar energy • Autotrophic or regionally autotrophic system • Conservation of energy through proximity • Cycling of matter • Integration of functions • Erosion control • Network coevolution
2. Zero Waste	• Cycling of matter • Filtration
3. Self-Regulation	• Negative feedback loops, facilitated by proximity and functional matching
4. Resilience and Self-Renewal	• Diversity • Panarchy (nested adaptive cycles); ecological memory • Positive feedback loops
5. Flexibility	• Networks

Source: Adapted from Bossel 1998.

Characteristics of Sustainable Societies

Sustainable socioecological systems as described by Bossel (1998) have all the above characteristics of ecosystems plus the following three additional characteristics based on study of traditional cultures and settlements:

6. Ethics based on strong emotional connections
7. Psychological fulfillment
8. Cooperative coexistence.

Ecosystems are characterized by abiotic and biotic components that form patterns and processes. Human social systems add extra dimensions to that equation. They include cultural, social, economic, and political structures and processes. By examining the patterns and processes (strategies) of indigenous cultures, as examples of sustainable socioecological systems, along with those sustainable ecosystems, we can discern how these systems meet their needs (characteristics) and sustain themselves.

It is important to note that drawing on the wisdom of indigenous and traditional societies does not mean that these societies were always socially and ecologically sustainable, or ideal. The strategies and characteristics discussed are generalizations, which certainly do not apply to every indigenous or traditional culture. Furthermore, while these cultures have much to teach us, unsustainable practices are also evident among these groups. Like all humans (and nonhuman animals), indigenous communities have impacted and shaped their environments—by hunting, by using fire, and through agricultural methods, for instance. But as Anderson argues, based on his research into resource management practices of traditional peoples, "No group, traditional or transformed, has a perfect relationship with its environment" (1996, 127). "However," he continues,

> all societies have something to teach. The great benefit of anthropology is that it can bring together the combined wisdom of people from all times and places. Today, we need all the wisdom we can get, and only by pooling a wide range of human experiences can we survive. (174–75)

Characteristic 6: Ethics Based on Strong Emotional Connections

Traditional and indigenous ethics and practices are sustained by felt connections that arise through continual, deep, and unmediated interactions with place, and by the stories, songs, and rituals that nurture these connections (Anderson 1996; Strang 1997; Abram 1997; Maybury-Lewis 1992; Turner 2005). These cultures focus on learning the story of the land and its patterns in order to relate to it properly and not harm the land (Kinsley 1995).

Anderson, in his book *Ecologies of the Heart: Emotion, Belief, and the Environment* (1996), finds importance in the fact that moral teachings of most indigenous and traditional societies incorporate a strong respect for the land and other living things, through powerful felt connections with the land and other beings:

> The common theme of all these traditional resource management ethics is not spiritual harmony with some disembodied and abstracted Nature, but actual personal and emotional involvement with the actual landscape and its nonhuman inhabitants. People interact with their surroundings. In all cultures, these surroundings become meaningful—not just as sources of food and shelter, but as sources of beauty, power, excitement, and other human values. In those cultures that endure and do not collapse, the meanings of nature are bound up in systems of respect and protection. Often, mutual obligations exist between people and the beings or forces they believe to exist in the wild. . . . (174)

Practices such as taboos and sacred groves provide powerful mechanisms for protecting species and habitats (Berkes and Holling 2002).

Generally, indigenous and traditional ethics are based on a view of the world as "somehow alive and animated by a single, unifying life force" (Knudtson and Suzuki 1992, 14). Humans are also seen as having responsibilities to look after the land and honor it:

> Native wisdom tends to assign human beings enormous responsibilities for sustaining harmonious relations within the whole natural world. . . .
>
> It regards the human obligation to maintain the balance and health of the natural world as a solemn spiritual duty that an individual must perform daily—not simply as admirable, abstract ethical imperatives that can be ignored as one chooses. The Native Mind emphasizes the need for reciprocity—for humans to express gratitude and make sacrifices routinely—to the natural world in return for the benefits they derive from it. (Knudtson and Suzuki 1992, 14)

Thus, traditional ethics (and the main world religions, as noted in chapter 1) are imbued with a respect and reverence for the land and other nonhuman beings.

Strong connections exist between members of indigenous/traditional cultural groups. Maybury-Lewis (1992, 87) argues that the "heart of the difference between the modern world and the traditional one is that in traditional societies people are a valuable resource and the interrelations between them are carefully tended; in modern society things are valuables and people are all too often treated as disposable." Ceremonial recognition of relationships is crucial, concludes Turner:

> Another significant concept is recognizing in ceremony—songs, rituals, dances, feasts—people's relationships with each other, across families, clans, communities, and generations, as well as with their other relatives—the animals, fish, trees, and all the other elements of creation. Implicit in this recognition is a sense of gratitude and appreciation for the gifts of the ocean, the land, and the ancestors. Ceremonies remind us of the importance of these connections and how critical they are to our survival and well-being. (2005, 231)

Characteristic 7: Psychological Fulfillment

Boyden (1992) derived his list of the universal health needs of humans, covered in chapter 1, from considering hunter-gatherer societies. It encompasses not only physical needs but also the less tangible, but nevertheless crucially important, psychological needs. The ways in which indigenous cultures meet these needs provide some guidance—again, not as examples of "perfect" societies but as common threads that could be revived in city communities.

Equitable, Cooperative Social Arrangements

Generally, traditional societies are relatively equitable and cooperative. Because communities tend to be small and tightly knit, food and materials are shared according to need. Economy arrangements are simple and directed to meeting needs. Traditional social arrangements may offer less freedom than those in modern societies but possibly a greater sense of security (Maybury-Lewis 1992). Optimizing freedom and cooperation is a key challenge for all societies.

Varied Activities for Creativity and Stimulation

Because they lack occupational specialism (except for age- and gender-based division of labor) and have plenty of time for pursuits besides obtaining food, members of hunter-gatherer societies engage in a wide variety of activities (Boyden 1992). These activities include ceremonies, rituals, making music, dancing, telling stories, and making artifacts such as spears, decorative ornaments, and message sticks.

A Sense of Meaning and Belonging through Traditions

Maybury-Lewis (1992) argues that people in tribal societies experience a sense of confidence that arises from feeling part of an endless flow that links their ancestors with their descendants (although this flow has in many instances been disrupted through colonialism). Art and stories are woven into the fabric of life that enable people to unify the cycle of birth and death.

Stories, songs, and language provide powerful tools to nourish connections between people and the land so that there is a sense of participation in a meaningful cosmos:

> Yet there remains another reason for the profound association between storytelling and the more-than-human terrain. It resides in the encompassing, enveloping wholeness of a story in relation to the characters that act and move within it. . . . we are situated in the land in much the same way that characters are situated in a story. Indeed, for the members of a deeply oral culture, this relation may be experienced as something more than a mere analogy: along with the other animals, the stones, the trees, and the clouds, we ourselves are characters within a huge story that is visibly unfolding all around us, participants within the vast imagination, or Dreaming, of the world. (Abram 1997, 163)

Characteristic 8: Cooperative Coexistence

While avoidance strategies may have been possible for much of human history, cooperation now is critical. The relationships among traditional cultures who could not avoid one another may shed some light on how cooperative coexistence might be achieved. Some key strategies could be the satisfaction of basic human needs, trading surpluses and exchanging gifts, and the development of cooperative alliances, like those developed between tribes in North America (Maybury-Lewis 1992).

Self-Regulating Communities of Place

Thayer points out that

> for most of our existence on earth, *Homo sapiens* banded together cooperatively to sustainably harvest the natural potentials of finite territories. Perception of the extent of the world and the size of its communities matched the ability of a particular group to derive livelihood from its world. Thus, the evolutionary survival of humanity has depended largely upon social cooperation in place. (2003, 55)

Communities grew their own food, tended animals, and lived in villages as small, cooperative settlements or as nomads following herds, harvesting wild crops, fishing, and hunting over territories based on systems of barter, reciprocity, and exchange of surpluses, or a combination of these strategies. Thus, they were communities of place, bioregional communities which survived by sustainable use of ecosystems.

Adaptive Learning and Environmental Feedback

Indigenous and traditional knowledge systems rely on adaptive learning practices of "learning by doing" and "the use of feedback from the environment to provide corrections for management practice" (Folke et al. 2002, 45). Knowledge is accumulated over generations of close interaction with the environment, and this knowledge is transmitted culturally, representing "institutional memory." Traditional communities have coevolved with their environment. Marten states that "centuries of trial-and-error cultural evolution have fine-tuned many aspects of traditional social systems to their environment" (2001, 97). Thus, their agricultural and harvesting practices over time matched ecological processes, supporting the regenerative capacities of ecosystems.

Research has shown that traditional societies appear to accept disturbances as intrinsic to ecosystem dynamics and so, instead of attempting to remove disturbances, they focus on managing the magnitude and frequency of the release phase of the adaptive cycle and rapidly moving into the renewal phase. In various ways, traditional societies help ecosystems to reorganize and recover, through maintaining and enhancing ecological memory (Berkes and Holling 2002).

Traditional management systems, according to Berkes and Holling (2002, 145), "interpret and respond to feedback" from ecosystems and include practices that copy disturbance at scales lower in the panarchy and those that sustain sources of renewal. These practices include the use of fire, small-scale clearing of patches, and pulse grazing, hunting, or fishing (in which periods of recovery punctuate land use). By mimicking small-scale natural disturbances, traditional societies build socioecological resilience, so enhancing the system's adaptive capacity to deal with larger-scale disturbances. Small-scale changes and careful observation of the impacts provide a basis for avoiding large-scale collapse of systems. This strategy, along with the decentralized structures, supports the resilience of such societies.

Summary of Characteristics of Sustainable Societies
The strategies for each of the characteristics of sustainable socioecological systems are summarized in table 5.2.

Bossel's Model Applied to CASE

In line with the previous discussion based on Bossel's work (1998), Cities as Sustainable Ecosystems can be seen as healthy (effective), zero waste, self-regulating, resilient, self-renewing, flexible, ethical, psychologically fulfilling, cooperative, and coexisting. The patterns and processes of sustainable ecosystems and sustainable socioecological systems provide us with ways to transform urban ecosystems toward sustainability. Changes need to occur to the patterns of movement of matter and energy within the city and its bioregion and, importantly, to the flow of information within the city and beyond—specifically, the restoration of feedback loops. This is the realm of cultural and social strategies.

City ecosystems are embedded in wider ecosystems, from the bioregional to the biosphere scale. CASE brings the focus back to the local and regional level so as to achieve sustainability at the global level. The strategies outlined in the previous sections provide a rich source of ideas for reshaping our cities. It is important to note that CASE aims to complement and sustain the natural processes provided by ecosystems (see table 3.1), by reshaping the patterns and processes of our cities—including urban form; design of infrastructure, architecture, and support systems; and institutions and social processes—to mimic and match sustainable patterns and processes in an integrated way.

The eight characteristics of Bossel's model are set out in table 5.3 with some of their implications for cities' social and institutional strategies and their urban form and infrastructure.

Nine possible strategies that seem to emerge from Bossel's model are elaborated below. They represent the kinds of strategies needed to create Cities as Sustainable Ecosystems.

1. Connective practices that nurture and sustain an ethic of care—for each other and for one's "life-place"

Table 5.2 **Characteristics and Strategies of Sustainable Societies**

Characteristics	Strategies
1. Healthy (Effective) 2. Zero Waste	• Renewable energy use • Low consumption and waste production • Local, needs-based, egalitarian economies • Maintenance of ecosystem functioning • Food production systems that incorporate strategies of sustainable ecosystems (e.g., diversity, nutrient cycling)
3. Self-Regulating	• Place-based communities allowing for self-regulation through closed feedback loops • Human population below carrying capacity
4. Resilient and Self-Renewing	• Adaptive learning • Democratic structures • Small communities with simple institutional structures • Maintenance of panarchies
5. Flexible	• Democratic, decentralized communities
6. Ethical	• Respect for land and people, sustained by strong emotional connections to place through continual engagement
7. Psychologically Fulfilling	• Equitable and cooperative social structures • Varied activities • Stories, rituals, and interaction with the land
8. Cooperative (Coexisting)	• Contentment through satisfaction of basic human needs • Cooperation and alliances • Gifts and trading of surpluses for peace initiatives

Source: Based on Bossel 1998

2. Visibility of the more-than-human world
3. Protection of cultural, economic, and ecological diversity
4. Local and bioregional economies of sustenance
5. Solar-based and ecological architecture
6. Sustainable design of support systems

Table 5.3 **Characteristics and Strategies for CASE**

Characteristics	Urban Social and Institutional Strategies
1. Healthy (Effective)	• Bioregional, needs-based economies • Local/bioregional self-sufficiency (food, water, and energy) • Promotion of conserver lifestyles by meeting needs with resource-intensive or nonmaterial satisfiers • Cooperative interactions • Stable populations
2. Zero Waste	• Conserver lifestyles—Reduce, Reuse, Recycle!
3. Self-Regulation	• Local and bioregional governance structures
4. Resilience and Self-Renewal	• Bioregional, place-based design • Local/bioregional economies • Polycentric institutions and adaptive management
5. Flexibility	• Civic participation • Partnerships and networks • Decentralized, polycentric structures • Place-based decision making (from regional down to precincts)
6. Ethics	• An ethic of care, nurtured through a process of reinhabitation
7. Psychological Fulfillment	• Cultivation of a sense of place through frequent, varied interactions with nature and bioregional celebrations • Meaningful livelihoods and flexible work patterns • Opportunities for creativity • Civic involvement in restoration activities, community service work, and community gardening
8. Cooperative (Coexistence)	• Peace initiatives and community development • Trade surpluses • Links between bioregions; global cooperation

Source: Based on Bossel 1998.

Urban Form and Infrastructure

- Sustainable agriculture; industrial ecology
- Walking-based cities with transit for energy efficiency
- Use of solar energy
- Compact urban form to minimize land use and maximize green space
- Protection and restoration of surrounding ecosystems through a system of static and dynamic reserves

- Closure of nutrient loops in food production
- Recycling of wastewater
- Closure of material loops in industrial systems
- Harnessing of waste heat
- Organic architecture to reduce heat-island effect
- Fuel conservation through walking and clean-energy transit

- Visibility of processes
- Integrated systems for water, energy, and food

- Compact buildings
- System of static and dynamic reserves, with reserves in city linked to bioregional system

- Polycentric urban design (linked ecovillages) with walkable centers

- Visibility of biodiversity and ecological processes in the city
- Walkable town centers

- Place-based design
- Compact urban design for easy access to activities

- Interregional linkages and biodiversity corridors

7. Polycentric institutions and adaptive management
8. Neighborhood and urban renewal
9. Cooperation through partnerships

Strategy 1: Connective Practices that Nurture and Sustain an Ethic of Care

Using the lessons from traditional societies, urban ethics needs to arise from direct engagement with the world and the use of stories, ceremony, and ritual. Ethics can be rediscovered from the deeper traditions of any place (Newman and Kenworthy 1999). To nurture such ethics and provide psychological fulfillment, cities should support practices that connect people to each other and their "life-places." This means fostering a positive relationship and commitment to place—"place attachment"—and a sense of belonging to one's human community and life-place—"community rootedness" (Beatley 2005, 30).

Thayer (2003, 3) argues that "the bioregion is emerging as the most logical locus and scale for sustainable, regenerative community to take root and to *take place*." Connectedness can serve to nourish our communities and life-places, but also ourselves, through a greater sense of belonging. It is crucial for building individual resiliency, especially in young people (Dent 2003). Connective practices can take the form of direct engagement, such as time spent outdoors in contemplation, gardening, walking, or doing restoration work individually or communally; or connectedness can take root through meaning-making practices such as festivals, celebrations, rituals, and the arts. The process of "reinhabitation" advocated by bioregionalists involves rebuilding this indigenous sense of connection to our bioregions, our life-places (Abram 1997).

As discussed earlier, stories, rituals, and other cultural practices served to connect people in indigenous societies with one another and the more-than-human world. Thus, art and creativity have a significant part to play in sustainability. These important aspects of human life have become the province of the "performer," and most people have become "spectators." In connecting art to sustainability, human experience is enriched too.

The design of public places can be critical to nurturing connective interactions. Many planners espouse the importance of walkable neighborhoods and pedestrianized spaces to facilitate these interactions (Newman and Kenworthy 1999; Newman 2007).

The process of engaging more with our local places and bioregions, and with each other, can nourish not only these places but also ourselves, through fostering a greater sense of belonging and community. Cultivating this sense of place is discussed further in chapter 6.

Strategy 2: Visibility of the More-than-Human World

The visibility of the more-than-human world and ecological processes is crucial to nurturing connections with the wider circle of life, as well as connecting us with the consequences of our activities, reawakening our appreciation of the flows of energy and materials that support us (Van der Ryn and Cowan 1996). This is one of the core principles of ecological design. Thus, urban environments can be redesigned to inform people about place and associated ecological processes, as Van der Ryn and Cowan suggest: "Weaving nature back into everyday life breaks down destructive dichotomies between the built world and wild nature" (163).

Visible flows of water need to be restored. Rather than using a conventional piped stormwater system, stormwater can be directed into swales and channels into gardens, or allowed to flow into constructed wetlands to purify the water for groundwater recharge before flowing into natural wetlands. Village Homes in Davis, California, holds 90 percent of stormwater runoff onsite through a system of swales and channels designed to drain water quickly or store it (Corbett, Corbett, and Thayer 2000). In Australia this approach, called water-sensitive urban design, is now becoming mandatory in some places. Wastewater recycling systems also can be made visible, as part of an integrated water management system at the neighborhood or community level (see chapter 9).

Food production in the city allows us to gain a greater appreciation of nutrient cycling and the role of diversity and cooperation in systems. Food production can occur at many levels: in buildings, in community gardens and city farms, and integrated into water purification systems (Hopkins 2000).

Box 5.1 **Water Recycling in Kolding, Denmark**

Perhaps the most spectacular of the Danish urban ecology projects is in the regional town of Kolding. Here a run-down inner-city block of some 145 apartments (in five-story traditional buildings) with an enclosed courtyard was transformed by a process that not only renewed the houses but created a beautiful water recycling system based on a "glass pyramid."

The wastewater from the complex is first treated by a small-scale primary and secondary waste treatment plant located underground. Then the water, which still contains some organic matter and most of its nutrients, is pumped to the glass pyramid using photovoltaic cells and a battery. Once in the pyramid, water passes into a series of ponds on the ground floor containing first algae, then plankton animals, and finally a fish pond complete with aquatic plants, which absorb much of the remaining material. Water is then pumped to the top of the pyramid where it trickles down over trays containing fifteen thousand plants that, when grown, are sold to a local nursery. The interior of the pyramid resembles an exotic greenhouse.

The water then passes out to a small wetland before it is allowed to run down a cascade to form a small creek through the common gardens and a children's water playground. This water is mixed with rainwater collected from the roofs and stored in an underground cistern. After it has been aerated through the cascade and creek, this water is used for toilets and washing machines in the buildings. Any excess water is percolated to the groundwater.

The complex also has solarized buildings, a solid-waste recycling center complete with a worm composting unit (which also takes sludge from the treatment process), and a community garden. The project was a partnership between the community and the local government, whose engineers and planners are keen to make Kolding a global leader in city sustainability.

Source: Based on Newman and Kenworthy 1999

Ancient Chinese and European cities incorporated green spaces in addition to being close to agricultural areas and forests. Chinese cities incorporated symbols of nature and were seen as part of a unity. Interestingly, Middle Eastern cities, being in arid regions, tended to have little internal green space but were surrounded by agricultural land. Mumford (1961) talks of the rise of the sky gods perhaps initiating a separation from nature. Certainly the walls and fortresses surrounding early cities became more common as their power increased. These fortifications may have fostered a sense of "the other" and a separation from the outside world. Surroundings that emphasize the human and exclude the wider circle of life may promote and reinforce this disconnection. Thus, the presence of open spaces in the city, as well as linkages to wild places outside the city, are vital.

Strategy 3: Protecting Cultural, Economic, and Ecological Diversity

Cultural, economic, and ecological diversity are valuable in themselves, but they are also crucial for the resilience of urban systems. Ecosystems provide valuable services that cannot be replaced through technology or even careful design. Indigenous cultures need to be recognized as a source of wisdom for sustainable ways of living, and these cultures and traditional ways should be safeguarded. The historic built environment is part of cultural diversity as well. Economic diversity provides options for change and ensures resilience in the urban system, as it copes with economic cycles of boom and bust that affect various economic functions and niches.

To protect ecological diversity, a linked network of representative reserves in the city and throughout the bioregion should be created, along with programs to enhance the diversity of gardens and support ecosystems in the bioregion (see chapter 3). These need to be sufficient to maintain vital ecological services, locally and bioregionally. For example, the city and bioregion need to be planned or transformed in observance of natural hydrological patterns. This approach would integrate existing reserves and national parks with managed landscapes, recognizing their interdependence.

Protecting and enhancing economic diversity in cities is discussed by Jacobs (1984) and builds on the same principle as biological diversity. Putnam (1993) has a similar approach to social diversity in cities and shows how it links back to economic and environmental diversity.

Strategy 4: Local and Bioregional Economies of Sustenance

In contrast to villages, cities have long been part of a global economy through their commerce with trading partners outside their bioregion. The industrial and modernist cities extended this to the large-scale exchange of goods, resulting in substantial resource flows. Increasingly, the economy of cities is based on information transactions, which offers cities the potential to reduce these physical resource flows and become more self-sufficient in the bioregion. As discussed previously, most ecosystems are essentially autotrophic. It is possible for cities to develop this characteristic through new solar technologies on every rooftop (as envisioned by McDonough and Braungart 2002). Cities should take their cue from indigenous cultures, who secured their energy needs locally and bioregionally, by employing a similar combination of rooftop solar and bioregional solar energy sources. Proximity of sources of sustenance cuts down on the energy required to transport them, and facilitates feedback loops. Thus, as argued by Berg (1992), cities need to be reconceived more as part of their bioregions, setting the context for sustainability and greater self-sufficiency. Basic human survival needs for food, energy, and water should fit the capacity of the bioregion to provide these resources. As Berry puts it,

> The only sustainable city . . . is a city in balance with its countryside: a city,
> that is, that would live off the net ecological income of its supporting region,
> paying as it goes all its ecological and human debts. (2000, para. 6)

This ecological balance was a key characteristic of early cities before the advent of fossil fuel use and motorized transportation.

One of the biggest problems with modern cities is the hidden nature of their impact. Through the separation of city dwellers from the impact of their activities, and a lack of connection with the wider circle of life, negative feedback loops have been disrupted. Thus, our consumption needs should be met as close to the point of production as possible in order to restore feedback loops that couple human needs to ecosystem capacity to deliver those needs. Ecological economist Herman Daly advocates keeping economic activities within the boundaries and limitations of ecosystems through bioregional economies. While acknowledging the merits of trade and commerce, Daly (1997) regards extensive trading activity in the context of globalization as problematic, as it is likely to lead to the overuse

---

Box 5.2 **The Garden City**

At the end of the nineteenth century, Ebenezer Howard put forward the idea of the Garden City (Howard 1965), which represents an important early attempt to reconnect city and country. The Garden City was envisaged as occupying 1,000 acres of land with around 30,000 inhabitants and surrounded by a greenbelt of about 5,000 acres. At the center of the city, Howard proposed a garden surrounded by important public buildings such as the town hall, the main concert hall, theater, library, and hospital, and encircled by further public parklands. Beyond this were compact housing areas (above present European levels and more than four times US and Australian levels) set in spacious grounds. Factories, warehouses, timber yards, dairies, and other production infrastructure were to be sited on the edge of the city, fronting onto a railway that connected to the main line leading to distant markets. Organic wastes from the city were to be used on the farms in the greenbelt. Pale copies of this vision were built into Garden Suburbs, which merely became car-dependent appendages to cities.

of natural resources beyond their capacity to regenerate and provide long-term service. One early attempt to reconnect city and country was proposed by Ebenezer Howard in the late nineteenth century in the form of the Garden City (see box 5.2).

Clearly, the closer the production of food to its consumption the better and the less energy required to transport it. Small-scale urban or peri-urban agriculture needs to be promoted. According to Hopkins (2000), biointensive gardening developed in the United States has recorded yields some two to sixteen times higher than commercial mechanized levels. However, as Hopkins admits, biointensive gardening is probably not sufficient to meet the needs of all city inhabitants. He suggests several ways to build links between the city and rural areas, including community-supported agriculture, farmers' markets, and consumer cooperatives, as outlined in chapter 2.

Reducing the use of resources is important to reduce pressure on ecosystems. Applying Max-Neef's analysis, we need to imagine different ways of meeting our needs, choosing less resource-intensive satisfiers. In developed cities, where per capita consumption levels are high, as mentioned in the Earth Charter (see chapter 1), the emphasis should shift away from consumption of goods to meet nonsubsistence needs to a greater focus on ways of being. Consumerism often acts as a substitute for real engagement with the world. The strategies discussed thus far in this chapter—processes of reinhabitation, a greater emphasis on community, and the visibility of the more-than-human world—could help counteract this.

Regionalization and localization of economies will bring power back to local and regional communities, thus facilitating cooperation, greater equity, and the opportunity to take responsibility for the health of bioregions.

Strategy 5: Solar-Based and Ecological Architecture

Cities are heavily reliant on fossil fuels. Energy needs can be increasingly met through harnessing solar energy (sunlight, wind, biofuels), or other local renewable sources such as geothermal or hydroelectric. Solar energy is renewable but finite, so energy conservation is still necessary. Energy conservation needs to be encouraged through passive solar design of buildings, use of low embodied energy materials, and energy-efficient appliances. The autotrophic cities outlined in chapter 2 are the models that show us how solar cities can work.

Peter Droege's *Renewable City* sets out a vision for the future city that is based on decentralized renewable energy sources linked together by a grid network utilizing the smart technology of control systems (Droege, 2007). This combination of IT with ET (information technology with environmental techonology) is the core infrastructure for future sustainable cities.

Architects such as Gaudi and Frank Lloyd Wright were early exponents of an architecture shaped and inspired by patterns observed in nature (Wines 2000). Gaudi modeled his structural systems in buildings on the intricate patterns of leaves, flower stems, and tree trunks, while Frank Lloyd Wright observed "soil erosion, rock formations, and climatic influences" to shape his designs and establish a connection between these processes and the built form (Wines 2000, 234). Ecological architecture, in contrast to conventional architecture that creates a separation between living and nonliving realms, seeks to build connections and integrate the two realms. Christopher Alexander (1979, 1987), in his books on pattern language, has extended this idea to show how organic patterns can help create more human- and community-oriented places as well.

Twenty-first-century architecture can be just as exciting and interesting if it is able to include ecological design at its foundation. McDonough (1992) developed the Hannover Principles (box 5.3), which spell out the philosophy behind design for sustainability, and the

---

Box 5.3 **The Hannover Principles of Design for Sustainability**

1. Insist on rights of humanity and nature to coexist in a healthy, supportive, diverse, and sustainable condition.
2. Recognize interdependence. The elements of human design interact with and depend upon the natural world, with broad and diverse implications at every scale. Expand design considerations to recognizing even distant effects.
3. Respect relationships between spirit and matter. Consider all aspects of human settlement including community, dwelling, industry, and trade in terms of existing and evolving connections between spiritual and material consciousness.
4. Accept responsibility for the consequences of design decisions upon human well-being, the viability of natural systems, and their right to coexist.
5. Create safe objects of long-term value. Do not burden future generations with requirements for maintenance or vigilant administration of potential danger due to the careless creation of products, processes, or standards.
6. Eliminate the concept of waste. Evaluate and optimize the full life cycle of products and processes, to approach the state of natural systems, in which there is no waste.
7 Rely on natural energy flows. Human designs should, like the living world, derive their creative forces from perpetual solar income. Incorporate this energy efficiently and safely for responsible use.
8. Understand the limitations of design. No human creation lasts forever and design does not solve all problems. Those who create and plan should practice humility in the face of nature. Treat nature as a model and mentor, not as an inconvenience to be evaded or controlled.
9. Seek constant improvement by the sharing of knowledge. Encourage direct and open communication between colleagues, patrons, manufacturers, and users to link long-term sustainable considerations with ethical responsibility, and reestablish the integral relationship between natural processes and human activity.

The Hannover Principles should be seen as a living document committed to the transformation and growth in the understanding of our interdependence with nature, so that they may adapt as our knowledge of the world evolves.

Source: McDonough 1992

Figure 5.2

The office building as a tree. Bill McDonough's concept of an ecological office has a green roof and a green wall on the shady side, like moss, with PV cells on the sunny side to make electricity.

Photo Bill McDonough

green buildings and green cities he has built since show it in practice. In particular he has demonstrated how a "photosynthetic roof" using either PV cells or growing plants can help a building be autotrophic, solar, and ecological in its architecture.

Strategy 6: Sustainable Design of Support Systems

Fresh air, food, and water, along with energy and shelter, are vital for human survival. All are obtained from ecosystems, either directly from natural ecosystems or from human-designed and managed ecosystems. Human-designed ecosystems still operate within a wider bioregion and, ultimately, the biosphere. Thus, they depend on the health of these natural systems to provide broader-scale processes such as energy capture, nutrient cycling, and the purification of water and air. The protection of biodiversity, then, is crucial.

Human-designed support systems—food production, energy production, water and wastewater treatment, transportation, and industrial systems—need to be transformed to attain the characteristics of sustainable ecosystems; in other words, they should be healthy, zero waste, self-regulating, resilient, flexible, and self-renewing. They also need to incorporate the strategies used by ecosystems and traditional cultures, discussed earlier, which include:

- Using sustainable energy sources, namely solar energy
- Closing material cycles
- Restoring feedback loops
- Building diversity
- Integrating functions
- Developing decentralized networks
- Applying cooperative approaches and looking for synergies
- Working with natural disturbance patterns and small-scale renewal processes

Currently, as Girardet (1992, 2001) points out, most cities are linear metabolic systems in which resources flow in and wastes flow out, unlike natural ecosystems in which resources are cycled in the system. Thus, cities need to close material cycles and adopt a more circular metabolism with the recycling of paper, glass, metals, and plastics, the treatment and reuse of wastewater, and the composting of organic wastes on local farm-land (see figure 5.3). For cities to be more autotrophic within their bioregions, their inputs and outputs should more closely match bioregional capacities. That is, more inputs should be gained locally and bioregionally, and wastes should be recycled at the local and bioregional scales.

In sustainable ecosystems, functions are integrated and proximal over local or biore-gional scales. The principles of ecological design, biomimicry, permaculture, and regen-erative design are all useful in this area. In industrial systems, there is considerable scope for different industries to cooperate, using wastes produced by one industrial process as the input for another process. These support systems need to be woven into the urban fabric and the wider bioregion. The emphasis needs to be more on localized rather than on centralized solutions—on solutions that reflect the characteristics of place such as water-sensitive urban design (see chapter 6).

Natural purification processes and biogeochemical cycles provide a model for manag-ing wastewater and stormwater (Ho 2002). Discharge of wastewater and stormwater beyond the natural purification capacity of an environment will result in the accumula-tion of organic materials (carbon), nitrogen, phosphorus, or other pollutants. Accumulation of nitrogen and phosphorus will lead to a high oxygen demand that, in turn, creates eutrophication of waters and consequent death of organisms.

The nitrogen and phosphorus in wastewater come from food consumed by humans. Fertilizers containing nitrogen and phosphorus are usually used to grow this food.

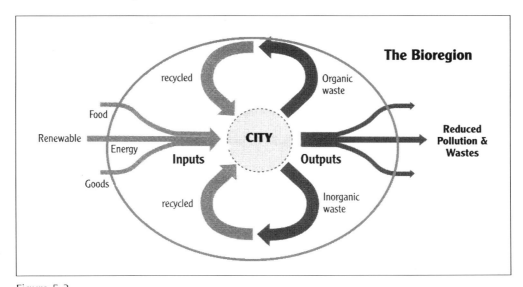

Figure 5.3

From linear to circular metabolism within the bioregion

Adapted from Rodgers 1997, based on Girardet 1992

These fertilizers are manufactured chemically, from atmospheric nitrogen and from phosphate rock. If the flow of nitrogen and phosphorus is one-way, from the atmosphere (for nitrogen) or rock mine (for phosphorus) into the river, depletion of a resource (mined phosphate rock) will occur in the long term, along with accumulation in and pollution of the river or estuary.

One way of managing the wastewater sustainably is by closing the material cycles locally. Nutrients in the wastewater can be reused to grow food. This approach reduces the need for chemical fertilizers and the amount of nutrients discharged into the river. The problems of resource depletion and water pollution are overcome by closing the material cycles. There's also a need to treat industrial wastewaters containing toxic substances separately, and not to mix industrial wastewaters with domestic wastewater. In addition, stormwater should be collected and treated separately, and infiltrated locally.

Food Supply in a Bioregional World

> In a bioregional world we would see much more of our needs met through a local and regional food supply system based on low input and organic agriculture. The food would be produced on local, efficient, mixed farms, producing a diversity of crops, and where animal manure can be used as fertilizer for crops. The food produced on these farms would be delivered through efficient regional packhouses to regional distribution centers for delivery to supermarkets, or direct supply to consumers. Composted food waste and sewage would be returned to these same farms to create a closed-loop cycle. (Desai and Riddlestone 2002, 68)

Food consumption and production need to be integrated, and a partnership approach should be encouraged so that production processes are driven by genuine human needs. Cities provide an ideal opportunity for developing small-scale intensive food production systems on cleared land and rooftops, which are integrated with stormwater and wastewater treatment, water harvesting, and renewable energy production and storage. With the high concentration of people, the opportunities for integrated research in cities are considerable. This will be discussed further in chapters 8 (Partnerships) and 9 (Sustainable Production and Consumption).

Strategy 7: Polycentric Institutions and Adaptive Management

Folke et al. (2002) argue that the challenge now, as the scale of human-induced change has increased, is to create institutional structures that fit ecological and social processes occurring at various temporal and spatial scales, and that address linkages across scales. These polycentric institutional structures facilitate diverse decision-making processes, which enable ideas to be tested at different scales, and they facilitate institutional dynamics that support adaptive management. Chapter 10 examines such governance at local and bioregional scales, as well as how links to global-scale governance can ensure that planetary processes are not neglected.

Adaptive management is an approach that recognizes the unpredictability of system dynamics and the ineffectiveness of top-down approaches. It brings together the methods of science, which focus on developing hypotheses and theories, with indigenous methods of "learning by doing" and responding to feedback, to build resilience of the socioecological system (Folke et al. 2002). By responding to changes and using feedback, adaptive management facilitates institutional and social learning, thereby adding to institutional and social memory.

Institutional memory provides a toolkit of possible responses for use in times of crisis or change (Bengtsson et al. 2002). Collaboration between experts and community should be encouraged, informing both and providing for a diversity of approaches. Safeguarding the knowledge of indigenous peoples is especially crucial. Alongside this is the need to monitor change. Folke et al. (2002, 10) recommend that indicators be developed to monitor "gradual change and early warning signals of loss of ecological resilience and possible threshold effects."

While adaptive management has arisen to address socioecological resilience, it appears to be a good model for facilitating social resilience, as it emphasizes inclusiveness, knowledge sharing, new approaches, and feedback response.

Civic participation in governance is vital to closing feedback loops, promoting, as it does, the free flow of information and interchange of ideas. It also supports resilience and flexibility in decision making. However, participation is also about engagement with our human communities and the more-than-human world, and, in this sense, it fulfills an important psychological need (Max-Neef 1992).

Empowerment and participation will be discussed further in chapter 7.

Strategy 8: Neighborhood and Urban Renewal

Just as ecosystems use small-scale disturbance for regeneration, cities could apply this approach through neighborhood renewal. At the neighborhood level, people can work together to reconnect with each other, restore public spaces, and work to make ecological processes visible and viable again. Voluntary replanting groups and recycling centers can form the beginning of such processes. Meaningful livelihoods can be created at this scale by developing home-based and local businesses that are part of a community economy or an ecovillage as discussed in chapter 2.

The resilience concept applies best to the scale of the neighborhood and, to some extent, to the economic character of a city. Old industrial centers like Pittsburgh, Manchester (England), and Melbourne have renewed themselves and facilitated new knowledge-based industries that have remade their cities. However, some economists (and ecologists) have extended this idea to suggest that cities do not need to plan for resilience, as the market will always enable other options to emerge. This has not always happened, as evidenced by Mayan, Easter Island, and other ancient settlements that suffered decline (Diamond, 2005).

To treat lightly such threats as the looming peak in world oil production, climate change, or bioregional pollution, and suggest that market-driven resilience will solve them is a fundamental denial of the other ecosystem principles, which suggest that cities should take action and plan for sustainability. In this way, humans contribute to system resilience, allowing for renewal and regeneration rather than shifting to another state less favorable to life.

Strategy 9: Fostering Cooperation through Partnerships
Partnerships are fundamental to how ecosystems and traditional settlements work. They enable the city to perform its social and economic functions and to work within its bioregional biocapacity. They can generate potent synergies for innovative change, including those needed for sustainability. These partnerships can work at all scales just as ecosystems do. Partnerships within the bioregion are a critical dimension outlined in this book. At the global scale, cities can partner through programs such as Cities for Climate Protection and the Water Challenge, both sponsored by the International Council for Local Environmental Initiatives (ICLEI). Partnerships will be discussed further in chapter 8.

The partnership between humans and the more-than-human world can be transformed to do less harm and more actively work with the rest of life in a mutually supportive way. Following the cooperative model seen in natural ecosystems and sustainable socioecological systems, human designs can be transformed to nourish not only human needs but also other life, as McDonough and Braungart point out:

> Natural systems take from their environment, but they also give something back. The cherry tree drops its leaves while it cycles water and makes oxygen; the ant community redistributes the nutrients throughout the soil. We can follow their cue to create a more inspiring engagement—a partnership—with nature. We can build factories whose products and by-products nourish the ecosystem with biodegradable material and recirculate technical materials instead of dumping, burning, or burying them. We can design systems that regulate themselves. Instead of using nature as a mere tool for human purposes, we can strive to become tools of nature who serve its agenda too. We can celebrate the fecundity of the world, instead of perpetuating a way of thinking and making that eliminates it. (2002, 155–56)

Thus, human activities need not be characterized primarily as taking resources for human needs, but also as contributing to the wider circle of life. Cities can help sustain and enrich our human and more-than-human communities in our bioregions and beyond.

Model 2: Ecosystem Succession Principles for City Form and Structure

Newman (1975) has created a model of how cities can learn from ecosystems to change their form and structure over time, based on ecosystem succession theory. He argues that the processes of succession observed in ecosystems after a disturbance, such as a fire or clearance, suggest how a city can become more effective in terms of its economic diversity, resource and information flows, and use of space; how its community can grow its social capital in terms of diversity and interconnection (networks); and how its environmental controls and governance can improve. More recent understandings of ecosystems indicate that they undergo disturbance at times to renew themselves and enable invigoration; then the process of succession begins again (panarchies). Similarly, in cities, the revitalization of older areas disturbed by a loss of economic function or the decay of buildings may enable a new phase in city development to occur that can utilize new technologies and create new urban options.

The model offers strategies in the following areas:

- **Energy and materials**: Pioneer ecosystems grow rapidly in energy flow, then stabilize, and materials become more and more tightly linked and conserved as they mature. The urban response would be to shift from growth in energy usage to energy efficiency, and from one-way flows of waste to recycling as the city matures.
- **Land and structures**: Pioneer ecosystems grow from low, dispersed structures to compact, mixed, diverse structures. Thus, cities need to move from a dispersed form to a structured, diverse, compact form.
- **Information**: Pioneer ecosystems grow rapidly from monocultures with few niches and mostly generalist species to a diverse interconnected system with much more complexity. Thus, cities need to shift from monocultures to networks of social capital and a diverse economy.
- **Control/governance**: Pioneer ecosystems grow from high resource vulnerability and system instability to greater internal control and system stability. Similarly, cities need to move from instability and resource vulnerability to effective governance and system stability.

Table 5.4 provides an additional summary. This model enables us to see that energy and materials growth can be decoupled from economic growth in cities, but only if the city is structured differently and is providing more extensive and diverse social and economic networks, information links, and effective governance. Further policy directions are illuminated in the third model.

Reshaping cities to achieve sustainability is a big challenge. Some solutions are provided by considering how ecosystems are reshaped by succession processes, as outlined in model 2. The differences between young and mature ecosystems offer some idea as to why cities should change. Whereas modern urban ecosystems are caught largely in the exploitation phase of the adaptive cycle, cities with sustainable socioecological systems would move quickly toward the conservation phase, while retaining flexibility to undertake renewal processes effectively. The key is to incorporate these characteristics into urban ecosystems, with strong participatory governance structures, functional feedback

Table 5.4   **Summary of the Ecosystem Succession Model**

	Young Ecosystem	Mature Ecosystem
Energy & Materials		
Gross productivity	Rapidly increasing	Stable and less
Net productivity	Rapidly increasing	Zero
Efficiency	Low	High
	• Wastage of energy and materials	• Waste organic matter an important energy source
	• Process inefficiencies	• Recycling of materials
		• Conservation in the use of materials
		• Processes more efficient
Trophic structure	Producers mainly	Balance of producers, consumers, decomposers, and integrative species
Space		
Spatial efficiency	Low	High
	Dispersed form	Compact form
	Low structural diversity	High structural diversity
	• Small structures only	• Structures both large and small
	• Lateral patterns only	• Lateral and vertical patterns (stratification)
	• Small variety in shape	• Large variety in shape
Information		
Community diversity	Low	High
	• Few functional niches	• Many functional niches
	• Generalists	• Specialists
Community organization	Low	High
	• Little interconnection	• Much interconnection
Governance		
Environmental control	Low	High
	• Resource availability external to biotic system	• Resource availability controlled within the biotic system
	• Climate unbuffered	• Climate buffered
	• System instability	• System stability

Source: Newman 1975

loops, and community neighborhood renewal schemes to better match adaptive cycles. All these approaches to creating more sustainable cities will be expounded in the other Melbourne Principles, but none will have much hope of success unless the transportation infrastructure priorities clearly support a sustainable model of transport.

City Strategy
Reduce energy in total
Reduce energy per unit of economic output
Recycle waste
More balanced economy (more high-level functions)
More functional diversity
More compact city
More diverse built forms
More diversity in community activities
More networks linking the diversity (social capital)
More effective governance to provide system stability

Model 3: A Human Ecology Approach to Understanding How Cities are Shaped

Since the advent of cities several thousand years ago, their patterns and processes have changed significantly. City economies are increasingly globalized, drawing in resources from across the biosphere, with consumption occurring far from the place of production. The costs to the environment and people are hidden from view. Cities concentrate power and, because of their large numbers of people, decision-making processes become invariably more complex. However, they are still shaped and structured by one fundamental driver: personal mobility.

The average travel-time budget is—and always has been, throughout urban history—around one hour per day. Called the Marchetti constant, this time allotment appears to be a principle for how people live in cities; they tend to prefer to travel on average half an hour for their main journey to and from home. It appears to have a biological basis in the time needed for the transition between productive work and recreational activity. People vary in how much time they like to make this transition, but the average is around half an hour and has been through centuries of urban living.

The Marchetti constant therefore dictates that cities can be no more than "one hour wide." This allows an average trip to be half an hour, and a maximum trip to be one hour. The time budget for mobility thus provides clear infrastructure and planning priorities for cities (see also box 5.4). This model, based on an expanded version by Newman and Kenworthy (1999), draws on human ecology and systems approaches to examine the shape and structure of cities. It is best understood in terms of how cities have changed through history while retaining this one major system characteristic of the hour travel-

Figure 5.4

Copenhagen is an example of a compact "mature" European city that has worked to prioritize walking and cycling so that only 27 percent use a car to go to work.

Figure 5.5

Old cities, such as Bern, Switzerland, are compact and walking-based.

Photos Jeff Kenworthy

time budget. Seeing the way that the urban system has historically been shaped by transport priorities should enable us to see how a more sustainable city can be shaped.

Walking Cities

The necessity of walking as the main mode of transport determined the urban form from the time the first cities were built between 10,000 and 7,000 years ago until the middle of the nineteenth century. The traditional walking city (see figures 5.4 and 5.5) featured high densities of between 100 and 200 people per hectare, mixed land use, and narrow streets, which could be walked at speeds of five to eight kilometers per hour. Therefore, these cities were small in total area, no more than five to eight kilometers across, to allow proximity to agricultural land and accessibility to all parts of the city with an average half-hour journey there and back.

The earliest cities appeared in the southern part of Mesopotamia and probably southwest Persia around the middle of the fourth millennium BC (Golany 1995). Golany claims that Mesopotamian cities were built according to the determining principle of the maximum number of people on the minimum amount of land so as to preserve land and facilitate easy social interaction. These compact cities also provided climatic benefits as they offered more shaded areas and less area exposed to direct sunlight. Little open space was provided in the city itself, but the open space (mostly agricultural land) surrounding the city was within walking distance from the center of the city. Agricultural plots around the city were tended by residents living near the edge of the city or in satellite villages, and were integrated closely with water and waste cycles.

Roseland (1997) identifies the presence of nature in the early city as an important feature: "Water and trees can be central to its streets and public spaces. Waste is recycled. Resources are used frugally. And most of all, there are productive rural land uses immediately adjacent to the city that are integrated closely into its functioning" (16). Rodgers (1997, 41) points out that, traditionally, the Chinese city and its agricultural hinterland were viewed as a totality. He mentions Shanghai as an example of a city that, even today, is mostly self-sufficient in vegetables and grain. However, the self-sufficiency of Chinese cities is being seriously undermined in "the rush to industrialize and urbanize," as is true in much of the developing world. Nonetheless, the main structure of many Chinese cities remains as walking cities.

Walking cities are being reinforced in the centers of most cities. Places like Vancouver have rebuilt their downtown using this principle; most people living there can walk to everything within half an hour.

Transit Cities

From around the mid-1800s in Europe and the New World, due to the pressure of population and industrial growth and the invention of trams and trains, the old walking-city form began to be superseded by transit-based cities. These cities were characterized by medium-density, mixed-use developments at the rail nodes and along the tram routes, and they could extend twenty to thirty kilometers within the average travel time budget (Newman and Kenworthy 1999) (see figure 5.6 below). At various nodes in the transit city, walking villages were formed, mostly around train and tram routes. These cities also created linear infrastructure of piped water, sewerage, and electricity lines. Agricultural and natural areas remained close between the corridors of linear development.

These cities have remained in many parts of the world and are still efficient and relevant to the requirements of livability and sustainability. However, cities reached a new frontier with the advent of large-scale automobile production and the provision of infrastructure for the automobile.

Automobile Cities

Since the 1950s, cities have been shaped largely by motorized transportation, particularly in North America and Australia (see figure 5.7). Car-dependent cities are characterized by low densities of between ten and twenty people per hectare. They are typically much bigger in area than transit cities and much more spread out, with people able to travel fifty kilometers in the

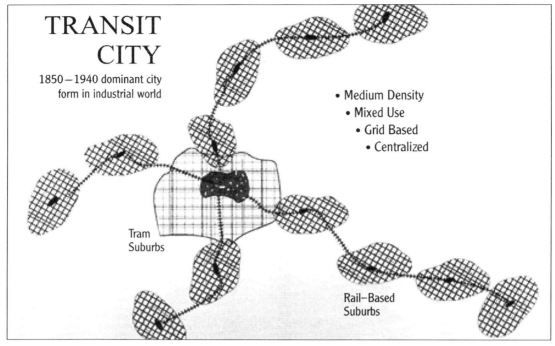

Figure 5.6

The transit city: "one hour wide" means twenty- to thirty-kilometer corridors.

average travel-time budget. The contrast in size between ancient cities and existing cities is marked (Morris 1994). In particular, apart from urban parks, there is generally little easy access to agricultural and natural lands, as the area between the linear corridors of the transit city has been filled in quickly by car-dependent suburbs whenever roads were provided.

This form of city occurred rapidly in the New World but is now occurring anywhere the highway infrastructure enables the city to be traversed more quickly by car than by public transport along corridors, or more quickly by car than by cycling or walking for local trips (see box 5.4).

Car dependence in automobile cities is associated with high ecological footprints and high economic costs. Automobile cities typically use more than 1,000 liters of gasoline per person per year on mobility (Atlanta, at 3,000, uses much more); transit cities use around 300 to 500 liters (Barcelona, at around 150, uses much less); and walking cities use less than 100 liters per person per year. Auto cities have per capita transport costs of 12 to 17 percent of their city wealth, compared to 5 to 8 percent in transit and walking cities (Newman and Kenworthy 1999). These high costs are due to the sheer space requirements of cars, as well as the expense of their purchase and use. Cars also have higher external costs, especially due to road accidents.

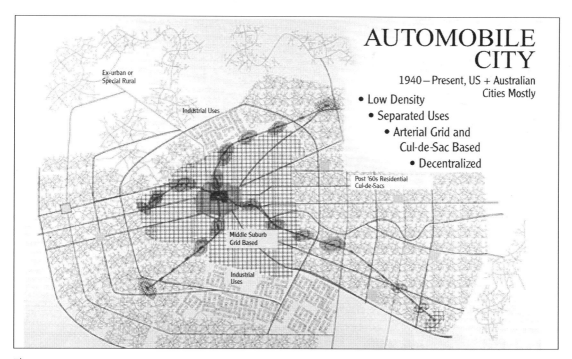

Figure 5.7

The automobile city: "one hour wide" means fifty kilometers across and in all directions.

Car-dependent cities also create a range of social problems. They undermine a sense of community by precluding the casual interactions that occur while walking and using public transport. The presence of cars makes streets unsafe for children. Urban vitality and public safety are compromised as the public realm is increasingly privatized. Social capital is diminished in the process and health is undermined by the lack of walking.

To sum up, the impact on ecosystem patterns and processes has dramatically increased as urbanization takes up more land, and the demands of urban populations place greater pressure on the ecosystems outside cities—all because of the need to accommodate people's average one-hour travel-time budget. The availability of cheap fossil fuels associated with automobile-dependent urban forms (induced by highway building) has led to sprawling cities with high ecological footprints and multiple social issues.

Comparing Walking, Transit, and Automobile Cities

Most cities today have some combination of all city forms, often in rings around the center. For example, Melbourne's outer fringe areas have two to three times more car use and two to three times less public transport and walking than the wealthy core and inner areas of the city.

Box 5.4 **The Limits to City Size**

Recent data shows that some megacities that were expected to see continued growth have begun to stabilize. The question can be asked: is this stabilization just temporary, or is some real limit to urban growth occurring?

One way to answer this is by looking at how the Marchetti constant applies to the issue. The Marchetti constant refers to the average travel-time budget for all cities of around one hour per person each day (Marchetti 1994). Some people travel more, some less. Data from cities of all types and sizes support this idea (Kenworthy and Laube 2001).

This travel-time budget has shaped urban form throughout history. It explains why, despite technological change, a city remains "one hour wide." It also suggests why a city may become dysfunctional beyond a particular size and spread. Cities with high density will be able to grow larger in population because they cover less area; various modes could still bring people to most destinations in under half an hour. Cities with lower density will reach their size limits sooner. For example, a city with an average transit or traffic speed of 40 kilometers per hour (kph) and a density of 100 people per hectare will start to become dysfunctional after it reaches a diameter of 40 kilometers and a population of 12 million. A city with 10 people per hectare will have a higher average travel speed (but not more than 50 kph), and hence would begin to experience transport dysfunction at around 2 million.

The other limit to city size can occur when cities overstretch their bioregional capacities. Cities can exceed the capacity of their watersheds to provide water sustainably. Similarly, the capacity of the bioregion to provide food, energy, and materials may be overstretched, forcing the city to rely more on imports. Cities can also exceed their airsheds if they produce more air pollutants than the bioregional air dispersion mechanisms can cope with. Environmentally sound technologies can provide only a partial solution. Reducing per capita consumption and stabilizing population size are the other parts of the equation.

Comparisons between cities show similarly large ranges in the amount of car use versus public or nonmotorized transport use (see figure 5.8a). There is no correlation in these transport patterns with average per capita wealth for these cities (see figure 5.8b). The wealthy Asian cities of Singapore, Tokyo, and Hong Kong have chosen to provide infrastructure for public transport despite being ten times wealthier than the developing Asian cities of Bangkok, Kuala Lumpur, Manila, Jakarta, and Surabaya. Similarly, European cities have half the car usage of US cities but higher per capita wealth.

The key to these differences (which lead to the significantly different patterns of gasoline consumption and sprawl shown in figure 4.1) is the relative speed of transit to traffic (see figure 5.8c). US and Australian cities have much higher traffic speeds than transit speeds; thus with the constraints of a travel-time budget, people will generally choose to drive. Only fast trains can compete with this infrastructure now. European cities and wealthy Asian cities have higher transit than traffic speeds and hence have much higher public transport usage. This will remain so only if they build no high-speed freeways. Such building is occurring in Tokyo and Hong Kong and will lead to greater automobile dependence.

Figure 5.8a

Use of public transport
(bottom circles) and non-
motorized transport (top
circles) in 1990

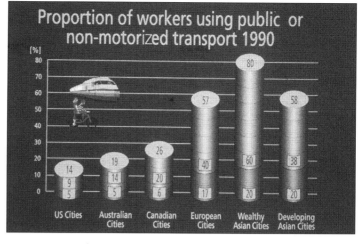

Figure 5.8b

Car use and average per
capita wealth (gross
regional product) in 1990

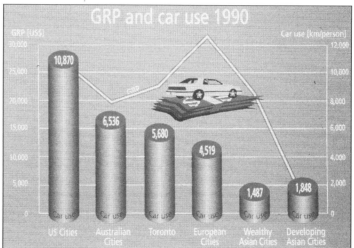

Figure 5.8c

Transit versus car speeds,
and their ratio, in 1990

*Sources: Newman and
Denworthy 1999.*

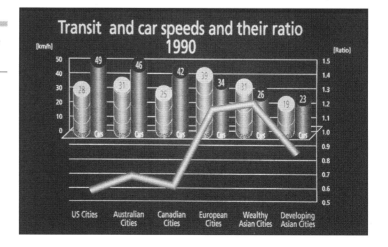

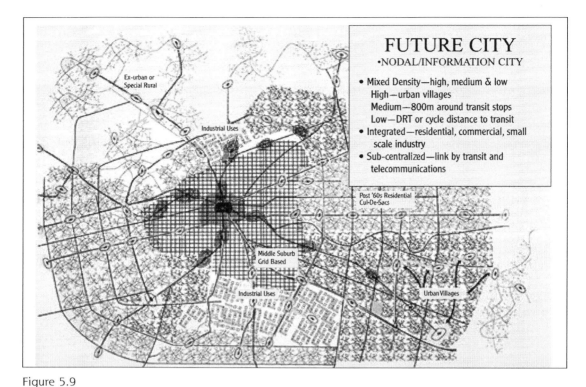

FUTURE CITY
•NODAL/INFORMATION CITY

• Mixed Density—high, medium & low
  High—urban villages
  Medium—800m around transit stops
  Low—DRT or cycle distance to transit
• Integrated—residential, commercial, small
  scale industry
• Sub-centralized—link by transit and
  telecommunications

Figure 5.9

Form of a sustainable city: centers linked by transit corridors throughout the old automobile city

The developing Asian cities have not developed quality mass-transit systems, so buses are stuck in traffic, despite having transit-based urban forms; hence city streets are filling up rapidly with cars as people try to minimize their travel times. Even in Bangkok, where average traffic speeds are just 13 kph, the transit speed is a noncompetitive 9 kph as there are no trains or busways. A new kind of automobile dependence that is traffic-induced rather than land-use-induced (as in automobile cities) has thus emerged. These cities can overcome automobile dependence quickly if they build sustainable rail systems or bus rapid-transit schemes that bypass the traffic. Curitiba and Bogotá have shown how to do this, though the city must have adequate space if buses are to be used.

The Implications of Model 3: Reshaping Cities as Networks of Urban Ecovillages
This leads us to the question of how cities can be reshaped to be less car dependent and, at the same time, integrate the other strategies discussed in the preceding two models. Newman and Kenworthy (1999) propose a sustainable-city model that features mixed-use urban ecovillages, linked across the city by transit, with low- and medium-density areas around these villages. Compact, mixed development facilitates walking and public

transport, thus affording the opportunity to restore vitality to the public realm and a sense of community (Newman 2001). The compact nodes would be surrounded by parks and integrated support systems—urban agriculture, and stormwater and wastewater management systems—with links to the wider bioregion. These nodes would serve as the knowledge and service centers of the new economy. Here people could meet in attractive, walkable centers and conduct the transactions that would fire the local, bioregional, and global economies. Urban ecovillages provide the appropriate scale for technology and metabolism to fit within bioregional capacities. The centers need to be networked by effective transit and telecommunications links as well as local community-oriented transport around the ecovillages (see figure 5.9).

Such an urban form cannot be developed if the city sprawls further or if highways are built, enabling cars to continue to outperform other modes of travel. Instead, it will require cities to provide fast, quality mass transit along corridors to the city center and across the city. A network of good public transport will then induce redevelopment of walkable urban villages around stations. These need to be built along ecological principles, thus providing local community sustainability options as well as a city structure with a much smaller ecological footprint. Ecological renewal of the suburbs between the nodes can occur, with adjacent local subcenters. Although remaining lower in density, the subcenters would provide options suitable for local bike, bus, or short car trips and the opportunity for viable, regional, fast mass transit.

Case Studies: Demonstrations of Ecological Development

While no city can be said to demonstrate all the characteristics and strategies outlined in these ecosystem-based models, there are many cities in which new or recent developments are heading in a more sustainable direction. A few of these are discussed in the case studies below. BedZED is a development in London that has adopted a bioregional approach. Bahía de Caráquez in Ecuador has declared its intention to become an ecological city, and the US organization Planet Drum, a pioneer in the bioregional movement, has been helping the city realize this vision. Christie Walk is a project in South Australia initiated by Urban Ecology Australia. The two final case studies look at Vauban, a model sustainable urban district in Freiburg, Germany, and Bogotá, an ecological leader in Latin America.

BedZED
Developed in partnership by the BioRegional Development Group and Peabody Trust, the Beddington Zero Energy Development (BedZED) in London is one of the most coherent examples of sustainable living in the United Kingdom.[3]

The development aims to contribute to the following:

• Meeting needs and dealing with impacts at the regional scale, including local processing and recycling of waste

Figure 5.10

BedZED, or the Beddington Zero Energy Development, is the first carbon-neutral land development in London.

Photo Tim Beatley

- Protecting greenbelts around cities and avoiding the loss of agricultural land
- Reducing environmental impact through sustainable design
- Supporting local economies and communities
- Improving quality of life.

Built on a brownfield site with a high-density mixed-use core, the development avoids compromising greenbelts while providing community facilities, open space, and private roof gardens. Energy, water, and some food systems, along with biodiversity, are integrated onsite. There is an emphasis on sourcing materials and energy from the local bioregion. Mixed tenure and affordable housing, along with a wide range of public facilities and onsite workspaces, provide the basis for a diverse local community and economy. Networking with local suppliers is promoted for economic sustainability, including bulk deliveries of groceries and links with local organic food growers. The development incorporates sustainable measures in all aspects of its design, including:

- **Zero-energy measures**, including use of passive solar design; active renewable systems such as photovoltaics (PV) and biomass-fueled combined heat and power (CHP); and visible energy meters
- **Water-saving measures**, including rainwater harvesting and graywater recycling for irrigation and indoor use; onsite sewage treatment, using sludge for food production and water for toilet flushing; stormwater management through porous landscaping and constructed wetlands; water-saving appliances; and water meters
- **Energy-efficient transportation**, including an emphasis on walking proximity achieved by high densities; a range of onsite public spaces and facilities, including a village square, café, childcare facility, and sporting facilities; a nearby train station; and a car club, offering members a pool of shared automobiles
- **Use of environmentally sound materials**, including recycled or reclaimed materials; low-embodied energy materials; and materials from local sources
- **Biodiversity enhancement**, including an ecopark with wetlands and wildlife habitats; development of drains into water features; extensive plantings of native species; and wildlife-friendly buildings such as bat roosts and sedum-planted roofs to attract insects (and thus birdlife)
- **Onsite food and crop production**, including permaculture gardens; lavender fields; urban forestry; and willow coppicing

By adopting sustainable lifestyle practices, the BedZED household is expected to have an ecological footprint of less than 2, compared with 6.19 for the typical UK household (see table 5.5).

Bahía de Caráquez, Ecuador: An Ecological City

Bahía de Caráquez is a city in Ecuador situated in the Guayas bioregion, featuring the Guayas River basin, dry tropical forest, and continuous human habitation for five thousand years. Following a series of devastating El Niño mudslides and a serious earthquake, Bahía de Caráquez officially declared itself an "Ecological City" in 1999 and commenced rebuilding in accordance with environmentally sound principles. San Francisco–based Planet Drum Foundation is helping the city realize this goal using a bioregional approach.[4]

Bahía de Caráquez has committed itself by law to become ecological and to demonstrate what a sustainable city can be in Latin America. Planet Drum helped create community awareness of issues there at a celebration announcing the eco-city declaration in January 1999. The organization has carried out a major bioregional project to revegetate a city barrio with native trees for erosion control against future mudslides and to create an urban "wild corridor." The next stage is working on additional revegetation of hillsides, water supply and purity, household ecology education, biological sewage treatment, alternative energy, and more.

The local government approved an ecological city plan in 2001, covering food, water,

Table 5.5 **Ecological Footprint (EF) for BedZED Development (in hectares/person, based**

		Car mileage	Car ownership	Public transport
Typical UK lifestyle	• Owns car • Vacations annually by plane • Recycles 11% • Eats out-of-season, highly packaged, imported food	0.9 (10,000 km/yr)	0.41	0
BedZED conventional lifestyle	• Owns car but takes public transport to work • Vacations annually by plane • Recycles 60% • Eats moderate-meat diet with some imported food	0.45 (5,000 km/yr)	0.32	0.3 (4,000 km/yr)
BedZED ideal	• Lives and works at BedZED • Recycles office paper • Doesn't own car (member of car club) • Vacations biennially by plane • Recycles 80% at home • Eats low-meat diet with local fresh food	0.09 (1,000 km/yr)	0.04 (20 people per car club)	0.3 (4,000 km/yr)
Global average				
Global available	Leaving 10% of bioproductive land for biodiversity			

energy, transportation, recycling, sewage treatment, wild habitat and species protection and restoration, education, human resources, business development, cultural initiatives, and municipal planning.

Peter Berg of Planet Drum says of the project:

Isn't it remarkable that the idea of an ecological small-sized city is coming out of the undeveloped world in South America? This model is certainly going to

on a four-person household)

Air travel	Electricity & gas	Water	Domestic waste	Office (energy & paper)	Food (incl. transport but not packaging)	Overall EF
0.3	0.45 (22,500 kWh/yr)	0.002 (140 liters/day)	1.7	0.8 (Nonrenewable energy, virgin paper)	1.63	**6.19**
0.3	0.1 (Waste wood CHP incl. landfill diversion credit)	0.001 (91 liters/day)	1.02	0.8 (Nonrenewable energy, virgin paper)	1.06	**4.36**
0.15	0.1 (Waste wood CHP incl. landfill diversion credit)	0.001 (91 liters/day)	0.34	0.16 (Closed-loop office paper scheme)	0.72	**1.9**
						2.4
						1.9

make sense in the so-called Third World, much of Asia, Africa, parts of Europe, and the rest of South America. Since a lot of the early work of how to put these things together is being done there, Bahía de Caráquez represents a kind of teaching institution for visitors and students to see how the transformation into an ecological city can be done. The implications of this kind of work in Bahia and other places can actually flow back to the developed world as well.[5]

Christie Walk, Australia

Christie Walk is a cohousing development on a two-thousand-square-meter block of land in inner-city Adelaide (see figure 5.11). It was built by the group Urban Ecology after years of struggle to obtain permission for their ecological innovations. Named after a long-time peace and environmental activist, the late Scott Christie, Christie Walk is a pilot project that demonstrates how communities can address the core issues for sustainable living in cities.[6]

The apartments, built of straw bales around a steel structure, have PV cells and a permaculture roof garden watered from graywater generated in the building. It is highly solar-oriented and insulated for reduced heating and cooling. The ongoing development of the project in the downtown area of Adelaide has included no parking, as people can walk and bike to everything.

Other ecological features include:

- Onsite sewage and graywater treatment, for reuse in local subsurface irrigation
- Onsite storage of stormwater, for use in flushing toilets
- Solar hot water
- Power from wind and photovoltaics
- Passive solar/climate-responsive design

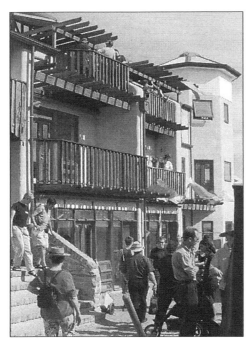

Figure 5.11

Christie Walk, a downtown ecovillage in Adelaide, Australia, features straw bale apartments with PV, water recycling, and no parking.

Photo Peter Newman

- No need for air conditioning despite Adelaide's desert climate
- Recycled, nontoxic materials with low embodied energy
- Pedestrian-friendly spaces
- Local food production
- Shared community garden
- Permaculture roof garden
- Reduced car dependency due to inner-city context.

Unlike many ecovillages, Christie Walk has found a solution for transport fuel by being placed in the center of town. This provides a more holistic demonstration of CASE than most of the rural-oriented ecovillages that save energy in buildings but not in transport.

Vauban, Germany

At the southern fringe of Freiburg, the land of a former French military base has been redeveloped as a model sustainable urban district. Vauban is home to five thousand inhabitants and six hundred permanent jobs. A community association was contracted by the city to include residents in the process and develop sustainability objectives, which have been upheld over the years.

The new district comprises mostly two- to four-story row houses and walk-up apartments, at an average density of ninety to one hundred units per hectare. The development incorporates various sustainability features. All buildings satisfy the Freiburg low-energy standard. Many of the buildings are new-generation timber-frame construction of up to four stories. Some buildings are passive solar designed; heating and cooling are largely achieved through building design, making the most of sunlight and natural breezes. Photovoltaics and solar-supported heating systems are featured on most buildings as well as intelligent ventilation and heat-capture devices. A new office block is a net exporter of electricity to the grid through its PV systems. A solar garage is the source for much of the residential power. Cars can be parked there at very high cost for those families who want one (half do not). The development is car-free in that cars are not allowed in unless they are for very short deliveries. The few streets are therefore filled with children playing, and a much higher proportion of the development has been set aside for natural areas, some of which are quite wild as the householders designed and manage them.

District heating and backup power is provided through a wood-based power plant. Most buildings have rainwater collection facilities and operate some applications like toilets and garden watering from them. A few buildings have included innovations such as a vacuum converter for sewage and organic waste, generating reusable biogas.

Vauban has been connected by light rail to the rest of Freiburg, and thus most travel is by walking, biking, and light rail. The children have considerable freedom as they are not worried by the constraints of traffic. An ecological suburb with a walking-city base, the project appears to be highly successful. Hundreds of people every day take tours of

Figure 5.12a–c

Vauban Ecovillage in Freiburg, Germany

Figure 5.12a

Vauban is a dense yet car-free ecovillage, which allows for much open space but short distances to urban activities.

Figure 5.12b

Most transport in Vauban is by light rail or bicycling. In the background is a central office complex, which exports power to the grid from its extensive PV system.

Figure 5.12c

Children are much freer in Vauban than elsewhere because there is virtually no traffic in the area.

Photos: Jan Scheuser.

Vauban to see how this new approach to city building was done and whether it could be translated elsewhere (Scheurer 2001).

Bogotá: Creating a Humane Eco-City

The former mayor of Bogotá, Enrique Peñalosa, has written about some of the programs he initiated to transform Bogotá into a more "humane city" as well as a more ecological one. In a presentation to the United Nations Asia-Pacific Leadership Forum, the mayor declared:

> Pedestrian and bicycle facilities are useful for recreational and transportation purposes, but they are a symbol as well of a society that respects human dignity. . . . We humans are pedestrians, walking animals. Just as fish need to swim, birds to fly, zebras run, we need to walk. Humane cities need to be made for walking. We also like to see people, be with people. . . . People walk and are with people in public spaces. . . .
>
> There is a conflict between a city for cars and a city for people. As a city becomes friendlier to motor vehicles, it inevitably becomes less humane.
>
> More than whether trains, tramways, buses, monorails are chosen, public transport success depends on density. High density makes possible low-cost, high-frequency public transport. High-rise buildings are not necessary for high densities. It is possible to achieve high densities with three-story and

four-story buildings. High-rise buildings dehumanize cities and tend to rapidly deteriorate with age.[7]

To realize this vision, the city of Bogotá implemented the following measures:

- A 45-kilometer greenway was constructed for recreational and transportation purposes, consisting of a linear park with bicycle paths. An 18-kilometer-long, 15-meter-wide tree-lined street was constructed for pedestrians and cyclists alone.
- More than 120 kilometers of main arterial roads are closed on Sundays between 7:00 AM and 2:00 PM. Cars are restricted twice a week for two peak hours in the morning and two peak hours in the afternoon. This scheme has reduced trip times and pollution levels.
- A car-free day is held once a year for the entire city.
- A large bicycle-path network has been established, and planning bylaws now require that all future roads must have adjacent bicycle paths.
- The TransMilenio, a bus-based transit system, has been implemented with two to four central lanes on main arteries devoted to buses. Feeder buses in ordinary streets take passengers to the trunk lines at no additional cost. This system has been transformative in providing an alternative to car use for trips along the main corridors.

Other ecological innovations were also introduced, including a series of green spaces designed by local communities (O'Meara Sheehan 2007).

Conclusions

The characteristics and strategies of sustainable natural ecosystems and traditional human settlements provide guidance in transforming cities into sustainable ecosystems. As well, two other models that build from an ecological base (ecosystem succession principles) and a human ecology base (travel-time budgets) show that ecosystem models can help shape our cities in practical ways. Some demonstrations of ecosystem-based urban planning are appearing in cities worldwide. The real test is in the ability of cities to make their own demonstrations. The application of the ten Melbourne Principles in a coherent, integrated, and comprehensive approach requires that the theoretical understandings of this chapter flow into those of the other nine. In addition, the practical strategies generated from the other principles must be constantly reviewed to see whether they really are helping to remake cities as sustainable ecosystems. Rebuilding cities using these principles can enable them to fit more easily into the bioregion and global ecosystem as regenerative urban ecosystems.

CHAPTER

6 | Sense of Place

PRINCIPLE 6
Recognize and build on the distinctive characteristics of cities, including their human and cultural values, history, and natural systems.

Elaboration: Each city has a distinctive profile of human, cultural, historic, and natural characteristics. This profile provides insights on pathways to sustainability that are both acceptable to the people and compatible with their values, traditions, institutions, and ecological realities.

Building on existing characteristics helps motivate and mobilize the human and physical resources of cities to achieve sustainable development and regeneration.

The Importance of a Sense of Place

> The places that we know and love can become the type of space that will nourish our lives at their deepest levels. Further, by reviving a sense of place we may be able to reactivate the care of the environment, which grows out of a sense of the sanctity and worth of particular places. (Lilburne 1989)

Cities are places shaped by their ecological context and historical processes. They combine human elements of buildings, infrastructure, and gardens with remnants of native ecosystems. Often cities have been built near water sources—rivers or the coast—and they have been shaped by this presence of water. Cities are also places where a complex array of human, political, economic, social, and cultural interactions occur, mediated by institutions and values. Place unites our social and ecological worlds. It is where real interaction occurs and stories unfold.

Thayer presents the idea of a life-place culture:

A life-place culture is an alternative mode for contemporary humanity that recognizes the limitations and potentials of the immediate regions in which people live and strives to relocalize the affections and actions of inhabitants in a manner that is socially inclusive, ecologically regenerative, economically sustainable, and spiritually fulfilling. The culture of reinhabitation is life-place culture: the rediscovery of a way to live well with grace and permanence, in place. (2003, 68)

A sense of place encompasses a feeling of connection to a place, a lived engagement with people and land, and an understanding and appreciation of the patterns and processes in time and space. Thayer proposes the hypothesis that

immersion in bioregional culture and attachment to a naturally defined region can offer a deepened sense of personal meaning, belonging, and fulfillment in life. Bioregional practice is a deep proposition, allowing the possibility of lifelong learning in and about one's own place. . . . It is a healing activity, allowing one to embrace the culture of nature and the nature of culture—to experience membership in a community including plants and animals as well as other humans. (71)

Sense of place needs to incorporate the indigenous context for any city. Every city's land area has a prehistory as well as more recent recorded histories. By understanding and recognizing the ancient attachment to a place that was part of indigenous culture, cities can begin to learn more about the new agenda, which demands such attachment be revived (Rose and D'Amico 2002; Sandercock 2003).

Developing connections with their bioregion allows people to celebrate a wider sense of belonging to a home-place or life-place that enfolds the city. It offers psychological enrichment and encourages sustainable practices, as people develop ties of affection for their life-places.

The challenge for our cities is to restore or reflect this sense of place. Designing for place is one of the core principles of ecological design:

Ecological design begins with the intimate knowledge of a place. It is small-scale and direct, responsive to local conditions and people. If we are sensitive to the nuances of place, we can inhabit without destroying.[1]

The distinctive pattern of life on Earth is diversity which occurs across space and time. Similarly, for much of human history, human cultures have matched natural diversity with a rich array of languages, worldviews, practices, and designs, which have, over time, generally sustained or enhanced biodiversity. Only in more recent times has the push for globalization led to the erosion of natural and cultural diversity and a shift toward a homogenous global consumer culture and urban form:

Standardization led to the homogenization of our communities, a blindness to history and the demise of unique ecological systems. A "one size fits all" mentality of efficiency overrode the special qualities of place and community. (Calthorpe and Fulton 2001, 44)

Timothy Beatley (2005) has published a major work on place—*Native to Nowhere: Sustaining Home and Community in a Global Age*—that arose from almost eight years of work "visiting and attempting to understand many innovative local sustainability projects and communities." He highlights the importance of creating places that allow communities to flourish and connections to biodiversity to develop. He argues against the tide of increasing homogenization of places, in which we lose the distinctiveness and diversity that make our lives interesting and meaningful. He discusses how places can be strengthened through understanding and reflecting history and heritage, through art and celebration, and through sharing institutions. Beatley argues for walkable places and walking cultures, and for landscapes, buildings, and infrastructure that teach. The book presents numerous North American and European examples.

Sustainability depends on systems being resilient, and this is achieved through diversity, which provides a wealth of different approaches to draw on in times of change. Thus, a sense of place needs to inform and inspire inhabitants of cities, including decision makers and planners. The way we design our cities and lifestyles, as well as our social and political processes and institutions, needs to match the distinctive patterns of place.

Strategies for Fostering a Sense of Place

Cities can reflect their own distinctiveness in five different but related ways:

1. Protecting important existing elements of their natural and cultural heritage
2. Designing to make historical and current social and ecological processes more visible
3. Connecting the urban form with the wider bioregion
4. Using cultural practices and the arts to nurture and deepen a sense of place
5. Discovering city "songlines."

These five strategies can become the basis for building a more effective sense of place.

Strategy 1: Protecting and Restoring Key Elements of Cities' Natural and Cultural Heritage

Ian McHarg's *Design with Nature* (1969) provided an ecological approach to understanding a city's natural environment. The overlay method he propounded, which is standard for landscape designers today, involves recognizing and protecting key ecological processes. This can be done in an existing city, for example, by restoring urban creeks used as stormwater drains and rehabilitating native vegetation. It can be applied at the bioregional level and the local level, identifying areas for protection and restoration as well as areas in which it is appropriate to build.

A city also needs to recognize its cultural features and this is best done by preserving important elements and making changes to the urban fabric that complement or enhance the character and human appeal of a place. Heritage controls are now commonplace, but they require constant vigilance and creativity to ensure that new building can enhance the character of the old. Invariably where this is done the economic value of the area is improved beyond that of the development itself. This extra value is due to the enhanced sense of place that heritage can provide.

Cultural heritage is also enhanced through iconic monuments and stories that are embedded into the urban fabric. In an old industrial area in Duisberg-Nord, Germany, a large park has been created amongst the factory ruins. Rather than seeing this industrial site as a place to avoid, park visitors now see it as critical to the history of the city. Water is an integral part of the design, as it was critical to the functioning of local factories. A large windmill pumps polluted water from the canal. The water is oxygenated before it is sent to the gardens and green spaces via elevated aqueducts. It then returns to the canals purified (Beatley 2005).

Similarly in Richmond, Virginia, which was the industrial and political capital of the South during the American Civil War, a new civil war museum has been constructed on the site of a derelict ironworks and armaments factory on the banks of the James River. Beautifully landscaped, the museum tells the story of the conflict of racism and of the destruction of Richmond. After touring the museum, visitors can walk outside and over an adjacent pedestrian bridge that takes them back in time with quotations from people as they faced the destruction of their city, including the bombing of the bridges. (See figures 6.1a and b)

In Fremantle, Australia, a statue in a public park commemorates three white settlers who were killed in an outback expedition "by warring blacks." Underneath this politically incorrect statue, a plaque has been placed that tells the story from an Aboriginal perspective. The juxtaposition of the two memorials allows people to relate to a sadder part of Australian history as well as see the need for new recognitions, which would not be the case if local authorities had simply torn down the old one. The history of place can thus be brought alive and made relevant to the present.

Strategy 2: Designing to Make Natural and Cultural Processes More Visible

> Design should tell a story about place and people—and be a pathway to understanding ourselves within nature.[2]

Visibility in urban design is crucial. In recent years many designers and planners have started to pay more attention to making ecological processes visually apparent in their designs so that the users may experience, learn about, and appreciate those processes. This approach includes climate-sensitive design of buildings, capturing stormwater on the surface of the land, restoring creeks that had been converted to drains, purifying wastewater in constructed wetlands, and other aspects of water-sensitive design. All

Figure 6.1a
The American Civil War
Center in Richmond,
Virginia, recounts a
painful but important
part of the city's history.

Photo Peter Newman

Figure 6.1b

Next to the civil war museum, an old bridge graphically outlines the bombing of
Richmond's bridges.

Photo Peter Newman

these design possibilities are termed "eco-revelatory design." Water, energy, and materials are the key elements of ecological processes. Communities of living things harness water, energy, and materials to sustain themselves and drive ecological processes. These processes need to be integrated into the urban fabric. Water provides the most visible connection between the urban ecosystem and other ecosystems in the bioregion.

Bioclimatic design uses shape, structure, orientation, choice of construction materials, and living elements to create buildings that respond to local climatic conditions optimally—keeping buildings cool in summer and warm in winter, and making the best use of natural light with zero or little input of extra energy (some may even export energy). Bioclimatic design can be as simple as the careful choice of plants to provide shade in summer and protection from winds in winter.

In Australia, the city of Albury in New South Wales has brought new life to local wetlands through the design of its wastewater treatment systems. During the warmer months the wastewater is used for irrigation, while in wetter months it is redirected to the Wonga Wetlands, located along the floodplain of the Murray River. Since the construction of the Hume Dam in 1919, the Murray River has not flooded as often, and even these floods have been of a lower intensity. This alteration to the natural flow has dried out many of the floodplain wetlands, destroying bird and fish breeding habitat. The Wonga Wetlands project was an opportunity for the city to revert to the original hydrological regime, as well as to educate the public about local ecological processes. Birds and other wildlife are now returning to the wetlands. Trails and bird blinds enable visitors to view the lagoons and wildlife without disturbing the birds or habitat. An environmental education center has been established, and the local Wiradjuri people have created a "living campsite" that serves as a cultural center.[3]

A similar wetlands development in northern California, the Arcata Marsh and Wildlife Sanctuary, highlights some of the positive potential of making natural processes more visible. Since 1986, this constructed wetland on the shores of Humboldt Bay, about 275 miles north of San Francisco, has provided secondary treatment of the city of Arcata's sewage water before discharge to the wider environment. Usually this treatment, which is required by law, is carried out in huge indoor treatment facilities. By creating a wetland to do the same thing, the city is able to provide not only this essential infrastructural service but also an educational and recreational site for the community. Arcata residents can observe their wastewater being treated biologically and providing habitat for fish and birds. The connection between wastewater and treatment is illuminated (Eisenstein 2001).

Water-Sensitive Urban Design

The term "water-sensitive urban design" (WSUD) was coined in Perth, Western Australia, where water is one of the key issues in city development. The aim was to devise and illustrate an approach to urban planning and design that incorporated water-resource and related environmental management into the planning process at various scales and time horizons (Water Sensitive Urban Design Research Group 1990). The term "sensitive" was selected because it encapsulates the different elements of concern to water management—water balance, water quality, and water consumption. It also highlights the need to make water more visible instead of hiding it in pipes.

The WSUD initiative has similar expressions in other cities, but in Perth it has produced a planning policy framework and comprehensive guidelines consisting of some eighty best planning and management practices. As stated by Newman and Kenworthy (1999, 248), these include the following:

Water Balance Objectives
- Maintain appropriate aquifer levels and recharge and stream-flow characteristics in accordance with assigned beneficial uses
- Prevent flood damage in developed areas
- Prevent excessive erosion of waterways, slopes, and banks

Water Conservation Objectives
- Minimize the import and use of scheme water
- Promote the reuse of stormwater
- Promote the reuse and recycling of effluent
- Reduce irrigation requirements
- Promote regulated self-supply

Water Quality Objectives
- Minimize waterborne sediment loadings
- Protect existing riparian or fringing vegetation
- Minimize the export of pollutants to surface- or groundwater
- Minimize the export and impact of pollution from sewerage

Environmental/Social Objectives
- Maintain water-related environmental values
- Maintain water-related recreational and cultural values
- Promote any necessary, site-specific water-sensitive objective identified by the appropriate resource management authority

Strategy 3: Connecting the Urban Form with the Bioregion

Protecting cultural and ecological features and making processes visible should be done within the wider bioregional context. Cities need to be recognized again as place-bound, embedded in ecosystems and bioregions, part of a life-community, part of an unfolding story of place. Rebuilding connections enriches our lives and our cities and strengthens our capacity to care for the places that sustain us. Bioregions embrace us, offering a sense of belonging and the possibility to shape unique identities for our cities and ways of living. They provide a basis for diversity and resilience. The extinction of place-oriented and bioregional-oriented experience in our cities diminishes our children and future generations, limiting their world.

The stories of the people and other inhabitants of our life-communities need to be woven explicitly into the physical and cultural fabric of our cities, restoring links to place and to our past. Sustainable lifestyles involve rebuilding a sense of connection with land and one another, coming home to the community of life, and seeing ourselves within a larger evolutionary story. Rebuilding connections and experiences can be done through physical patterns and through creative arts and practices. Bioregional celebrations become critical to the future sustainability of a city. The focus of this third strategy is on physical patterns, and the next strategy will take up the role of the arts.

Building connections from city to bioregion requires a good knowledge of the bioregion, developing profiles of place. Planners need to inform themselves of the stories of place to integrate them into new developments and regeneration programs. As Sandercock (2003, 210) argues, "Local communities have grounded, experiential, intuitive, and contextual knowledge that is more often manifested in stories, songs, and visual images than in typical planning sources. Planners need to learn and practice these other ways of knowing."

Profiles of Place

Collecting, linking, and disseminating information about the social, cultural, historic, and natural characteristics of the city and bioregion provide a solid basis for designing sustainable solutions, along with specific site analysis. Cities within a bioregion could work together to compile this information, drawing on indigenous, local, historical, and scientific sources. This information could be organized and presented in the form of a database (see the GIS and ethnoecology databases discussed below) or a bioregional map (see the discussion in strategy 4, on the arts).

Ecotrust, a nonprofit organization in the Pacific Northwest of North America, has developed a comprehensive and ecosystem-level geographic information system (GIS) consisting of biophysical, social, economic, and cultural databases. The organization is attempting to fill an information gap left by government resource management agencies, which have gathered large quantities of data but have no mandate to make the data available to the public. Ecotrust compiles the data across political and agency jurisdictions to create regional and community databases based on watershed boundaries. This information will help conservationists, researchers, foresters, farmers, fishers, business people, investors, planners, policymakers, and citizens better understand the dynamics of the "Salmon Nation" bioregion and make informed choices about future natural resource management and economic development.[4]

Researchers in anthropology and ethnobotany at Fort Lewis College in Durango, Colorado, have created the Ethnoecology Database of the Greater Southwest to preserve and share information about the traditional cultures and natural environment of the southwestern United States. The Greater Southwest bioregion, which extends into northern Mexico, is considered the third most diverse bioregion in the world.

According to one of the student researchers at Fort Lewis College, what distinguishes the Ethnoecology Database is its bioregional ethnographic collectivism:

> The term *bioregional ethnographic collectivism* . . . describe[s] the pooling of ethnographies of several cultures that are related, based on the bioregion from which they originate. It is a way of organizing and understanding cultures based on their adaptive strategies to a common bioregion (the land) from which they generate their material culture. It examines the common material foundations for cultures and their unique ways of altering the landscape to fit their specific needs.[5]

In its current form, the Ethnoecology Database includes topics such as art, culture, chemistry, images, interviews (oral history), literature, medicine, organizations, phenology, textiles, and traditional ecological knowledge. Users can search for particular plants by species, common name, or utility. Although the primary function of the database is as a research tool for students, its creators hope that it will also assist community members in their efforts to become sustainable.[6]

Greenway Linkages

> A community's sense of belonging to a life-place (i.e., its levels of attachment to and concern for the welfare of the natural region) is directly proportional to its ability to access the representative character and spaces of that region. . . . There is a necessary connection between direct life-place experience and true belonging. (Thayer 2003, 84–85)

Greenways, or wildlife corridors, link reserves in the city with those in the wider bioregion. These linkages can be used to protect biodiversity, maintain hydrological patterns, or accommodate infrastructure. In Zurich several stormwater pipes have been dug out and refashioned into vegetated creeks, which now serve as natural corridors linking the city from its center to its surrounding forests.

Heritage and nature trails provide linkages between the city and its wider environment, offering local residents a means to explore and appreciate the natural and cultural heritage of their bioregion. Trail signage could include not only factual information, but also community art, poetry, and stories. Portland, Oregon, whose system of trails is outlined below, is typical of many American cities that have made a feature of nature or heritage trails in and around their urban areas.

In the Portland metropolitan area, which includes Vancouver, Washington, an ambitious project has been established to protect a regional web of parks and green spaces linked by river and stream corridors and a system of trails. In Portland, "bioregion" actually means something in terms of governance, as voters approved the creation of a regional planning body to manage regional transport and bioregional issues such as biodiversity corridors. This metropolitan service district, known as Metro, works with residents and local governments to ensure that people have access to nature close to home, as well as new ways to get to work, school, or shopping.

When originally conceived a century ago, Portland's trail system was going to be forty miles long, encircling the city. The metropolitan area has grown substantially since then, and plans for a regional system of trails and greenways have grown with it. The 1992 Metropolitan Greenspaces Master Plan envisioned a network that would include twenty-five cities and four counties within the Portland/Vancouver metro region. Today, plans call for an eight-hundred-mile network of land trails, water trails, and greenways. Nearly 30 percent of the land-based trails are complete.[7]

Strategy 4: Using Cultural Practices and the Arts to Celebrate a Sense of Place

Numerous cultural practices and forms of creative expression can be used to deepen a sense of place, including seasonal and bioregional festivals; restoration work; arts initiatives such as exhibitions, poetry readings, and storytelling; and bioregional mapping.

Bioregional Mapping

Bioregional mapping offers a process for compiling knowledge in a more graphical form. It is a process that can inspire communities and encourage them to build connections with place and one another. This, in turn, can motivate and mobilize community action. Mapping bioregions, along with ecoliteracy initiatives and bioregional celebrations and festivals, can reawaken a sense of place.

Stories can be a significant part of bioregional mapping:

> To restore any place, we must also begin to re-story it, to make it the lesson of our legends, festivals, and seasonal rites. Story is the way we encode deep-seated values within our culture. . . . By replenishing the land with our stories, we let the wild voices around us guide the restoration work we do. The stories will outlast us. (Nabhan 1998)

Bioregional Celebrations

Most cities have some kind of festival designed to foster a better sense of place. Not all make enough of their bioregional context. In Australia each of the main cities has recently developed festivals that are much more bioregional in character. Hobart has its Mountain Festival and Brisbane its River Festival. Both make a feature of creative expressions of what the local natural icons mean to people.

The Putah-Cache Bioregion Project sponsored by the University of California–Davis includes an art and literature component to celebrate and promote a sense of place. Each year the project appoints several artists and writers in residence, who are "expected to do work that responds to the geography, biology, and culture of the combined watersheds of Putah Creek and Cache Creek." These resident artists and writers present their work to the bioregional community in exhibitions and readings, including the annual Watershed Arts Festival, and have their work published in pamphlets and posters.[8]

Strategy 5: Discovering City "Songlines"

> Pre-colonial Australia was the last landmass on earth peopled neither by farmers nor by city dwellers but by hunter-gatherers. Along a labyrinth of invisible pathways, known to us as Songlines, the Aboriginals traveled in order to perform all those activities that are distinctly human—song, dance, marriage, exchange of ideas, and arrangements of territorial boundaries by agreement rather than by force. The Songlines, in Aboriginal culture, are what sustain life. The task of a new planning imagination is to search for the city's songlines, for all that is life sustaining, in the face of the inferno. (Sandercock 2003, 227–28)

Leonie Sandercock (2003) discusses the critical importance of stories for cities and the way that the sharing of stories can bring people together and help them shape new collective stories. She argues that stories and storytelling are central to planning practice, acting as a catalyst for change. These stories can become the same meaningful mechanism for belonging to a city used by country-dwelling Aboriginal people when they devised "songlines": information about place stored in the form of songs that are learned from childhood, which can be sung to reveal features of the countryside. Songlines can take many forms in today's digital world, but they need to reflect the original idea of layers of information—from practical to deeply spiritual—about a place and the journey through it. They can facilitate connections between city dwellers and their bioregions, linking city and country, and providing a tangible broader context for city life.

In indigenous cultures, the feeling of a sense of place was supported by lived engagement with the more-than-human world, the presence of which was more immediate and omnipresent than it is in most modern cities. Songlines, along with rituals, ceremonies, and other cultural practices, gave meaning to interactions and nurtured connections.

In many indigenous cultures, land and community are linked, giving a sense of belonging and participating in a greater story. A similar sense of place and belonging is evident in Western traditions in grassroots spirituality and practical, organic ideas about place such as the natural history movement, the human ecology movement, and the urban ecology movement (Newman and Kenworthy 1999).

Every city occupies land that has some kind of indigenous story or stories attached to it. By recognizing this attachment through place-names and by telling these stories publicly in works of art and in buildings, current city inhabitants can become part of that story and develop a similar sense of place. As well as its indigenous history, a city's local and social histories are also central to its identity, evoking a sense of belonging. So these stories, too, need to be told and integrated with the indigenous story. Cities with a strong sense of place have made highly visible their natural history and their indigenous and local histories. They are creating a new songline, particularly when expressed in a heritage trail that can tell the story of the landscape and the town together.

By discovering where old Aboriginal songlines still exist and understanding what they mean for present-day urban life, the city of Perth is beginning to open up new possibilities for heritage trails. Most cities just need to re-create the meaningful corridors that once existed, that tell a story that contributes to their city's identity and sense of place. But most cities will also have much more history of the original inhabitants than is generally known by the public, which tell how they existed there with little technology and an acute awareness of their bioregional place.

Conclusions

Sense of place is one of the most powerful concepts in the CASE approach to sustainability. Cities can build a sense of place by protecting important environmental and cultural features; designing *with* natural processes not against them; connecting the urban form with its bioregion; using education and the arts to inform and dramatize a sense of place; and discovering and incorporating their "songlines."

A sense of place needs to inform and inspire inhabitants of cities, including decision makers and planners. The way we design our cities and our lifestyles, our social and political processes, and our institutions needs to match the distinctive patterns of the places in which we live. Cities can be both ecologically and socially regenerative through activating their sense of place.

Empowerment and Participation

PRINCIPLE 7
Empower people and foster participation.

Elaboration: The journey toward sustainability requires broadly based support. Empowering people mobilizes local knowledge and resources and enlists the support and active participation of those who need to be involved in all stages, from long-term planning to implementation of sustainable solutions.

People have a right to be involved in the decisions that affect them. Attention needs to be given to empowering those whose voices are not always heard, such as the poor.

The Importance of Empowerment and Participation

Sustainability rests on the ability of people to participate in decision-making processes and to contribute to the well-being of their communities. Empowerment means developing people's confidence to participate, especially marginalized groups such as women, indigenous people, the poor, the disabled, and the illiterate. It means giving people the tools to participate in decision-making processes and developing processes that respect different ways of being in the world. Empowerment is about giving a voice to all people and fostering involvement in civic life. This inclusion of a diversity of perspectives increases the resilience of societies, providing a wider range of solutions and responses to challenges and change. Empowerment celebrates diversity and directs it into common-good outcomes.

Cultural and institutional changes are crucial to reducing the impact of human activities in cities on ecological and social dimensions. However, ultimately creating healthy communities involves a process of empowerment whereby citizens recognize their own capacities and responsibility to generate the changes they want. Civic participation provides a powerful tool for moving toward sustainability by restoring the feedback loops, which, in their current disrupted state, engender inaction and resistance (J. Moore 1997). Anderson echoes this point, stressing the powerful role of the individual:

Culture . . . is not a straitjacket or an unchanging body of tradition. It is the result of countless human decisions. Culturally coded knowledge systems are "emergent phenomena": they are not totally predictable from those countless decisions. But these systems do not decide, nor do they act. Only individuals (alone or in organizations and groups) can do that. Actions, and the results of actions, lead to changes. (1996, 129)

Participation in decision making helps people appreciate the complexities of issues and feel a sense of ownership toward the outcome. It encourages people to take responsibility and care for their human communities and wider life communities.

Empowerment is about enabling people to take more control of their day-to-day lives and to make their own decisions about their surroundings (Lopes and Rakodi 2002, 122). For disempowered communities, this process usually needs to be initiated by outside forces operating with a more egalitarian vision of society, aiming at facilitating powerless people to organize and take further action themselves. Lopes and Rakodi identify a key role for external agents as "giving powerless people access to a new body of ideas and information, and raising their consciousness and awareness that the existing network of relationships is unjust." Through the empowerment process, low-income groups gain access to new realms of knowledge and can start to make new personal and collective choices for their lives. Developing a belief in their capacity to achieve desired outcomes enhances people's self-esteem, raises awareness of the forces shaping their lives, reduces the likelihood of poverty, frees people from mental and physical dependence, and opens new spaces for collective participation and dialogue (Paulin, 2006).

Empowerment is important not just because it is a human right, but also because the issues of sustainability are far too complex and difficult to resolve without involving as many different views as possible in a creative strategic conversation. Aristotle called this "second-road thinking," based on the insight that complex problems require voices of difference. Many scholars similarly have recognized that complex problems often are not solved by pure logic or science or engineering, as these approaches focus on efficiency, and how to make "what is" more efficient. They cannot easily shift to creating solutions that are not just efficiency gains. Innovative solutions to extremely complex or "wicked" problems—like those to do with sustainability—require unimagined approaches and different ways of thinking. A diversity of backgrounds and experience can generate insights into an issue not considered by those immersed in the issue and those whose advice comes chiefly from manuals of previous best practice. Empowerment can create opportunities for innovation, though only if a diversity of people is actively engaged.

Lessons from Sustainable Systems
The emphasis on diversity is based on the same network structure that characterizes ecosystems, in which all parts of the ecosystem play a role in its overall function. The capacity to act and participate in the system is facilitated by the ecosystem's struc-

ture. Food webs and other functional associations are decentralized networks in which no one species dominates—at least not for long before the system flips to another state. Indigenous cultures accumulated their knowledge of resource management through adaptive learning—learning by doing—which ensured participation. Political structures were often relatively small and simple; nations were sometimes formed through alliances, as with some American Indian tribes. These alliances were based on protocols of interaction but left the power for looking after homelands in the hands of the tribes.

Similarly, cities need to build on this organic structure. Close networks of people tied to a local place form the basis of a community. Communities, in turn, are linked together as part of a bioregion. Empowerment ensures that these community and bioregional aspects of a city are given a voice. Changes to governance structures will be discussed in chapter 10.

Defining Empowerment

Lopes and Rakodi (2002) present a set of nine indicators of empowerment:

1. Self-confidence levels of community members
2. Capacity of the community to organize itself
3. Capacity of the community to understand and reflect on the reality of the environment in which they are living
4. Capacity of the community to set goals
5. Capacity of the community to develop plans
6. Capacity of the community to implement plans
7. Capacity of the community to create networks
8. Capacity of the community to communicate effectively
9. Capacity of the community to evaluate outcomes of its activities

Empowerment is also described as deliberative democracy. Carson and Hartz-Karp (2005) characterize deliberative democracy as a process that requires the following:

- Influence: capacity to influence policy and decision making
- Inclusion: voices representative of population, diverse viewpoints and values, equal opportunity to participate
- Deliberation: open dialogue, access to information, space to understand and reframe issues, respect, and movement toward consensus

It is these elements—inclusion, deliberation, and influence—that address the power relationships and values to be expressed, thus informing the development process. How we make decisions becomes as important as what we decide. Moreover, if we are to make decisions that represent all the people, then addressing the power differentials between groups becomes critical. This is particularly important when the voice of some groups in our society, such as indigenous people, is unlikely to be carefully heard or heeded.

Strategies for Empowerment and Participation

Empowerment and participation go hand in hand. City governments need to develop strategies for empowering people through transformation of structures and processes to enable people to participate in decision making.

"Environmental citizenship" has been promoted by the United Nations Environment Program (UNEP) since 1992. Now UNEP and its International Environmental Technology Center (IETC) are promoting the concept as a means of encouraging use of environmentally sound technologies in developing countries. It refers to the responsibility that we all have to care for the environment and use the Earth's resources sustainably. The UNEP/IETC guidebook on the subject (Casanova 2003) presents three basic principles of environmental citizenship:

- Environmental conservation is a paramount duty of citizenship that all citizens must be aware of.
- Governments have a responsibility to make people aware of their environmental rights and duties and to provide them with appropriate conditions that let them enjoy their rights as well as exercise their duties as environmental citizens.
- Cooperation and collaboration between governments and their citizens to conserve the environment are keys to achieving environmental sustainability. (Casanova 2003, 2)

The guidebook goes on to identify three key building blocks of environmental citizenship:

- An informed citizenry—"the best guarantee of environmental stewardship"
- An enabling of government—to support its citizens in environmental activities, to support public policies that protect the environment, and to support political freedom
- Partnership—between local governments and citizens (Casanova 2003, 3)

This chapter will discuss the following strategies for empowerment in cities:

1. Committing to empowerment and participation
2. Empowering people through education and healing circles
3. Using different levels of engagement for different urban functions
4. Engaging the most disempowered
5. Developing a resource base for empowerment

Partnerships will be discussed further in chapter 8.

Strategy 1: Committing to Empowerment and Participation

Each level of government in a city region needs to be committed to empowerment and to implementing effective participatory processes. General commitment to participatory processes was expressed by the mayors and city officials of the world who signed the "Local Government Declaration to the World Summit on Sustainable Development" in Johannesburg in 2002 (see appendix A):

> [We reaffirm] our commitment to the principles of sustainable development, including solidarity, transversality (integrating the economic, social, and environmental dimensions), participation of civil society in decision making, and responsibility to future generations and disadvantaged populations.

In Western Australia government officials decided in 2001 soon after elections that they would try to establish processes that promoted empowerment and deliberative democracy whenever possible. Guidelines for this were established, along with an Office of Citizens and Civics.[1] However, not all ministers took the approaches seriously, and some were quickly led into top-down decisions when advised by their senior public servants. One minister who did take the process seriously was Minister for Planning and Infrastructure Alannah MacTiernan, who committed to taking all her contentious issues through deliberative processes. She outlined her reasons for taking this approach as follows:

> My concern is that we are increasingly functioning in a climate where making good decisions becomes very difficult. . . . The media wants clear black and whites. . . . it wants outrage, not considered partial disagreement. . . . This mitigates against good governance. In my view, we need to "retool democracy" —to establish systems where we genuinely encourage community involvement in decision-making—where we present government not as the arbitrator of two or more opposing camps, each of whom are provided with incentives by the process in hardening their position, but as the facilitator of bringing divergent voices together to hammer out a way forward. (MacTiernan 2004)

MacTiernan has taken on a range of processes and some forty-two projects, from contentious high-rises to the location of a community center and the resolution of a highway noise issue. The most extensive process was the Dialogue for the City exercise described in chapter 1, which established a green vision for the city of Perth. Most of these projects have been assessed and were found to have had good outcomes in which public support was obvious, making them more likely to be sustainable.[2]

Resource material from Sarkissian, Hirst, and Stenberg (2003, 12) shows what can be done in any community, and the authors suggest the following criteria for assessing the effectiveness of participation processes:

- Timeliness: participation should occur at the stage in a project when citizens can still make a difference, rather than as a tokenistic gesture at the end of a process
- Involvement of a cross-section of the community
- Outcomes that are community-focused not self-interested
- Interactive and deliberative processes in which big-picture questions are considered
- Striving for consensus
- High likelihood of recommendations being adopted
- Skilled, independent, and flexible facilitation

- Open, fair, and accountable processes
- Cost-effectiveness

Most cities that have seriously committed to empowerment on their decisions can demonstrate these outcomes.

Strategy 2: Empowering People through Education and Healing Circles

Empowerment is part of the larger process of building cultural capacity, or cultural sustainability:

> Cultural sustainability means creating a political and community culture that sustains itself in such a way that active citizen participation is seen as an ever-present feature of the policy process. Cultural sustainability in this context is a very important precondition to increase responsibility for social and environmental sustainability.[3]

People need to be empowered to be part of decision-making processes. Citizenship, as mentioned in the previous section, depends on informed citizens. Thus, education is a crucial aspect of empowerment, especially for women and the poor. Ecological and social literacy are both vital to encourage informed participation. However, marginalized groups may not feel confident or safe to participate because of their circumstances and historical issues. In some places people are afraid to speak out because of fear of attack. In the transition to more democratic structures, time is needed to heal the wounds of persecution and establish relationships of trust and mutual respect.

Traditionally, dialogue has been used by indigenous peoples for healing (Clarkson, Morrisette, and Regallet 1992). One effective tool is the healing circle that provides a space for people to release their pain and to support each other through the process. In the American Indian context this process rests on the principles of "respect, non-interference" and recognition of the spirits of the elders and "the creator" to guide participants through the process. The sacred pipe is handed around and each person has the chance to talk with care and respect, without interruption. The rest of the group listens closely thus providing a space for people to express their feelings and feel validated, with often the pain of one individual being echoed by other people in the group.

Strategy 3: Using Different Levels of Engagement for Different Urban Functions

Different levels of community participation exist with different empowerment outcomes. Robinson (2002) has suggested four levels based on increasing levels of risk or complexity (see figure 7.1). The goal is to try to achieve empowerment through partnership (see chapter 8). City governments need to choose the appropriate level of engagement for the particular issues at hand.

The range of different techniques for empowerment include the following procedures:[4]

- **Planning cells, or citizen juries**: Bodies of randomly selected jurors, who are asked to deliberate on complex or contentious issues. The jurors cross-examine expert witnesses, deliberate, and make recommendations that the government has already agreed it will substantially act on.
- **Consensus conferences**: A jury process, which the public may attend and contribute to at various points. The Danish Parliament has incorporated such conferences into their operations.
- **Deliberative polls**: The polling of randomly selected citizens who are paid to attend a high-profile (often televised) event. The citizens are polled on the contentious issue before and after an extensive dialogue involving experts. One such event was held in Texas, where energy utilities asked people their views about

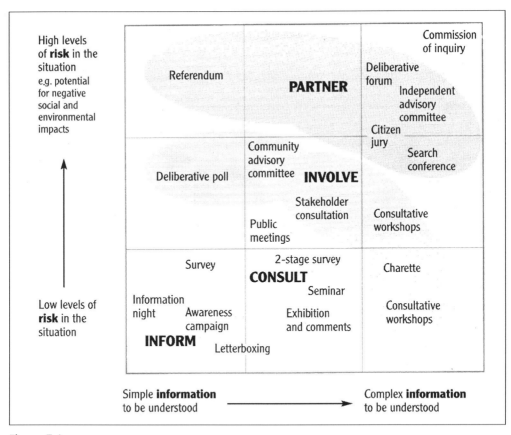

Figure 7.1

Participation processes for different levels of risk and complexity

Robinson 2002, 4

future power options; the strength of feeling for renewable energy was such that the utilities then began making legislated targets for renewables.

- **Participative budgets**: A mass process of deciding on budget priorities through direct consultation of the public. Developed in Pôrto Alegre, this technique has now spread to over seventy cities across Brazil.
- **Consensus forums**: Daylong conferences in which care is taken to involve stakeholders and at least a third of randomly selected citizens, to enable a group voice to represent common-good outcomes. These forums are effective when participants know that government will act on their conclusions.
- **Multi-criteria analysis workshops**: A decision-making process involving carefully selected experts and stakeholders, as well as randomly selected citizens (usually drawn from electoral rolls). Participants must deliberate on various options through selecting criteria, weighting them, and then processing the options to see which one generates most consensus. This process works well on siting of infrastructure or contentious land uses.
- **Twenty-first-century town meetings**: A dialogue process for a large group of citizens (usually 300 to 5,000) on large strategic directions (e.g., AmericaSpeaks held one with 5,000 people on options for Lower Manhattan after 9/11). These events utilize technology so that small groups sitting around networked computers can enter their conclusions and then get immediate feedback on how their opinions compare to those of others. By seeing broad conclusions immediately, people leave feeling that the majority message has been received.
- **Enquiry-by-design charettes**: A technique created by New Urbanist professionals who wanted to find a way of circumventing the interminable planning processes for new developments. At these charettes, innovations can be discussed without threat to due process, and community involvement can be sought at the early stages in planning. Local government professionals, experts, consultants, and community are brought together for two days to sketch out possible development options that could be considered for a site. Because of dialogue, the variety of options that arises is usually far greater than if a single expert had been consulted. Because of the broad consensus, there is ownership and commitment to implementing the ideas.

Strategy 4: Engaging the Most Disempowered

Empowering women, youth, and the poor is crucial to addressing poverty and sustainability. Some innovative initiatives have been started that target these disempowered groups—such as Urban Basic Services for the Poor, Child-Friendly Cities, the Partnership on Youth Empowerment in Africa, and a community-based watershed management project in Brazil.

Urban Basic Services for the Poor (UBSP) is a program in India that engages the urban poor, especially women, in enhancing their communities and personal circumstances, with the broader aim of general neighborhood and city improvement. Established in the 1960s, UBSP now involves over 465 cities and towns across the country and reaches about ten million urban poor. The empowerment of women has been closely associated with reductions in population growth rates, thus contributing to sustainability in multiple ways.

Up to 40 percent of the total urban population in India lives in poverty, and women constitute the majority of the urban poor. Because their role in decision making is low, due to patriarchal values reinforced through tradition, religion, and other social institutions, women have had limited opportunities for employment and a lack of access to credit—contributing to an intergenerational cycle of female poverty and deprivation.

Many of the participating women have said that before UBSP they stayed in their homes and could not interact with outsiders. Now, through UBSP's training and guidance, they are more confident and unafraid to make their needs known both within and outside their homes.[5]

Tranter and Malone (2003, 18) argue that "democratic behavior is learnt through experience; so children must be given a voice in their communities so they will be able to, now and in the future, participate fully in civil society." This right to participate is declared as part of UNICEF's Child-Friendly Cities initiative.[6] The program supports projects in various countries, including several youth parliaments in Albania, Georgia, and elsewhere.

Another program that targets youth is UN-Habitat's Partnership on Youth Empowerment in Africa.[7] Working with other international organizations, UN-Habitat has launched this educational and media initiative at the city scale. It attempts to foster a culture of prevention and values of citizenship among youth as a way of realizing the Millennium Development Goal of improving the lives of one hundred million slum dwellers—many of whom are African youth—by 2015. The first step is to develop training and capacity-building materials to meet the needs of at-risk youth in selected cities in Africa.

In the metropolitan area of São Paulo, Brazil, the Community-Based Watershed Management project (CBWM) in the city of Santo André is attempting to protect and rehabilitate fragile urban watershed areas by engaging and assisting the poor and marginalized who have come to occupy those lands in informal settlements. According to de Castro and McNaughton (2003, 1), the project incorporates participatory action research, social impact assessment, community economic development, gender planning, and environmental education. Bioregional mapping is an important part of the approach, serving as "an accessible method of community empowerment" (de Castro and McNaughton 2003, 9).

The CBWM project has formulated a framework for watershed management based on community participation and learning by doing. Top-down methods applied under the military dictatorship that ruled Brazil from the 1960s to the mid-1980s were unsuccessful in dealing with the settlement of environmentally sensitive watershed areas by low-income families. Water quality for the metropolitan region deteriorated, along with the quality of life for low-income settlers. With the decentralization of power that followed the approval of the country's new constitution in 1988, control of urban management functions has shifted back to the municipal level. The government of Santo André, a city of about 665,000 people, is now committed to a high degree of public participation in urban planning. Thus it designed the CBWM project to include a wide range of stakeholders in the conceptualization and implementation of planning guidelines, including groups such as low-income communities, women, and "illegal" residents, who have been excluded from decision-making processes in the past (Castro and McNaughton 2003, 3–5).

Among the factors contributing to the success of CBWM are the three tools that the project has applied to community development and land-use decision making: Environmentally Sensitive Areas (ESA) methodology, the charette process, and bioregional mapping. Together they constitute a holistic participatory process (de Castro and McNaughton 2003, 7).

The purpose of ESA analysis is to identify the various types of sensitive areas, create maps for each type, and then bring the map layers together in a meaningful way to show environmental constraints. The interests of local stakeholders are reflected in the types of sensitive areas and the way in which they are integrated. These results are used to develop zoning and community development maps, as well as to screen specific project proposals during environmental impact analyses.

The charette process is a design exercise, as outlined above, that takes a broad, inclusive approach to difficult problems, generating illustrations that show the implications of particular planning policies. In the CBWM project, the main goal of the charette was to develop "compelling visions of what a sustainable community in the watershed might look like in order to inform future land use, urban design, and environmental policy for the whole area" (de Castro and McNaughton 2003, 8). One outcome of the charette was a publication titled *Sustainable Watersheds: Urban Landscape Design for Low-Income Settlements*.

The third tool used by CBWM in land-use planning—bioregional mapping—draws on the knowledge of the people who live in a place. De Castro and McNaughton describe bioregional mapping as "a strategy for building locally controlled and self-reliant economies that are closely tied to the use and sustainability of the surrounding ecosystems" (2003, 9). Through the process of developing maps collaboratively, "people strengthen their community self-identification and increase awareness of existing biophysical, socio-economic, and cultural resources and values within the community" (10). Participation of community members can vary from consultative to self-directed involvement. Whatever process is adopted, de Castro and McNaughton note that it is crucial for community members to feel actively involved in order to encourage community stewardship. Collaborative bioregional mapping can provide the basis for community visioning (see chapter 1), and it can help build positive connections between decision makers and members of the local community. It improves the capacity for communication on issues such as land use, environmental awareness, and tourism.

Strategy 5: Developing a Resource Base for Empowerment
The Co-Intelligence Institute suggests more than twenty ways to achieve a stronger, wiser, more resilient, and more engaged community.[8] These include asset mapping, listening projects, friendship webs, indicator projects, and open space conferencing. A sim-

ilar set of techniques can be found on deliberative-democracy specialist Janette Hartz-Karp's website.[9]

In a series of books titled *Community Participation in Practice*, Sarkissian, Cook, and Walsh (1994–2005) outline the theory and practice of conducting public participation processes. The first book, *A Practical Guide*, discusses the principles of community participation and some key participatory techniques. A checklist of approaches is presented and detailed further in the *Workshop Checklist*, the final section of which explains how to evaluate the effectiveness and appropriateness of participatory processes. The *Casebook* presents case studies of projects undertaken in Australia. The *Handbook* provides resources for carrying out public participation processes. A more recent addition to the series, *New Directions*, builds on these previous publications and incorporates the work of other theorists and practitioners as well as reviewing participatory practice in Australia and in the rest of the world.[10]

Community toolkits, such as the Green Communities Assistance Kit developed by the US Environmental Protection Agency, can inspire and guide community action.[11]

The anti-freeway movement that has developed in many cities across the world is a potent example of community empowerment and participation. Newman and Kenworthy (1999) and Newman (1999) tell several stories of urban areas like Greenwich Village in New York City, which would have lost its vibrancy and community structure had it not been for the citizens, led by Jane Jacobs, who stood up to the freeway plan of Robert Moses. When Jacobs later moved to Toronto, she helped in the fight to stop the Spadina Expressway, which would have cut a swath through the inner city. Instead of building this or any other expressways, Toronto went for public transport and has created one of the least auto-dependent cities in North America. Similar stories can be told of Portland, Vancouver, and most European cities, all of which had large motorway plans dreamed up for them by international traffic-planning consultants. Common to many of these stories of citizen-based action to stop freeways has been the importance of key women who have helped create a different dream for their cities. The anti-freeway movement is about taking hold of the future from elitist engineers (usually men, so the phrase "taking toys from the boys"

Figure 7.2a

"Future car" at a street fair in Vancouver to stop a freeway

Photo Peter Newman

Figure 7.2b

Shrine to Jane Jacobs at the Vancouver street fair

Photo Peter Newman

Figure 7.3

Overcoming the road lobby will require public participation.

was often heard in these debates) and instead presenting a dream of how other options such as light rail, traffic calming, and urban villages can provide a softer, more human kind of city.

Conclusions

Empowerment is crucial to CASE. The issues dealt with are complex, and they cross traditional boundaries of knowledge—meaning that "experts" can be found wanting. Such issues require cities to engage with a diversity of opinions and backgrounds. People from the edges of a city—from backgrounds that do not usually lead to decision-making roles—are particularly important to consult, because they may have solutions unimagined by those at the center. Cities need a new leap of the imagination beyond normal professional practice if they are to be sustainable and regenerative. Voices of difference will be needed to stimulate such imagination.

8 | *Partnerships*

PRINCIPLE 8
Expand and enable cooperative networks to work toward a common, sustainable future.

Elaboration: Strengthening existing networks and establishing new cooperative networks within cities facilitates the transfer of knowledge and supports continual environmental improvement.

The people of cities are the key drivers for transforming cities toward sustainability. This can be achieved effectively if the people living in cities are well informed, and can easily access knowledge and share learning. Furthermore, people working with each other through such networks can enhance the energy and the talents of people.

There is also value in cities sharing their learning with other cities, pooling resources to develop sustainability tools, and supporting and mentoring one another through inner-city and regional networks. These networks can serve as vehicles for information exchange and can encourage collective effort.

Cooperative Networks in Nature

In recent years, biologists and ecologists have begun to shift their metaphors from hierarchies to networks and have come to realize that partnership—the tendency to associate, establish links, cooperate, and maintain symbiotic relationships—is one of the hallmarks of life. (Capra 2002, 99)

Biology has often provided analogies for political life. Social Darwinism was one of the cul-de-sacs of this trend that is now seen as a mistake, as it led to concepts of the "master race" and eugenics that violated humanitarian principles. Drawing its focus from Darwin's ideas about evolution being based on survival of the fittest, Social Darwinism thus emphasized competitive relationships in economic, social, and political spheres.

However, in recent times cooperative relationships have been attracting greater interest by biologists; there is growing recognition that these are a vital, if not more important, feature of natural systems. Cooperative or symbiotic relationships are being documented and are emerging as a critical pattern in the functioning of ecosystems. In the same way, cooperation is vital to how we organize human relations and institutions in cities.

Pollination is one example of a symbiotic relationship whereby the pollinator (a bird or insect) feasts on the nectar of a flower, spreads the pollen, and helps the plant to reproduce. Similarly, animals eating fruits gain sustenance and help distribute the plant's seeds. Cooperative relationships abound in ecosystems. Temporally they are understood in terms of coevolution in ecological theory. As observed in permaculture, elements of a system often perform many different functions that support the other elements. For example, trees provide shade for plants and animals, prevent erosion, provide food and habitat for animals, and contribute to climatic control. In some places, such as rainforests, trees actually attract rain. Decomposers in the soil gain sustenance from plant and animal wastes, and in turn make nutrients available again to plants, as well as eliminate waste from the system.

Sahtouris (1998) identifies a "repeating pattern" in evolution "in which aggressive competition leads to the threat of extinction, which is then avoided by the formation of cooperative alliances." If competitive relationships were the rule, then systems would eventually self-destruct. Thus, evolution can be viewed as a progression toward ever greater cooperation. People and institutions in cities need to harness the life-affirming power of cooperation. This cooperation needs to be expressed at all levels of city operations—at the global, bioregional, and community scales.

Networks are gaining recognition as the basic pattern of life:

> At all levels of life—from the metabolic networks inside cells to the food webs of ecosystems and the networks of communications in human societies—the components of living systems are interlinked in network fashion. (Capra 2002, 228)

The dynamics of networks is emerging as a major new area of research.[1]

Cooperative Networks in Cities (Social Capital)

Capra (2002) notes that social functions and processes are being organized increasingly around networks and that social networks are becoming a critical source of power. Thus, the growing awareness of the value of cooperation in ecosystems is paralleled by a growing awareness in cities about the importance of social capital.

Since Robert Putnam (1993) examined the foundations of wealth in Italian city-regions, there has been growing understanding that networks of trust and support enable an economy to work. Cities that create partnerships based on developing their mutual interests of business, government, and community are the cities that thrive in all aspects of sustainability.

Social capital is formed through the everyday life of cities—in the associations of professionals, recreational clubs, religious and spiritual organizations, cultural activities, and all the myriad neighborhoods and support structures. Those cities that encourage active participation in civil society are those that develop the trust and recognition of mutual interests necessary for any important projects. The social interactions between people from different sectors are the glue of a city.

Awareness of the importance of social capital has reached boardrooms and is motivating firms to become involved very directly in their communities as part of their corporate social responsibility. Sustainability recognizes the importance of building social capital from the grassroots level. The role of government in facilitating social capital for sustainability is to develop partnerships.

Defining Partnership

Partnership goes much further than mere participation. It implies joint initiatives, joint ownership, and joint benefits from development programs and projects, not just participation in the initiatives of another. (Wakely 1997)

Recognition is growing that cities cannot make effective changes toward sustainability without active partnerships within or among the business, government, and civil sectors at the neighborhood, citywide, and bioregional levels. Any sustainability solutions, especially top-down measures, are rarely successful unless they involve partnerships that can ensure they are enacted. Carley argues that a coherent partnership approach can integrate top-down and bottom-up strategies:

Recent research which examined participation in "nested" urban development partnerships in city-regions found that, in addition to horizontal integration of government with civil society and business, vertical integration of action and policy between the levels of neighborhood, city, urban region, and nation is also a prerequisite to sustainable development. This "chain" of initiative and partnership is only as strong as its weakest link.

It is also the case that while some aspects of large, complex cities are best managed at the strategic, citywide, or city-regional level, many other aspects of urban development are more effectively devolved to the local, neighborhood level. . . . A key to improved integration is to link regional, citywide, and local initiatives in a systematic development framework, recognizing that guidance and decisions at the level of the region can have profound impacts on the viability of community development initiatives. (2001, 12)

Furthermore, cooperation can occur between different cities in a bioregion and beyond. These networks allow the exchange of knowledge and skills, and also the development of collaborative solutions. Cooperation makes the task of building sustainability easier. Partnerships need to operate horizontally across different sectors and also vertically across different levels—from national to regional to the local neighborhood and even household level, as Carley (2001) suggests. Moreover, in line with the bioregional concept of the city as an ecosystem, partnerships need to be encouraged between urban and rural communities, and in a psychological sense between the human and more-than-human communities.

Genuine cooperative partnerships depend on the following factors:

- Sharing of power
- Trust
- Effective communication
- Shared or complementary vision and goals
- Symbiosis (mutual benefit)
- Adequate resources

Partnerships for sustainability, linking cities around the world, are increasingly showing that cooperation can be more powerful in solving problems than competition.

Strategies for Creating Partnerships in Cities

Partnerships are facilitated by in-person meetings, but innovations in communications technology—particularly videoconferencing and the internet—widen the options for the linking of people. The notion of partnerships in cities can be framed in terms of six strategies, each focusing on a different type of cooperation:

1. Government-initiated partnerships
2. Business-initiated partnerships
3. Community-initiated partnerships
4. Bioregional partnerships between urban and rural communities
5. Research partnerships
6. Intercity partnerships

Strategy 1: Government-Initiated Partnerships

To some extent, all partnerships are affected by the structures and processes of government that establish legislative boundaries and have the power to provide financial support, infrastructure, and information. As a writer for the Global Development Research Center points out,

> Partnerships do not simply happen. There is a clear need for a macro level framework to be developed, which will bring together disparate resources and stakeholders working toward sustainable urban areas.[2]

In a UNEP/IETC publication, Casanova (2003) has identified seven principles of building partnerships, which governments should follow to promote environmental citizenship:

1. Contacting key persons
2. Communicating the purpose
3. Community visioning
4. Confidence building
5. Collective action
6. Creating external links
7. Continuing support.

Similarly, the Bremen Initiative—a global campaign established in 1999 to foster partnership between municipalities and businesses—has developed a series of guiding principles:

- Mutual respect
- Efforts to understand each other's mission and mandate, framework conditions, aims, and objectives
- Receptiveness to needs and concerns of the weaker partner (e.g., small enterprises in large cities and small towns with large companies)
- Clear and open communication
- Consideration of the social, cultural, environmental, as well as the global impact of policies, projects, and decisions
- Transparency of decision making.[3]

Environs Australia is an organization that provides support to local governments interested in promoting sustainable development.[4] It recognizes the significance of developing a partnership network that facilitates collaboration, exchange of ideas, and the creation of a shared sustainability vision. Through its Sustainability Business Partnerships program, Environs encourages local government councils to work with businesses who are committed to providing sustainable products and services. Partners must demonstrate that they meet the following sustainability criteria:

1. **Commit to Sustainability**
   Make a formal commitment to helping society achieve sustainability as part of core business.
2. **Open and Accountable Operations**
   Have a publicly available environment policy and periodic performance report. This will provide the following information:
   - ever breached environmental legislation?
   - report on the areas of influence rather than direct impact
   - sources of investment (particularly logging industries, mining, tobacco, defense, and gaming)
   - any form of quality assurance and accreditations (e.g., ISO 14001)
   - actions to boost public commitment to achieve sustainability

3. Provide a simple life-cycle analysis of product(s) and service(s):
- sources of materials and processing agents
- have in place a design for the environment system (if the product originator) or "selection for the environment" system if a reseller
- engage in open consultation at implementation and, if required, be responsive to product modification
- provide details of membership and/or contributions to any industry associations, lobby groups, or campaigns

4. Provide Environmental Criteria

Provide, where relevant, the following environmental criteria:
- use of recycled materials and waste prevention
- product reusability
- durability
- energy efficiency
- life-cycle costs (primarily sources and transportation costs)
- low biodiversity and ecosystems impact and a commitment to support the development of biodiversity-inclusive Life-Cycle Assessment (LCA) methods and purchasing assessment systems

5. Provide Social and/or Governance Criteria

Provide, where relevant, information on good governance and social responsibility activities.

6. Advance Implementation of Local Action on Sustainability

Offer a product or service that allows councils or their communities to implement and extend local sustainability actions.

7. Be of Value to Local Governments

Offer a product or service that is of value to councils implementing or promoting environmental and sustainability aims.

8. Attain Accreditation and/or Recognition of Corporate Sustainability Performance

ISO 14000 is the existing accreditation system, but a number of systems for fuller sustainability accreditation are being developed and will be available to governments to enable them to ensure they are complying with world best practice on sustainability.

9. Provide Feedback

Provide feedback on partnership results (market penetration, product modification, a successful case study, etc.).

Governments in cities are developing codes of conduct, principles of operations, and "sustainability covenants" with professional organizations and individual businesses, in order to embed their mutual interests in sustainability and to create opportunities for stretch targets (Government of Western Australia 2003).

Strategy 2: Business-Initiated Partnerships

Business alliances can create accreditation systems; allow for industrial ecology solutions; develop corporate ethics; provide assistance to communities; and develop sustainable practices, labeling, and self-regulation.

Business usually plays a dominant role in city-regions, even in places like China but especially in America and Europe, where business leadership can transform the problems of sustainability into opportunities to make profits through innovative solutions. In towns that have particularly dominant businesses as in mining regions, or in cities with industrial complexes, industry needs to form partnerships with local communities to ensure that it can leave a legacy of economic, social, and environmental benefit. Frequently such partnerships are driven by the need for cooperation among all parts of a region in order to achieve goals on waste, pollution, and other environmental concerns. But increasingly these groups are also finding social goals to address, such as occupational health and safety issues, local employment and training (especially of indigenous people), and local procurement.

Global issues such as greenhouse gases, oil consumption, and biodiversity increasingly require business to form partnerships that can effect transformative change for cities worldwide. The World Business Council on Sustainable Development (WBCSD), which brings together 150 of the most innovative companies in the world, has been set up to do this.[5] At the World Summit on Sustainable Development in Johannesburg in 2002, the WBCSD and Greenpeace formed a partnership to show how together they could talk governments into moving more quickly on global sustainability issues. Certainly key industries and corporations (such as BP) have shown that they could meet the Kyoto commitments much faster than government, but there are also many that are not yet interested in changing their fundamentals for global sustainability.

In Mexico the WBCSD formed a partnership with the government and the World Resources Institute to reduce greenhouse gases. By bringing innovative corporate members into such a partnership, the organization hopes that other businesses will follow their example. The WRI/WBCSD Greenhouse Gas Protocol seems to be doing just that. The WBCSD was able to immediately get commitments from key companies in the cement, petroleum, and iron/steel industries, which emit 30 percent of Mexico's greenhouse gases. The next phase will be to enlist further support from industries that are responsible for 80 percent of Mexico's greenhouse emissions. The program has introduced emissions accounting, best-practice greenhouse gas reduction technologies and management, carbon trading, and a network of support. The next place to establish such a partnership will be the Philippines, and interest has been expressed also in China, India, South Africa and Brazil. These emerging economies will soon have cities whose global innovations in climate protection will be leading the world.

A similar partnership in the United States was established in 2007—the Global Roundtable on Climate Change—to enable major US industries to begin taking responsibility for collectively being the world's biggest contributor to greenhouse gases. The roundtable is seeking partnerships with government to establish a cap-and-trade system for reducing carbon.

A number of corporate sustainability/environmental performance evaluation models now exist that act as transparent "filters" of businesses' ability to incorporate sustainability principles and practice into corporate structures and activities. These include the SAM Group's Dow Jones Sustainability Index, the Australian Conservation Foundation's Good Reputation Index, the Business Council of Australia's Statement of Strategies for Sustainable Development, and the Earth Index. Depending on the size and nature of a business, partners are encouraged to gain assessment and accreditation to such indexes.

A business-initiated partnership in the Kwinana industrial area in Western Australia is showing how industry can get involved with the regional community and help shape visions for a more sustainable form of industrial development (Verstegen 2003). The thirty or so major industries in Kwinana, a complex in the southern suburbs of Perth, formed the Kwinana Industries Council (KIC) and the Kwinana Community-Industries Forum (KCIF). The council and the forum have facilitated an active dialogue among community, industry, and local and state government stakeholders. The bimonthly forum is the largest and most comprehensive of its type in Australia, allowing community members or groups to raise current issues with industry and government in a responsive forum aligned with such values as openness, honesty, goodwill, representative participation, and integration. The forum was developed to address the lack of trust among industry, community, and government sectors in the Kwinana industrial region. It has now gone beyond its original conflict-resolution role to articulate a powerful vision and mechanism to achieve integrated decision making and codevelopment among community, industry, and public sector stakeholders. Significant social capital and capacity for sustainable development is associated with these relationships.

Some of the outcomes from this partnership have been:

- The development of an extensive industrial ecology process whereby waste from one industry is used as a resource by another. Over one hundred linkages have been established.
- The development of a combined wastewater recycling system in partnership with the state government, which takes the main sewer and treats it for use as industrial process water. The reuse of this wastewater has freed up some 10 percent of Perth's water supply.
- A greening of Kwinana project that has seen extensive landscaping implemented around industries and the conservation of remnant bush.
- Significant reductions in wastewater discharges, to the point at which marine ecosystems have now recovered and are rebuilding to preindustrial ecosystem health.
- An air quality monitoring and hotline system for immediate reporting of problems, which parallels a sulfur trading scheme that has seen pollutants affecting ambient air quality maintained at or below required levels.

- A training program for local youth to help them acquire jobs and apprenticeships, and a program for professionals to receive sustainability training.

Social capital and capacity building on the part of industrial development stakeholders can catalyze a breakdown of the misconception that social, environmental, and economic goals are inevitably in conflict. These new forms of decision making require a significant departure from the industrial development paradigms of the past, as they require industry commitment to community involvement and partnership building in the local region.

Strategy 3: Community-Initiated Partnerships

Communities can initiate partnerships to stimulate change through participatory processes, to raise awareness of sustainability issues, to empower marginalized groups, and to create new ways of living and making a living. Community groups can work together to build better understandings of the concerns, fears, and hopes of different sectors and to build common visions and solutions. They could develop sustainability plans and indicators, or collaborate on actual projects.

Networks across these different sectors are crucial and can be facilitated through empowerment processes (discussed in chapter 7) and effective governance (discussed in chapter 10). Such networking leads to holistic decision making and sharing of different perspectives and ideas to develop more effective strategies for sustainability. Sharing information at the bioregional level should be done through personal contact, although cybernetworks can facilitate information sharing over more distant scales.

Surface Transportation Policy Partnership and Other Pro-Transit Partnerships

In 1991, US transportation funding systems were dramatically changed when Congress passed the Intermodal Surface Transportation Efficiency Act (ISTEA). This new bill ended the restriction of federal transportation funds just to highways and allowed other, more sustainable modes to be funded if cities wanted to reprioritize. Suddenly cities had a chance to create a more sustainable future for themselves, but the highway lobbies hadn't seen this legislation coming. Where had ISTEA come from? The bill was written by the Surface Transportation Policy Partnership (STPP), which had formed from more than a hundred sustainable transport groups from across America. They gave the bill to New York Senator Daniel Patrick Moynihan, who willingly introduced it to Congress, where it was passed. ISTEA has been reauthorized three times with almost completely unanimous support, as communities find it much better to have a say in transportation priorities. Transit and bike/walk projects have risen rapidly to consume over 20 percent of the funds and have led to a small revolution in US cities (though they have a long way to go to catch up to European cities in these areas). The STPP remains a potent lobbying force for sustainable transport in Washington, DC.[6]

Many other cities have developed partnerships over transit systems. In 1979 the city of Perth, Australia, took the first steps toward closing its rail system down. A nongovernment organization (NGO) called the Friends of the Railway was formed and rapidly developed strong community support sufficient to reverse the government's course. From there the NGO's vision of a more rail-oriented city has been progressively adopted by the government, which has gradually electrified and extended the system to all corridors. Initially skeptical about the rail project, the business community has grown to see it as a major advantage for the city and has committed to developing transit-oriented villages around stations. In fifteen years patronage has gone from seven million per year to fifty million, with a doubling expected in the next five years (Newman and Kenworthy 2007).

GreenCityBlueLake, Northeast Ohio

A grassroots group, EcoCity Cleveland, is promoting a regional vision for northeast Ohio under the banner of GreenCityBlueLake. The GreenCityBlueLake website,[7] established by EcoCity Cleveland, aims to support the growth of a network for sustainability, providing a space for sharing stories and developing partnerships:

> We need a bold sustainability agenda that inspires us to move into the future in innovative ways. This agenda must be regional in scale. And it must be created by a broad network that transcends regional divisions and leverages the activities of many partners.

Figure 8.1

Perth's new rail system: a partnership of community, government, and business for a more sustainable city

Photo New Metro Rail

The GreenCityBlueLake initiative will facilitate community discussions and strategic planning and action for sustainability in northeast Ohio. The industrial past of Cleveland has left its scars, so EcoCity Cleveland hopes to see different kinds of industrial activity emerge in the region. Its members are looking for new types of leadership, new ways of working together, and new approaches for energy, water, food, health, land development, transportation, building, business, education, and the arts. The group contends,

> The challenges of the twenty-first century are rushing upon us. This work can drive innovation, attract talent, and make Greater Cleveland a greener, healthier, and more prosperous place for all.[8]

WA Collaboration

The WA Collaboration in Western Australia is an alliance of nongovernment, social, and environmental groups including unions, indigenous groups, social welfare, church, and conservation groups that provides a forum for presenting community views on sustainability.[9] It is based on a similar national group, the Australian Collaboration, though the WA group has more extensive membership. It was established when the state government began to develop a sustainability strategy. The WA Collaboration brought the NGO community into a unified lobby group to achieve a coherent input into the strategy.

Following an extensive community involvement process, including a Sustainability Summit, it issued a report in 2003: *The Community Sustainability Agenda: Creating a Just and Sustainable Western Australia*. The Collaboration has continued to provide informed advice to various agencies implementing the Western Australian State Sustainability Strategy, ensuring there is a continued voice from this unique partnership of civil society groups.

Global Ecovillage Network

Ecovillages are by definition community based (see chapter 2). The Global Ecovillage Network (GEN) is an organization that promotes the development of ecovillages worldwide. GEN offers a forum in which people and communities "dedicated to restoring the land and living 'sustainable plus' lives by putting more back into the environment than they take out" can share their ideas, experiences, and technologies.

Its members include large groups like Sarvodaya (11,000 sustainable villages in Sri Lanka); EcoYoff and Colufifa (350 villages in Senegal); the Ladakh project on the Tibetan plateau; ecotowns like Auroville in South India and Nimbin in Australia; small rural ecovillages like Gaia Asociación in Argentina and Huehuecoyotl, Mexico; urban rejuvenation projects like Los Angeles Ecovillage and Christiania in Copenhagen; permaculture design sites such as Crystal Waters in Australia, Cochabamba in Bolivia, and Barus in Brazil; and educational centers such as Findhorn in Scotland, Center for Alternative Technology in Wales, and Earthlands in Massachusetts.

GEN's primary aim is to support and encourage sustainable settlements across the world through the following:

- Internal and external communications services, facilitating the flow and exchange of information about ecovillages and demonstration sites
- Networking and project coordination in fields related to sustainable settlements
- Global cooperation and partnerships (as with the UN Best Practices program, EU Phare, European Youth For Action, and the UN Economic and Social Council).[10]

A more recent initiative has sought to take the concepts developed by the Global Ecovillage Network and apply them to cities. The Urban Ecovillage Network has emerged in North America with the aim of engaging "urban neighborhoods throughout the world in the process of reinventing how we live in cities, to be more ecologically, economically, and culturally sustainable."[11]

Strategy 4: Bioregional Partnerships between Urban and Rural Communities

The transformation of cities toward sustainability—the city as ecosystem within a bioregion—requires the nurturing of partnerships between urban and rural communities. The goal is to create symbiotic relationships whereby rural communities gain financial security and support for caring for the land, while urban communities are assured of a supply of produce by sustainable (and ethical) methods. Such links between city and country encourage greater responsibility to the land and each other, and integrate production and consumption, thereby closing feedback loops.

Place-based ownership models of industry—such as consumer cooperatives, and community and employee ownership—bring power back to local communities. These models of regional economic security are also supported by ecological modes of stakeholder representation in regional development decision making. With a vision reflecting the developer's needs as much as community concerns, empowered communities would be proactive in regaining viability and vitality through sustainable industrial development and employment opportunities, while regional environmental and health issues would be replaced with appropriate and profitable technology. These kinds of partnerships are strengthening in the agricultural sector.

Figure 8.2

Farmers' market in Charlottesville, Virginia

Photo Peter Newman

Community-Supported Agriculture

Partnerships between farmers and consumers were first established in Japan in the 1960s by a group of Japanese women concerned about the application of pesticides, the rise in processed and imported foods, and the decline in farming populations. Called *teikei*, meaning "partnership" or "food with the farmer's face on it," this system involved direct consumer support for local farmers on an annual basis. The system has been taken up in other places such as Europe and North America.

In the West this concept has been dubbed community-supported agriculture (CSA), an approach that contributes to a sustainable agricultural system by:

- Providing farmers with direct outlets for farm produce and fair compensation
- Fostering sustainable land stewardship by supporting farmers to make the transition toward minimal or zero chemical inputs
- Strengthening local economies by keeping food dollars in local communities
- Linking producers with consumers directly, allowing people to have a personal connection with their food and the land on which it was produced
- Making nutritious, affordable, wholesome foods widely available to community members.

There are over a thousand CSA farms in the United States and Canada. Box 8.1 explains more about how CSA systems work.

City Farms

Many cities have developed city farms that form a bridge between the city and its bioregion. These city farms provide an opportunity for city people—especially children and the disempowered—to become involved in agriculture. They offer demonstrations of technology and sustainable urban living, and they usually have clear links to their bioregions with development of nurseries for replanting in the regions (Newman and Kenworthy 1999). They can be an important part of the "city as ark" concept outlined in chapter 3.

In subtropical Brisbane, Australia, a community group has transformed four hectares of flood-prone city parkland into a diverse, organic "food forest."[12] Northey Street City Farm was established in 1994 to demonstrate permaculture. In the process of growing food, project leaders have also successfully cultivated community and sustainability awareness. The farm is now part of the Australian City Farms and Community Gardens Network.

Northey Street City Farm is home to hundreds of exotic and native fruit and nut trees, in addition to the vegetables, herbs, and flowers tended by farm staff and community volunteers. As the permaculture plants became established, various breeds of poultry were introduced and rotated through the area. Water features such as ponds were developed for aesthetic purposes, microclimate moderation, ecological restoration, and pest management. They attract birds, frogs, and beneficial insects into this urban landscape. Bird and bat boxes have been constructed and placed high in the trees.

People of all ages, backgrounds, and abilities work side by side at the farm. Schoolchildren regularly visit to participate in educational programs about the environment and urban sustainability. Many young unemployed people have gained valuable hands-on training through the farm's permaculture accreditation programs. University

Box 8.1   **What Is Community-Supported Agriculture and How Does It Work?**

Community-supported agriculture (CSA) is a partnership of mutual commitment between a farm and a community of supporters that provides a direct link between the production and consumption of food. Supporters cover a farm's yearly operating budget by purchasing a share of the season's harvest. CSA members make a commitment to support the farm throughout the season, and assume the costs, risks, and bounty of growing food along with the farmer or grower. Members help pay for seeds, fertilizer, water, equipment maintenance, labor, etc. In return, the farm provides, to the best of its ability, a healthy supply of seasonal fresh produce throughout the growing season. Becoming a member creates a responsible relationship between people and the food they eat, the land on which it is grown, and those who grow it. Members can't choose out-of-season produce, but by receiving what is in season the chance to be closer to the cycles of the bioregion are greater.

The mutually supportive relationship between local farmers, growers, and community members helps create a generally more stable farm economy in which members are assured the highest quality produce, often at below retail prices. In return, farmers and growers are guaranteed a reliable market for a diverse selection of crops.

Money, Members, and Management

A farmer or grower, often with the assistance of a core group, draws up a budget reflecting the production costs for the year. This includes all salaries, distribution costs, investments for seeds and tools, land payments, machinery maintenance, etc. The budget is then divided by the number of people for which the farm will provide, and this determines the cost of each share of the harvest. One share is usually designed to provide the weekly vegetable needs for a family of four. Flowers, fruit, meat, honey, eggs, and dairy products are also available through some CSA.

Community members sign up and purchase their shares, either in one lump sum before the seeds are sown in early spring, or in several installments throughout the growing season. Production expenses are thereby guaranteed, and the farmer or grower starts receiving income as soon as work begins.

In return for their investment, CSA members receive a bag of fresh, locally grown, typically organic produce once a week while the season enables growing to occur. This means only occasionally throughout the winter in colder climates and year-round in milder zones. Members prefer a wide variety of vegetables and herbs, which encourages integrated cropping and companion planting. These practices help reduce risk factors and give multiple benefits to the soil. Crops are planted in succession in order to provide a continuous weekly supply of mixed vegetables. As crops rotate throughout the season, weekly shares vary by size and types of produce, reflecting local growing seasons and conditions.

CSA programs vary considerably as they are based on farm or garden location, agricultural practices, and specific farm and community goals and needs. Memberships are known to include a variety of community members including low-income families, homeless people, senior citizens, and differently abled individuals. If provided, an extra fee typically is charged for home delivery. Most CSA programs invite members to visit the farm and welcome volunteer assistance. Working shares are an option in some cases, whereby a member commits to three or four hours a week to help the farm in exchange for a discount on membership cost. Apprenticeships are growing in popularity. For some farms they are an integral component of a successful operation. Apprenticeships offer valuable hands-on education.

Property arrangements tend to be quite flexible. Beyond private ownership, there is leasing of land with lease fees factored in as a regular budget item. CSA is also an excellent opportunity for holding land in some form of trust arrangement. *(continued on page 182)*

Box 8.1   *(continued from page 181)*

Every CSA program strives over time for a truly sustainable operation, both economically and environmentally. Networks of CSA have been forming to develop associative economies by growing and providing a greater range of products in a cooperative fashion. Some CSA programs provide produce for local restaurants, roadside stands, or farmers' markets while building farm membership, or in many cases, in addition to it.

Distribution and Decision Making

Distribution styles also vary. Once the day's produce is harvested, the entire amount is weighed and the number of pounds or items (e.g., heads of lettuce, ears of corn) to be received by each share is determined. Some CSA programs have members come to the farm and weigh out their own share, and leave behind any items they don't want at a surplus table. Other farms have a distribution crew to weigh items and pack shares to be picked up by members at the farm or at distribution points.

Several advantages to the direct marketing approach of CSA, in addition to shared risk and prepayment of farm costs, are the minimal loss and waste of harvested farm produce, little or reduced need for long-term storage, and a willingness by members to accept produce with natural cosmetic imperfections.

A core group made up of the farmers or growers, distributors, key administrators, and several CSA members can be the decision-making body for a CSA program. This group often determines short- and long-range goals, prepares the budget, conducts publicity and outreach, organizes events, etc. Annual meetings, a member newsletter, and occasional surveys are some basic means of communication between the farm and its members.

Source: Community-supported agriculture, University of Massachusetts–Amherst,
http://umassvegetable.org/food_farming_systems/csa

students have undertaken onsite research. Currently the farm is working in partnership with a local Aboriginal group to develop the bushfood gardens (edible indigenous plants) and document this information.

Northey Street City Farm has sparked related community initiatives and events, such as an organic farmers' market, nursery of edible plants, community green-waste recycling center, creek cleanup, catchment management, bush rehabilitation, campaigns against GMOs and food irradiation, bicycle rallies, and sustainable living festivals. It has inspired almost a dozen other communities in the region to create their own public gardens and contributed to a noticeable rise in ecoliteracy in the city of Brisbane.

Strategy 5: Research Partnerships
Sustainability requires an integration of different disciplines and modes of inquiry that lends itself to a collaborative approach. Partnerships between different research institutions have a major role to play in developing more sustainable urban solutions. Computer and telecommunications networks expand the opportunities for easier communication between the different parts of such research partnerships. The various teams of

people that are needed for problem solving in a city and its bioregion need to be pulled together for research dialogues that can provide innovative solutions. This is not made easy due to professional silos and can only be overcome by partnerships.

Funding by sustainability groups, as outlined earlier, is the best incentive for such partnerships to form. Research partnerships need not involve only "experts" but also the community in adaptive management processes whereby both groups can learn from each other and produce more imaginative solutions. The research done by natural resource management partnerships, which builds on the community science of farmers and conservationists, can be replicated in research partnerships within cities on technology, management, design, and lifestyles for sustainability.

Many universities are establishing research centers on sustainability. Most are forming strong partnerships with business and some with government, but few are forming partnerships with community. The challenge of sustainability research is to form partnerships with all three sectors.

Strategy 6: Partnerships between Cities

Cities have traditionally competed with each other economically, but sustainability is increasingly bringing them together to partner on solving their deeper problems. This partnership can occur in formalized sister-city relationships; through associations such as ICLEI (Local Governments for Sustainability, originally known as the International Council for Local Environmental Initiatives); and through new linkages such as the proposal to share in procurement of innovative, sustainable technologies, which came out of the 2004 UN Sustainable Development for Cities Conference in Hong Kong.

International Partnerships

Local Agenda 21 and ICLEI's Cities for Climate Protection campaign and Water Challenge campaign all provide global links between cities.[13] They remain among the most significant outcomes to have emerged from the 1992 UN Conference on Environment and Development (Rio Earth Summit), which produced the first unified call for sustainable development by the nations of the world. Local government realized it would need to help lead this agenda, and ICLEI was given the charter to create global programs that link cities in their attempts to find sustainability solutions.

Other international networks between cities are also emerging, such as the PLUS Network (Partners for Long-term Urban Sustainability, originally known as the +30 Network).[14] The PLUS Network has a core membership of around thirty cities, sharing their experiences, expertise, and tools to undertake very long-term (60- to 100-year) planning for urban sustainability. The network's peer exchanges allow members to assess results, reduce development costs, and compare their progress to benchmarks and to one another. Lessons from the core group are shared with other cities through ICLEI. The International Center for Sustainable Cities in Vancouver, Canada, founded the network and serves as its secretariat.

In 2005 the Large Cities Climate Leadership Group (also known as C40 Cities) formed, and together with the William J. Clinton Foundation they have committed to sustainability through partnership on climate issues.[15] Member and affiliate cities have begun to set up a collective "buyers club" to improve prices on the purchase of new sustainable technologies such as hydrogen fuel cell buses, electric rail, photovoltaics, wind power, energy efficiency systems, and innovative waste treatment systems. By banding together, economies of scale can be created to reduce the price of and hasten the transition to sustainability.

European Sustainable Cities and Towns Campaign

A major urban sustainability collaboration has emerged in Europe called the European Sustainable Cities and Towns Campaign.[16] It began at a conference in Aalborg, Denmark, in May 1994, at which a charter was drawn up, the Charter of European Cities and Towns Toward Sustainability. It stated:

> We understand that our present urban lifestyle, in particular our patterns of division of labor and functions, land-use, transport, industrial production, agriculture, consumption, and leisure activities, and hence our standard of living, make us essentially responsible for many environmental problems humankind is facing. This is particularly relevant as 80 percent of Europe's population live in urban areas.
>
> We have learned that present levels of resource consumption in the industrialized countries cannot be achieved by all people currently living, much less by future generations, without destroying the natural capital.
>
> We are convinced that sustainable human life on this globe cannot be achieved without sustainable local communities. Local government is close to where environmental problems are perceived and closest to the citizens and shares responsibility with governments at all levels for the well-being of humankind and nature. Therefore, cities and towns are key players in the process of changing lifestyles, production, consumption and spatial patterns.

The Aalborg Charter provided a framework for implementing sustainable development and committed local authorities to conduct Local Agenda 21 processes. Almost two thousand local authorities are participating in the campaign, and ten networks of cities and towns committed to sustainability have been formed. A decade later at the fourth European Sustainable Cities and Towns Conference, one hundred cities signed a pledge called the Aalborg +10 Commitments.[17] Signatories agreed to carry out baseline environmental reviews of their cities within the first year. Targets for action on a range of environmental issues had to be identified within the first two years. Cities must also monitor progress toward the targets and prepare regular public reports.

The Aalborg Commitments from 2004 opens with the following statement:

> We, European local governments united in the European Sustainable Cities &
> Towns Campaign, assembled at the Aalborg +10 Conference, confirm our
> shared vision of a sustainable future for our communities.
>
> Our vision is of cities and towns that are inclusive, prosperous, creative,
> and sustainable, and that provide a good quality of life for all citizens and
> enable their participation in all aspects of urban life.

The commitments are grouped under the following themes:

- Governance
- Local management toward sustainability
- Natural common goods
- Responsible consumption and lifestyle choices
- Planning and design
- Better mobility, less traffic
- Local action for health
- Vibrant and sustainable local economy
- Social equity and justice
- Local to global.

Sister Cities: Partnership between Zurich and K'un-ming

Most local governments have sister cities, but few put these partnerships to work for sustainability. K'un-ming in China and Zurich in Switzerland are an exception.

From 1995 to 2005, the city and region of K'un-ming was marked by rapid urban growth and a strong trend toward modernization. The economy is expected to continue to expand strongly and the city's population to double by 2020. Such a pace of growth normally leads to a situation in which social, environmental, and cultural heritage issues are increasingly neglected.

Due to these dramatic circumstances, the city partnership between Zurich and K'un-ming, which had begun in 1982, developed gradually from a cultural exchange into an intensive technical cooperation between the two cities, aimed at steering the strong development of K'un-ming toward a more sustainable path. With the involvement of the Swiss Development Cooperation and the ORL (National, Regional, and Local Planning) Institute at the Swiss Federal Institute of Technology, three phases of the overall project for the K'un-ming Urban Development and Public Transportation Masterplan (KUDPTM) have been carried out. The main contents of KUDPTM were regional development, traffic management and public transportation, urban landscape planning, and networking and dissemination.

Main successes were the implementation of the first bus rapid-transit system in China and the now ongoing efforts to establish a strong regional rail system. Furthermore, the project-based collaboration during the last nine years has strongly contributed to the improvement of the urban planning and management skills of K'un-ming's officials, especially when dealing with sustainability issues (Feiner et al. 2002).

Conclusions

Partnerships are increasingly being recognized as a vital aspect of sustainability. In cities, partnerships can be initiated by governments, business, or the community, and involve one or more of these different sectors. Partnerships need to occur between cities and their bioregions too. Research partnerships can help produce more creative and innovative solutions. Cities can also partner with each other to exchange information and technologies and create economies of scale. The path to sustainability and regeneration in cities is certainly a shared one.

Sustainable Production and Consumption

PRINCIPLE 9

Promote sustainable production and consumption through appropriate use of environmentally sound technologies and effective demand management.

Elaboration: A range of approaches and tools can be used to promote sustainable practices. Demand management, which includes accurate valuations of natural resources and increasing public awareness, is a valuable strategy to support sustainable consumption. This approach can also provide significant savings in infrastructure investment.

Sustainable production can be supported by the adoption and use of environmentally sound technologies that may improve environmental performance significantly. These technologies protect the environment, are less polluting, use resources in a sustainable manner, recycle more of their wastes and products, and handle all residual wastes in a more environmentally acceptable way than the technologies they replace.

Environmentally sound technologies can also be used to drive reduced impacts and enhance value along a supply chain and to support businesses embracing product stewardship.

Integrating Production and Consumption

We have got to remember that the great destructiveness of the industrial age comes from a division, a sort of divorce, in our economy, and therefore our consciousness, between production and consumption. Of this radical division of functions we can say, without much fear of oversimplifying, that the aim of producers is to sell as much as possible and that the aim of consumers is to buy as much as possible. (Berry 2001, 77)

Sustainable production requires us to develop whole new ways of producing goods and services with far fewer resources and close to zero waste. However, sustainability is about more than just technological changes. As Desai and Riddlestone (2002, 29) point out, "Technology will not save us from having to confront the simple issue of limits to consumption." Technological fixes alone are inadequate to sufficiently reduce the ecological footprints of cities. For instance, in the United States, Japan, and Germany, despite efficiency gains over the past twenty years, the total and per capita use of materials in these countries has risen overall (Day 1998). Day argues that "the goal of sustainability is slipping further from our grasp." Sustainable consumption patterns are the other part of the equation.

Transforming our consumption and production patterns rests on bringing the processes of consumption and production together to enhance awareness of the impacts that these patterns have on human communities and ecosystems, in other words, restoring feedback loops between the city and its bioregion. Only in this way can exploitive relationships turn into regenerative ones. Bioregional and local economies provide the key to restoring these feedback loops, and matching our consumption and production patterns better to bioregional capacities. They provide the appropriate context and scale for meeting human needs, developing consumer and producer partnerships, and enabling people to exercise their civic responsibilities. Furthermore, we need to tap into the wisdom of the natural world and human creativity to envision different ways of living, producing, and consuming.

Sustainable Consumption

Reducing consumption of resources by the wealthy citizens of the world and focusing on meeting the basic needs of the poor is vital to sustainability. The level of a city's consumption reflects demographics, per capita demand for goods, and the resource intensity of those goods. These factors are in turn shaped by cultural worldviews, ethics, and values; the flow of information; economic, political, and social constraints; and personal perceptions of the capacity to create change. Changing the consumption patterns of wealthy nations will require a shift in urban values to reflect sustainability concerns. A key to reducing consumption levels is bringing consumption and production processes closer together through the regionalization and localization of economies. This brings power back to local and regional communities, thereby facilitating cooperation and greater equity, restoring feedback loops, and making people responsible for the health of ecosystems and bioregions. The empowerment of people to participate in decision making, and the formation of cooperative partnerships between communities, governments, and businesses are crucial elements in the process of reenvisioning ourselves as citizens rather than just consumers.

Human needs can be satisfied in many different ways. The key is to find synergic satisfiers that are the least resource intensive (perhaps requiring no goods) and that are produced by processes that mimic those of natural ecosystems. To move toward sustainable consumption, the focus needs to be on meeting genuine human needs and stabilizing populations. Evidence suggests that birth rates are lower in cities than in rural areas, so cities may assist in this stabilization process. Ecovillages, both in cities and rural areas, can help build the economic and social security crucial to lowering birth rates. By finding simpler, more sustainable ways of living, we can meet the challenges that lie ahead:

> Our evolutionary intelligence is now being tested. The choices made within this generation will reverberate into the deep future. Although human societies have confronted major hurdles throughout history, the challenges of our era are genuinely unique. Never before have so many people been called upon to make such sweeping changes in so little time. Never before has the entire human family been entrusted with the task of working together to imagine and then consciously build a sustainable, just, and compassionate future. Seeds growing for the past generation in the garden of simplicity are now blossoming into the springtime of their relevance for the Earth. May the garden thrive. (Elgin 2003)

There is scant literature on the issue of sustainable consumption. The works by Clive Hamilton (2003, 2005) and Thomas Princen (2005) are an exception. In *The Logic of Sufficiency*, Princen examines the need for appreciating limits in our society. He suggests that the sweepingly pervasive concepts of "efficiency" and "cooperation" are valuable in guiding our economy but have no sense of limits in them. While he acknowledges that efficiency and cooperation are culturally intuitive, having evolved to ensure the very survival of early human settlements, Princen warns that in a modern context of critical environmental threats and displaced risks and consequences, unfettered interpretations and applications of efficiency and cooperation can serve to undermine sustainability. As intuitive and popular as these principles are, both suffer from "normative neutrality," he argues. "One can find efficiencies in harvesting a forest so as to save trees just as well as one can find efficiencies to get every last bit of fiber from an acre of timberland. One can cooperate to protect a forest just as well as one can cooperate to clear-cut it" (Princen 2005, 16). Efficiency and cooperation, therefore, as valid and relevant as they can be, are no more than the means by which we may strive to meet defined objectives. And they are certainly not synonymous with sustainability or ecological rationality simply by merit of being potentially beneficial.

Conversely, Princen alleges that sufficiency is, by definition, consistent with the principles of sustainability and ecological rationality, in that it actively allows for development to be naturally constrained by both biophysical and social limits to growth. He proposes that sufficiency, though commonly perceived as being synonymous with "lack" and "sacrifice," actually has the potential to nourish and replenish on many levels—ecologically, socially, and economically.

Recognizing that "economic sufficiency" could be a hard sell in the Western world, infatuated as we are with economic primacy and maximization, Princen details numerous examples of what could be described as "the business case for sufficiency." Through such proven examples, he demonstrates that by respecting natural limits through sufficiency and ecological rationality, business can invoke a profitable and perpetual financial return on investment.

The voluntary simplicity movement has some currency as a lifestyle more in keeping with sustainable use of the world's resources. Princen has tried to show that a similar movement is needed in business.

While the remainder of this chapter looks first at strategies for sustainable consumption and then separately at strategies for sustainable production, the key point is for cities to formulate programs that integrate both types of strategies. Thus the strategies discussed below should be seen as necessarily complementary and integrated approaches to reducing what we consume and changing how we produce consumable products, simultaneously.

Strategies for Sustainable Consumption

Strategies for sustainable consumption include:

1. Encouraging voluntary simplicity individually or communally through simplicity circles
2. Initiating education programs for demand management
3. Initiating sustainable procurement programs at all levels of government and in private corporations and organizations
4. Backing the "slow movement"

Strategy 1: Voluntary Simplicity

The voluntary simplicity movement is gaining ground in Western countries, promoting conserver lifestyles that demonstrate the possibility of having a high quality of life with reduced resource use. Voluntary simplicity attacks consumerism at its heart, the motivation to consume, which can be caused by a multitude of other needs and which can never be truly satisfied by amassing material goods. Thus voluntary simplicity seeks to help people find other nonconsumptive ways of addressing their needs. It has been taken up by concerned citizens on an individual basis, and by those who have joined together in simplicity circles to provide support and inspiration for each other in the search for simpler ways of living.[1] The processes of gathering and sharing experiences help nurture community connections. Groups may organize events to meet social, creative, and spiritual needs, such as holding seasonal festivals, sharing meals, creating a community garden, walking together, or conducting talks and soirees.

The simplicity movement has been growing over the last two decades. It gained attention when Duane Elgin published his seminal work *Voluntary Simplicity: Toward A Way of Life That Is Outwardly Simple, Inwardly Rich* in 1981. As Linda Breen Pierce explains, "Voluntary simplicity is not about doing without. In fact it's just the opposite—it's about having enough: enough intimacy with others and with nature, enough sense of purpose and fulfilling work, enough fun and joy." It is the lack of these qualities that people in cities have been encouraged, through subtle media messages and broader cultural values, to meet through consumption. "Voluntary simplicity is about living life fully, of experiencing life as a whole human being. It's also about caring for the Earth and people throughout the world who truly do not have enough."[2]

A growing body of knowledge suggests that we view the current overconsumption in society as a sickness. Hamilton and Denniss (2005) call it "affluenza." Jessie O'Neill, a licensed therapist and author of *The Golden Ghetto: The Psychology of Affluence*, has started the Affluenza Project as a way of offering therapy for this sickness. She says,

> Individually, affluenza is a dysfunctional relationship with money/wealth, or the pursuit of it. Individual and cultural symptoms are: an inability to delay gratification and tolerate frustration; a false sense of entitlement; loss of future motivation; low self-esteem; loss of self-confidence; low self-worth; preoccupation with externals. Sudden wealth syndrome and sudden poverty syndrome are both parts of the greater "dis-ease" of affluenza.[3]

Although there are deep reasons why people overconsume, there are also deep motivations for living simply. Pushes and pulls toward this way of life seem equally compelling for rich and poor alike. Most people are not choosing to live more simply from a feeling of sacrifice; rather, they are seeking deeper sources of satisfaction than are being offered by a high-stress, consumption-obsessed society. To illustrate: while real incomes doubled in the United States in the past generation, the percentage of the population reporting they are very happy has remained unchanged (roughly a third); at the same time, divorce rates have doubled and teen suicide rates have tripled. A whole generation has tasted the fruits of an affluent society and has discovered that money does not buy happiness. In the search for satisfaction, millions of people are not only "downshifting" or pulling back from the rat race, they are also "upshifting" or moving ahead into a life that is, though materially more modest, rich with family, friends, community, creative work in the world, and a soulful connection with the universe (Hamilton 2003).

Voluntary simplicity is not a policy that can be developed first by governments and business; it is a policy that depends on the values of civic society. Thus voluntary simplicity movements need to be encouraged by churches, lifestyle groups, universities, professional associations, and the media. However governments and business can encourage voluntary simplicity through their own examples, in the lifestyles of their leaders, in procurement policies, and by demand-management strategies.

Strategy 2: Demand Management

Demand management seeks to educate consumers about ways of achieving their needs without so much damaging use of unsustainable resources. Householders and businesses can meet their needs for heat, light, cleanliness, gardens, safe goods, or accessibility without the need for more fossil fuel power stations, more dams, more mountains of waste, and more freeways. Demand management seeks to meet current needs without damaging the next generation's ability to meet their needs because we have used up most of their options.

In developed countries, local government initiatives have started to help communities become more aware of their resource use and find ways to reduce resource consumption (UNEP/IETC 2003). Approaches such as "reduce, reuse, recycle" have become popular, though the focus has tended to be on recycling and to a lesser extent on reusing and reducing. The key point is that reducing resource use does not have to mean reducing quality of life. Indeed, the Factor Four agenda (von Weizsäcker, Lovins, and Lovins 1997) suggests we can simultaneously halve resource consumption and double wealth. At the very least, we can ensure that livability is improved, while resource use is reduced (Newman and Kenworthy 1999), which still amounts to a reversal of historical trends.

Household and corporate demand-management schemes have proliferated, as people and managers have discovered that it is possible to save money while doing the right thing for the future. TravelSmart is a program begun by the Western Australian government to reduce the demand for increased traffic capacity, which was beginning to challenge not only fiscal limits but also the quality of urban life in Perth.[4] The program, devised by sociologist Werner Brog, works through local governments and a team of trained people who contact householders first by phone and then by home visits, during which family members talk through their travel needs and how they could perhaps meet them with less private vehicle use. The program has seen an average reduction in car use of 15 percent, with some places reaching 30 percent (Ashton-Graham and John 2005). A benefit-cost ratio of 14 to 1 was found. The TravelSmart Workplace program has helped many businesses create green travel plans, and it has been adopted by all Australian cities and many cities in other countries.

Based on TravelSmart, a new household sustainability program in Western Australia uses the same approach but includes energy, water, waste, travel, and gardens in one integrated program.[5] Cities like Portland and Seattle have created similar integrated programs for volunteers to attend. In the Perth area, householders have shown a real demand for advice on how to live lighter on the land, including one private-sector program called EcoSmart[6] and one from local government called Living Smart.

Living Smart is a community sustainability education program set up by the City of Fremantle and Murdoch University. It has been effective in reducing resource consumption and empowering people by informing them and helping them set goals (Sheehy and Dingle 2003; Raphael et al. 2003). The program brings people together in small groups to raise awareness of sustainability issues and the implications of overconsumption. It has generated change by giving people the necessary knowledge and skills to make their homes more sustainable—and save money in the process.

A key feature of the program's approach is helping families set goals on sustainability. The topics covered include water, waste, energy, chemicals, gardens, health, taking action, and simple living. At the close of each session, participants talk in small groups about what they learned and the kinds of changes that they could make. Then each person "sets a goal to change or improve their behavior in the topic area" (Sheehy and Dingle 2003, 5). The goals set for each topic are presented in a wall chart "to motivate participants by showing what others are doing and what they are able to achieve as a group." At the start of each session, time is spent discussing progress toward goals. Participants are able to share any benefits and difficulties they are experiencing.

Evaluation of the pilot Living Smart program demonstrated that the workshops and goal-setting approach not only improved participants' knowledge noticeably, but also genuinely changed behavior patterns.[7] Overcoming the sickness of overconsumption will be much easier if it is a shared journey.

The important next step in integrated household sustainability programs will be to make them not voluntary but mainstream, so that the majority of citizens can benefit from the improved lifestyles, and the community can benefit from the reduced resource consumption. This step will require government commitments.

There is an important role for the media in cultural change to reduce consumption. Two "reality" TV shows in Australia have demonstrated what can be done. In 2007 *EcoHouse* and *Carbon Cops* were national success stories as Australians learned how families struggled to reduce their energy, water, waste, and travel. They saw how this involved a simultaneous change in lifestyles and adoption of new technologies. But mostly they saw that sustainable production and consumption was feasible and fun, creating new opportunities for families in the cities of the future.

Strategy 3: Sustainable Purchasing Programs

Unsustainable consumption is not only about how much we consume but also about the quality of the goods consumed. By examining more carefully the environmental and social qualities of consumer goods, we can begin to change the impacts of consumption.

Governments and institutions can set an example of more sustainable consumption by adopting purchasing programs based on sustainability. As Mastny points out,

> The world's institutions are significant consumers, spending enormous sums on goods and services to help them run efficiently and achieve their missions. These purchases range from durable goods like office equipment and fleet vehicles to important services like electric power, custodial cleaning, and catering. (2003)

Because of both the scale of their buying and the visibility of their activities, institutions are important players in the movement to build more sustainable markets. Diverting even a small portion of institutional spending to more environmentally sound products and services can send a powerful message to the marketplace. It can also reduce the overall footprint of institutional consumption, bringing widespread environmental and economic benefits. In European cities the EU directive on sustainable procurement[8] has enabled many places to demonstrate innovations in purchasing policies.

The vast majority of purchasing, however, is from ordinary people who make decisions on what they buy based on simple factors such as the price and how quickly it can be purchased. "Fast and cheap" is the basis of globalization and takes no account of local economies, local or bioregional ecologies, or the needs of local communities. The challenge of making cities more sustainable is to recognize that these other dimensions are important. But how can you challenge "fast and cheap"?

Strategy 4: Slow Movement

The slow movement is a growing phenomenon that has paralleled the sustainable cities movement and is similarly beginning to make linkages to sustainability. The slow movement challenges the emphasis on speed and global markets by promoting reflection and ethical action to achieve something that can be appreciated only if it is slow and local. The movement has focused on three issues in particular: slow food, slow cities, and slow traffic.

Slow Food

The slow movement began as the slow food movement, which started in 1989 in Italy as a response to industrial fast food culture. A worldwide network has developed from local *convivia*, promoting the slow food message through events and educational programs.

Slow Food is a nonprofit, ecogastronomic, member-supported organization that was founded in 1989 to counteract fast food and fast life, the disappearance of local food traditions, and people's dwindling interest in the food they eat, where it comes from, how it tastes, and how our food choices affect the rest of the world.[9] The formal movement, whose official symbol is a snail, has over eighty thousand members across the globe, but many millions more now find the philosophy attractive.

The Slow Food Manifesto, written in 1989 by founding member Folco Portinari and endorsed by fifteen countries, summarizes the movement's philosophy:

> Our century, which began and has developed under the insignia of industrial civilization, first invented the machine and then took it as its life model.
>
> We are enslaved by speed and have all succumbed to the same insidious virus: Fast Life, which disrupts our habits, pervades the privacy of our homes and forces us to eat Fast Foods.
>
> To be worthy of the name, *Homo sapiens* should rid himself of speed before it reduces him to a species in danger of extinction.
>
> A firm defense of quiet material pleasure is the only way to oppose the universal folly of Fast Life.
>
> May suitable doses of guaranteed sensual pleasure and slow, long-lasting enjoyment preserve us from the contagion of the multitude who mistake frenzy for efficiency.
>
> Our defense should begin at the table with Slow Food. Let us rediscover the flavors and savors of regional cooking and banish the degrading effects of Fast Food.

In the name of productivity, Fast Life has changed our way of being and threatens our environment and our landscapes. So Slow Food is now the only truly progressive answer.

That is what real culture is all about: developing taste rather than demeaning it. And what better way to set about this than an international exchange of experiences, knowledge, projects?

Slow Food guarantees a better future. . . .

Slow Cities

The slow city movement, or Cittaslow (from "slow city" in Italian), takes the slow food philosophy and applies it to the way we design and manage cities. Its proponents have developed a set of characteristics that define a slow city; only cities that meet the criteria can join the official Cittaslow network. One criterion in particular is controversial, as it specifies that cities should not be bigger than fifty thousand people. One of the movement's founders, Stefano Cimicchi, explains:

We want the [Cittaslow] association to become a player at the European level to make sure that the [EU] constitution . . . takes into account the reality of small towns and cities. Scholars, town planners, and sociologists have recognized that the most human dimension to live in is that of the small agglomerates of no more than fifty thousand inhabitants. The model for the ideal city is the late-medieval and Renaissance one, with the piazza functioning as a center of social aggregation. Europe has to remember its roots and acknowledge the historical role its cities have played in the construction of its identity.[10]

This criterion has attracted some criticism. There are no simple answers about city size and its relation to quality of life and sustainability, but conversations about these questions are important to have (see chapter 5). There is little doubt, however, that the big cities of the world need the slow city movement as much as small ones.

The approach to slow cities is summarized in the Cittaslow Charter (see box 9.1).

Slow Traffic

The slow traffic movement began in Germany and the Netherlands in the 1970s, when several historic towns found that modernist road standards could not be applied to their cities without destroying them. Instead of speeding up traffic and increasing road capacity, they showed that cities worked better when they calmed traffic, put a cap on road capacity, and then emphasized walking, biking, and transit (Newman and Kenworthy 1999).

Traffic calming challenges every fiber of a traffic engineer's training. Hence it usually has been implemented primarily in historical areas; rarely will one see good examples in new areas. But that has begun to change as the approach to cities becomes more and more about sustainability rather than achieving efficiency for cars. Traffic has become a symbol of all that is wrong with the global city, and as highway engineers build more

Box 9.1 **Cittaslow Charter**

Towns and cities that want to join the Cittaslow network are expected to make a series of commitments. A Cittaslow ("slow city") is one which has a desire to:

- implement an environmental policy which nurtures the distinctive features of that town or city and its surrounding area, and focuses on recycling and recovery
- put in place infrastructure that will make environmentally friendly use of land, rather than just put up buildings on it
- encourage the use of technology that will improve the quality of air and life in the city
- support the production and consumption of organic foodstuffs
- eschew genetically modified products
- put in place mechanisms to help manufacturers of distinctive local produce which get into financial difficulty
- protect and promote products which
    - have their roots in tradition
    - reflect a local way of doing things
    - help to make that particular area what it is
- facilitate more direct contact between consumers and quality producers through the provision of designated areas and times for them to come together
- remove any physical obstructions or cultural obstacles that might prevent full enjoyment of all that the town has to offer
- make sure that all inhabitants—not just those involved in the tourist trade—are aware of the fact that this is a Cittaslow, focusing particularly on the next generation by encouraging learning about food and where it comes from
- encourage a spirit of genuine hospitality toward guests of the town

A Cittaslow will also make a commitment to:

- promote the network's ideas, and publicize any projects undertaken in their fulfillment
- apply Cittaslow principles in their own jurisdictions (where compatible with local circumstances) and welcome inspections by the Network to check that this is happening
- contribute any ideas which may be of general interest and usefulness to the Network

Any town or city which commits itself to these principles will be encouraged to:

- use the Network's logo and call itself a "Cittaslow"
- allow anyone, whether in the public or private sector, contributing to the Network's aims, to use the logo
- take part in all events organized by the Network and make use of its internal organization and facilities

Source: Cittaslow, www.cittaslow.org.uk; Slow Movement, www.slowmovement.com

traffic capacity, the problem compounds. A CASE city requires that traffic be reduced at its source. Only in this way will gasoline consumption be reduced and cities begin to be more sustainable in their transport. Slower traffic consumes more fuel per vehicle but makes the cities overall use less fuel as drivers switch to other modes and reduce how far they drive. Data on cities from around the world show a clear relationship between slower traffic and less fuel (Newman and Kenworthy 1999).

Traffic calming reduces the speed of traffic wherever possible by enabling other road users to have space. Thus sidewalks are widened, cycleways included, and some traffic lanes replaced by transit lanes and light-rail tracks. Some freeways such as the Embarcadero in San Francisco have been removed and replaced by tree-lined boulevards, which are more suitable for transit and walking as well as traffic. These mixed roads are now called "complete streets."

Some cities have made a deliberate attempt to remove all large signs designed to be read by drivers at speed. This approach, called "naked streets," improves street aesthetics and slows down cars, as drivers no longer have easy cues to guide them through at speed. Other road users thus have a better chance on the road. This approach is part of what David Engwicht calls "mental speed bumps."[11] Evidence from the United Kingdom and elsewhere indicates reductions in traffic accidents wherever this approach has been taken.

The idea of naked streets has already become a reality in the small Dutch town of Makkinga (population 1,000). A sign by the town entrance reads *Verkeersbordvrij*: "free of traffic signs." Cars move unhurriedly over granite cobblestone streets that have no stop signs or traffic lights, just roundabouts. The streets also have no direction signs,

Figure 9.1

Kensington High Road in London is an example of the "naked street" approach to traffic management.

Photo Peter Newman

parking meters, stopping restrictions, or painted lines to guide traffic. Pedestrians and cyclists join more easily into this traffic flow.[12] Slow traffic and slow cities have a role to play in the creation of less-resource-consuming cities.

Sustainable Production

Human production converts renewable and nonrenewable resources into products and services to meet human needs and wants. These resources come directly from ecosystems or from living beings in human-designed systems. The ongoing health of our own systems relies on the health of the wider ecosystems within which they are embedded. Sustainable production is not just a technological issue. As mentioned at the start of this chapter, consumption and production processes need to be integrated.

New, innovative technologies and eco-efficiency gains are required to meet both the challenge of CASE and human needs for all. The agenda for eco-efficient sustainable production has been set by von Weizsäcker, Lovins, and Lovins (1997) as Factor Four—double wealth and halve resource consumption—or even Factor Ten—double wealth and five times greater resource efficiency. The United Nations and the World Business Council on Sustainable Development have set a high target for industrialized countries of a tenfold reduction in consumption of resources by 2040, along with rapid transfers of knowledge and technology to developing countries. While this sustainable production agenda is a huge challenge, it is important to remember that throughout the Industrial Revolution of the past two hundred years, human productivity has increased by 20,000 percent.

However, there is little point in trying to make production more efficient and cleaner if the goals of production, and the system within which production occurs, are unsustainable. The problem is called the Jevons Paradox after the nineteenth-century economist, who successfully predicted that increasing the efficiency of burning coal would lead to increased, not decreased, coal use due to greater consumption. A more recent example involves the automobile industry, where increased efficiency in burning gasoline has been diluted by cheaper fuel and vehicles, leading to greater vehicle use. However, in recent years both efficiency and use have gotten worse. Despite forty years of technological development of automobiles, the fleet fuel average of many cities throughout the world has worsened. This decrease in fuel economy is due to aging vehicles and particularly to the increase in large four-wheel-drive vehicles (SUVs) that consume far more fuel than improved-technology small sedans. In addition, the number of cars has risen, and the vehicle miles traveled in most cities has continued to increase on a per capita basis—thus fossil fuel usage has also risen further.

It is imperative to adopt an integrated approach to all technological development, as there is no technological magic bullet that will create sustainable cities. Local and regional systems of production that involve partnerships between consumers and producers and between cities and rural areas will need to be encouraged, along with changes in the types of technologies used and the integration of these technologies.

Strategies for Sustainable Production

Strategies for sustainable production can be added to those for sustainable consumption and include:

5. Bioregional and community technology: making the scale of technology appropriate to bioregions and communities
6. Biomimicry: using nature to help with innovation
7. Eco-efficiency and industrial ecology: promoting industry cooperation to reduce wastes and costs
8. Integrated technologies for support systems: finding new ways to achieve synergies in food, energy, water, and waste systems.
9. Technology assessment: developing sustainability criteria to evaluate technologies

Strategy 5: Bioregional and Community Technology

New technology that helps create sustainability—such as renewable energy and innovative water and waste systems—operate best at a combination of bioregional and community scales. Bioregionally linked energy and water systems fit the solar bioregion and bioregional watershed. However, they comprise mostly a series of linked small-scale systems that work best at a community level. The city, as a network of ecovillages, provides the structure to facilitate technology on a community scale. Mimicking nature, our food, energy, and water management systems can be integrated on the local and bioregional scale through a decentralized approach. Communities in partnership with businesses can drive technological development and innovation, empowering them in the process and ensuring that technologies are developed to meet genuine human needs. The need for public participation in technological development is critical, to ensure that questions of ethics and sustainability are addressed and that technological change is not driven by profit alone.

This scale of technology is the solution first suggested by E. F. Schumacher in *Small Is Beautiful* (1973). It is still powerfully relevant to all cities but thus far has been applied only in Third World villages. In cities of the developing world, community-scale technology can build on the level of the neighborhood to provide water, sewerage, energy, solid-waste management, and even local transport. The technology is available, but as most Third World cities are built on old village structures of five hundred people, it is important that the management system also be available (see box 9.2 on the Malang sewerage system). The use of information technology control systems can now enable small scale environmental technologies to be managed locally and integrated bioregionally into grid systems. Some commentators believe this combination of IT and ET is the basis of the new fifth-cycle economy (Hall 1998; Hargroves and Smith 2005).

Strategy 6: Biomimicry

My guess is that *Homo industrialis*, having reached the limits of nature's tolerance, is seeing his shadow on the wall, along with the shadows of rhinos,

Box 9.2 **Malang Sewerage System: Community-Scale Eco-technology**

The Embong Brantas Project was a small-scale community technology (SSCT) demonstration project implemented in the Embong Brantas community in East Java, Indonesia. The project commenced in 1994 and represented the fruit of a collaboration between Murdoch University in Perth, Western Australia, and Merdeka University in Malang, East Java. The project aimed to test Australian small-scale domestic wastewater technology for its applicability in the local Indonesian context.

The Embong Brantas is a squatter community along the Brantas River in the center of Malang municipality. Malang is a city of 800,000 people, and the Embong Brantas is a *kampung* (local urban village) of approximately 5,000 people. The demonstration project was directly involved with a smaller subgroup of 100 people in the Embong Brantas community who had no toilets but used the river.

The Technologies

Two toilet blocks were built to provide for the local community, which is on a highly constrained site as in most squatter towns. Two small-scale Australian treatment systems, Ecomax and BioMAX, were squeezed into the village under new ablution blocks so that no distribution pipes were required.

The BioMAX system is an onsite treatment system that utilizes anaerobic and aerobic methods to meet the standard discharge criteria for BOD5 (biological oxygen demand over a 5-day period) and suspended solids of 20 mg/l (milligrams per liter) and 30 mg/l. The final treated water can also be used to irrigate surface coverage such as small shrubs and ground cover. About 2,000 BioMAX systems of differing capacities have already been installed in several different countries, including Australia, South Africa, and Indonesia.

Ecomax is an innovative high-performance sewage treatment system developed in Western Australia in 1989. It treats waste by filtering it through a soil-amended filter. The system has the following notable features: very high phosphorus and nitrogen removal, high removal of BOD and suspended solids, disinfection without chemical addition, heavy metal removal, gravity-driven process, very long life, negligible maintenance, and no moving parts.

The benefits of both systems are that the effluents either are discharged to the ground or can be reused for local community gardening. This is more beneficial compared to large-scale conventional sewage treatment plants, which generally discharge to a watercourse. Both technologies are also considered to be more advanced sewage treatment systems than current conventional systems.

The Process

The Center for Environmental Management and Technology (CEMT) at Merdeka University was established by Murdoch University and Merdeka University in July 1996 as a result of an International Symposium on Environmental Technology. The speakers at the symposium envisaged the idea of applying small-scale Australian domestic wastewater technology to a small pilot project in an Indonesian community. CEMT, which is made up of academics from the two universities, was then charged with coordinating the project and securing funding.

(continued on page 202)

Box 9.2 *(continued from page 201)*

Workshops were held with stakeholders, many of whom were reluctant to work in a squatter settlement. CEMT also conducted a survey to evaluate stakeholders' social and political acceptance of the project. The results showed a very optimistic attitude toward participation in the project, but also a general lack of knowledge about the technology and how it would be operated and maintained. An environmental education program was then set up by CEMT to address this problem. The local community was then able to manage the system and has continued to do so.

By the end of 1997, agreement by the local community, government agencies, and the Australian Agency for International Development (AUSAID) had been secured, along with agreement for joint funding by all parties. In March 1998, the local government, through the Regional Development Planning Board and the Public Works Department of Malang Municipality, built the retaining wall for the two types of Australian technologies. A small-scale BioMAX wastewater treatment system was then installed in the Embong Brantas community in November 1998. In 1999 an Ecomax system was installed.

Lessons Learned

- The importance of environmental education within the local community and local agencies in order to (1) build environmental awareness of the issues and (2) encourage stakeholders to participate in the implementation and ongoing management and maintenance of the SSCT project. A partnership approach with the local community, local agencies, and the university (CEMT) provided a way of sharing knowledge and encouraging local ownership, mutual participation, and joint funding opportunities.
- The value of ensuring that the local community and relevant agencies actually want the project, have a positive attitude toward it from its outset, and are interested in both its initial implementation and ongoing management and maintenance. Women play a critical role in this process. Using a stakeholders' workshop and a survey during the early stages of this project helped foster positive attitudes and gave the local community a sense of ownership in the project.
- The need to be constantly looking for ways to improve and make the technology more appropriate to the local context, to ensure that it can be maintained and managed in the long term by local communities and local agencies.

The project represented the collaborative efforts of the local government, university, and community. The project succeeded in technical terms, but more importantly it showed how a local community can manage its own sanitation system and be proud to do so.

Source: Newman and Suriptono 2000

condors, manatees, lady's slippers, and other species he is taking down with him. Shaken by the sight he, we, are hungry for instructions about how to live sanely and sustainably on the Earth. The good news is that wisdom is widespread, not only in indigenous peoples but also in the species that have lived on Earth for longer than humans. . . . After 3.8 billion years of research and development, failures are fossils, and what surrounds us is the secret to survival. (Benyus 1997, 1–3)

Biomimicry is the use of natural patterns as the basis for design. The nine principles of biomimicry are given in box 9.3, along with permaculture principles, which are also based on observation of natural systems. In *Biomimicry: Innovation Inspired by Nature*, Benyus (1997) outlines many examples of applying nature's designs to the manufacturing of materials and the processes of production itself. The development of penicillin was based on the study of how fungi protect themselves against bacteria. Recent biomimicry ideas include:

- Development of desalination membranes based on the functioning of kidneys
- Use of mother-of-pearl as a model for durable, lightweight biocomposite materials, with applications including artificial bone
- Creation of a water-based "super glue" based on the analysis of five mussel proteins that enable the foot of a blue mussel to adhere to surfaces underwater
- Development of pigment-free colors through the discovery that butterfly wings create iridescence through structure not pigmentation, thus enabling the production of sunlight-readable digital screens.

Industrial ecology (see below) is a biomimicry concept based on the process of waste recycling that occurs naturally in ecosystems. A wealth of case studies, illustrating the lessons that can be learned from nature to design new materials and processes, are provided online by the Biomimicry Institute.[13]

Strategy 7: Eco-efficiency and Industrial Ecology

Industrial ecology and industrial metabolism are concepts for new patterns of industrial production. Essentially, they aim to mimic the material recycling aspect of an ecosystem. Material flow management is crucial to these approaches, which focus on minimizing environmental impact through increased efficiency and source reduction—preventing or reducing waste where it originates, at the source.

The following represent six principal elements of industrial ecology/metabolism:

1. Creation of industrial ecosystems: maximizing use of recycled materials in production, optimizing use of materials and embedded energy, minimizing waste generation, and reevaluating "wastes" as raw material for other processes.
2. Balancing industrial input and output to natural ecosystem capacity: understanding the ability of the larger natural system to deal with toxics and other industrial wastes in typical and catastrophic situations.
3. Dematerialization of industrial output: reducing materials and energy intensity in industrial production.

4. Improving the metabolic pathways of industrial processes and materials use: reducing or simplifying industrial processes to emulate highly efficient processes found in nature.

5. Systemic patterns of energy use: promoting the development of an energy supply system that functions as a part of the industrial ecosystem and that is free of the negative environmental impacts associated with current patterns of energy use.

6. Policy alignment with a long-term perspective of industrial system evolution: cities and nations working together to integrate economic and environmental policies.[14]

A range of tools may be used in the design of industrial ecologies such as life-cycle analysis, material flows analysis, and energy and exergy analysis. The ZERI Brewery (see box 9.4) and the Kwinana project (see chapter 8) are both examples of industrial ecology.

Verstegen (2003) cautions against industrial ecology as a purely technological initiative, arguing that it may be counterproductive to achieving sustainable production and consumption for the following reasons:

- Interdependence among industries decreases the flexibility to change and fosters path-dependent development.
- Therefore, resource exchange networks may perpetuate unsustainable industries by encouraging industrial codependencies (as in Verstegen's example of a coal-fired power plant in Kalundborg, Denmark).
- Improved efficiency of economic system components tends to stimulate greater consumption and thus can undermine the sustainability of the system as a whole (the Jevons Paradox).
- Adaptability in complex systems declines with greater efficiency.
- Complex interdependent systems with extended "food chains" are unstable in variable environments.
- A tendency to look for future development opportunities can stimulate greater resource use rather than meeting needs of the community.
- Efficiency-driven industrial growth does not result in increased employment opportunities for the regional community.
- Industrial symbiosis does not in itself encourage a greater level of community participation in industrial development and decision-making processes.

An expanded sense of industrial ecology would recognize that industry and society are inextricably linked and would emphasize fostering partnerships and networks to manage resources in more sustainable ways. Drawing from the ecological metaphor, this can be achieved by identifying and fostering symbiotic networks among and within community, business, and government. The key element here is not engineering solutions, but rather the social capital and creativity generated by people. This approach would include questions of human needs and how best to meet them, along with how production processes

---

Box 9.3 **Lessons from Nature: Biomimicry and Permaculture**

Lessons of Life's Wisdom	Biomimicry Principles	Permaculture Design Principles
• Life favors self-organization • Life is frugal and sharing • Life depends on inclusive, place-based communities • Life rewards cooperation • Life depends on boundaries • Life banks on diversity, creative individuality, and shared learning	• Nature runs on sunlight • Nature uses only the energy it needs • Nature fits form to function • Nature recycles everything • Nature rewards cooperation • Nature banks on diversity • Nature demands local expertise • Nature curbs excesses from within • Nature taps the power of limits	• Observe and interact • Catch and store energy • Obtain a yield • Apply self-regulation and accept feedback • Use and value renewable resources and services • Produce no waste • Design from patterns to details • Integrate rather than segregate • Use small and slow solutions • Use and value diversity • Use edges and value the marginal • Creatively use and respond to change
Source: Korten 1999	*Source: Benyus 1997*	*Source: Holmgren 2002*

---

link into wider economic and social systems. Thus, industrial ecology ideally brings together consumption and production processes, rather than treating production separately.

Strategy 8: Integrated Technologies for Support Systems

The principles of ecological design, biomimicry, permaculture, and regenerative design can be applied to the design of sustainable support systems or sustainable infrastructure for cities. Sustainable technologies may be defined as technologies that meet the following criteria:

- Meet genuine needs
- Are optimally efficient and clean
- Are developed by participatory science
- Function as part of integrated systems using the lessons from nature within sustainable systems (landscapes, cities, bioregions)

Currently the systems that provide us with food, water, energy, and waste management are often administered separately. As discussed earlier, functions within sustainable ecosystems are integrated and proximal. Food, water, and energy are captured and stored, and wastes are recycled by the system. These "support" systems are all part of the ecosystem as a whole.

To put this in practice, cities would need to create decentralized support systems,

Box 9.4 **The ZERI Brewery**

A traditional brewery produces not only beer but also organic waste streams. Because this waste is organic, its polluting effect is not like that of industrial poisons; however, the sheer quantity of waste-water produced makes it a problem. Today's breweries sometimes use more than twenty liters of water per liter of brewed beer. Much of the grain used to make the beer is also wasted. Only a small percentage of the nutrients are used in the production process; the rest are left untouched in the spent grains after brewing. Occasionally the spent grains are used for animal feed, but this is not an optimal use, as the spent grains are tough for animals to digest. The result is indigestion and added amounts of methane gas emitted into the atmosphere by the animals. Thus, the waste in a traditional brewing system generates very little (if any) value, and it may actually have negative value if the brewery must pay to get rid of the wastewater and spent grains.

The Zero Emissions Research and Initiatives foundation, or ZERI, has devised an alternative approach to the technology of brewing that reflects the approach to material recycling taken by ecosystems. In order to maximize the value of the brewery's inputs, ZERI looked for the best possible ways of using the generated waste in a cascading, integrated manner.

Spent grains, rich in fiber and protein, are an excellent substitute for flour in bread. When mixed with other fibers, such as rice straw, they become an ideal substrate for the growing of mushrooms. Using ZERI's approach, a brewery can generate additional value from its grain in the form of mushrooms or bread. (The world market for mushrooms is already larger than that for coffee.) The advantage of growing mushrooms on the spent grains is that mushrooms will make the spent grains more digestible to livestock and will also increase the grains' protein content—which in turn increases the animals' growth and quality of meat.

Next, the waste from the livestock is flushed into a digester with the wastewater from the brewery. The digester generates two outputs: biogas and a nutrient solution. The biogas is stored in gas tanks and can be used by the brewery or sold. The nutrient solution flows into shallow basins where algae, through photosynthesis, digest it. These algae that have grown and multiplied on the nutrients then flow into a pond and become feed for fish. The fish pond itself emulates nature with different species living at different depths, functioning much like any wild lake without the need for antibiotics.

enabling food, water, energy, and waste management processes to be integrated. This is the goal of permaculture design, and this approach can be employed effectively for the design of infrastructure support in cities. Computer networks can be used to facilitate the integration of community- and bioregional-scale technologies and to monitor decentralized systems. Thus, the city infrastructure would form a set of nested and networked systems as in an ecosystem.

Case studies are given of integrated food production systems that enable waste to be recycled and energy to be saved due to the local urban production system. Small-scale urban agriculture can produce higher yields than commercial mechanized farming. Hopkins (2000) indicates that biointensive gardening developed in the United States has recorded yields some two to sixteen times the commercial mechanized levels. The Cuban example below illustrates the viability not only of producing organic food but also of recycling wastes and saving energy through reduced freight transport.

Box 9.4   *(continued)*

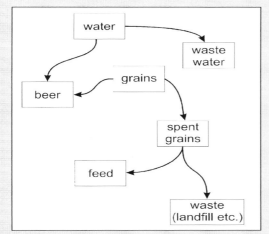

Figure 9.2a

Traditional brewery flow diagram

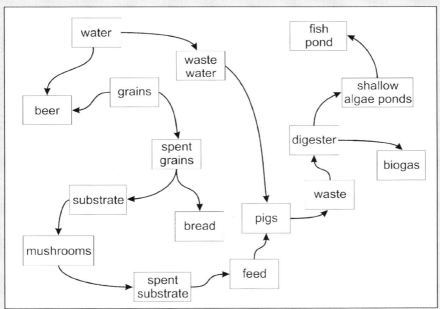

Figure 9.2b

ZERI brewery flow diagram

By generating value in a cascading scheme, ZERI's system uses all the nutrients and fiber from the spent grains, as well as the wastewater from the brewing process. "Waste" becomes a valuable resource to create more jobs, more income, and a better environment.

Source: Case studies, Zero Emissions Research and Initiatives, http://www.zeri.org/case_studies_beer.htm

A 1999 report demonstrates that organic farming—often regarded as an insignificant part of the food supply—can feed virtually a whole country. Titled "Cultivating Havana: Urban Agriculture and Food Security in the Years of Crisis," the report found that in Cuba, a large proportion of the foods people eat daily are grown without synthetic fertilizers and toxic pesticides. The author, Catherine Murphy, works with the Institute for Food and Development Policy, or Food First, a Californian group dedicated to promoting sustainable farming.

According to the report, after the collapse of the Soviet Union in the late 1980s Cuba lost Soviet aid, which provided them with modern agricultural chemicals. Thus 1,300,000 tons of chemical fertilizers, 17,000 tons of herbicides, and 10,000 tons of pesticides could no longer be imported. Urban agriculture was one of Cuba's responses to this shock; the government intensified the previously established National Food Program, which aimed at taking thousands of poorly utilized areas, mainly around Havana, and converted them into intensive vegetable gardens. Planting in the city instead of only in the countryside decreased the need for transportation, refrigeration, and other scarce resources.

By 1998, over 8,000 urban farms and community gardens were established, run by over 30,000 people in and around Havana. The Food First report describes urban agriculture as a significant component of the Havana cityscape, and the model is now being copied throughout the country with production rising steeply. Today, food from the urban farms is grown almost completely with active organic methods. Havana has banned the use of chemical pesticides in agriculture within city boundaries.[15]

Millions of people die each year from diseases caused by poor sanitation and urban waste. Usually this is caused by human waste contaminating water supplies and food. Hence if urban agriculture is to be developed, cities must be very careful about managing human wastes. If we are to close cycles by using wastes to grow food, it is imperative that this be done in ways that prevent microbial and chemical contamination from occurring. The following example of urban organic farming and urban aquaculture for food and wastewater management, drawn from a UNEP/IETC sourcebook on wastewater management (Ho 2002), addresses these matters.

The largest, single wastewater-fed aquaculture system in the world lies to the east of Calcutta, India, in an area called the East Calcutta Wetlands. The wastewater-fed fish ponds occupy an area of about 2,500 hectares within a 12,000-hectare waste recycling region, which also includes cultivation of vegetables on wastewater and garbage, and paddy fields irrigated with fish pond effluent. The system has been developed over the past sixty years by farmers who learned by experience how to regulate the intake of raw sewage into ponds to culture fish.

Drainage and preparation of the ponds for fish culture is carried out during the coolest months. Primary fertilization involves filling the ponds with raw sewage and allowing them to undergo natural purification for twenty to thirty days before fish are stocked. Secondary fertilization involves introducing small amounts of wastewater—periodically in small ponds and almost continuously in large ponds—to maintain growth of plankton to feed the fish. The primary cultured species are Indian major carp, Chinese carp, and tilapia.

The area of wastewater-fed ponds in the East Calcutta Wetlands has declined over the past thirty years, mainly due to urban expansion. Currently they provide employment for seventeen thousand poor fishermen and produce twenty tons of fish daily. Much of the harvest comprises small fish that are purchased by poor urban consumers. Besides this food, the wetlands provide a low-cost, natural wastewater treatment and reuse system for a city that lacks conventional wastewater treatment plants. The low-lying fish ponds also provide stormwater drainage and a "lung" for Calcutta.

An improved wastewater-fed aquaculture system inspired by the traditional practices of the East Calcutta farmers has recently been implemented as part of the Ganga Action Plan, which aims to improve the water quality of the Ganges River. An integrated wet-land system (IWS) for wastewater treatment and resource recovery through aquaculture and agriculture has been developed to date in three smaller cities in the Calcutta metro-politan area. The challenge in replicating the East Calcutta Wetlands experience has been scaling it down to an appropriate level. Whereas the Calcutta municipal system gener-ates about 750 million liters of wastewater daily and the total resource recovery area covers about 12,000 hectares, smaller municipalities have a wastewater load of less than 50 million liters per day and much smaller areas of available land for nutrient recovery.

Resource recovery at the new IWS sites has been achieved with different levels of suc-cess, but all three provide important lessons for the challenge of transferring traditional, ecologically sound knowledge to an acceptable technological option for wastewater treat-ment policy makers, planners, and engineers. At the Titagarh-Bandipur IWS, a series of three ponds were constructed in a derelict wetland. Effluent from the fish ponds is used to irrigate about twenty-five hectares of rice fields, with an average production of three tons per hectare without use of chemical fertilizers. About two hundred farming house-holds benefit, but improved distribution of treated effluent would almost double the number of beneficiaries. The irrigated area is slated to expand in the future with increased wastewater flow from the municipality.

An important feature of the IWS is the participation of stakeholders: the Calcutta Metropolitan Water and Sanitation Authority, the local village authorities, the fish farm-ers who lease the ponds, and the rice-farming households are all involved in the project. Agenda 21, the UN's 1992 blueprint for sustainable development, emphasized the need to institutionalize the participation of stakeholders in environmental improvement projects —in this case empowering a rural community to manage its own wastewater treatment and reuse. Another crucial feature is the implementation of a revenue-generating mech-anism that should ensure adequate management of the system.[16]

The use of waste in a food production system must always be sympathetic to public health. Traditionally wastewater has been gathered around cities and reused only after sufficient time has elapsed for human contaminants to be naturally removed. Excess wastes were flushed into the rivers but only if the value in those wastes was mostly removed for agriculture. The use of the bioregion for waste treatment was feasible as long as its capacity to treat was not exceeded. Throughout the world, as cities have grown, the increase in waste has far outstripped natural capacities. Cities everywhere have to find ways of treating and reusing waste. Approaches that use new technology to totally remove waste are now practicable, but a CASE approach would try to reuse waste as much as possible in the bioregion for agricultural production and ecological regeneration. Often public health authorities have tried to ban all use of waste for agriculture, which means that water and waste are not used efficiently or ecologically. Although human health is optimized in this approach, it is generally not sustainable as there is not enough water and organic fertilizer to enable bioregional agriculture to proceed ecologically. As a result, cities tend to extract water and produce food in largely unsustainable ways. Thus approaches will require new technologies and management systems that integrate public health and environmental engineering with ecologically sound planning (Ho 2002).

One such approach is the use of wastewater in aquaculture. Largely anecdotal evidence does not show a significantly increased risk to public health from consumption of wastewater-fed fish. However, according to Ho (2002), scientifically based data to support this are almost entirely lacking. Microorganisms, particularly viruses and bacteria, die at a rapid rate in wastewater-fed ponds, which explains in part why fish from such systems do not seem to increase disease greatly. Trematodes pose a serious risk in East Asia if fish harvested from nightsoil-fed ponds are eaten raw. Toxic substances (heavy metals and organics) pose a threat if industrial waste is allowed into the waste stream. Thus, fish and other aquatic organisms cultured in wastewater should be monitored regularly to ensure that concentrations of contaminants stay within safety limits. However the use of wastewater for agriculture needs to be seen more positively as a solution to waste treatment, to water supply, and to bioregional agriculture.

Another successful example of this type of systems integration, again drawn from the UNEP/IETC sourcebook (Ho 2002), is the wastewater-fed system of agriculture and aquaculture to the south of Hanoi, the capital of Vietnam. About one-third of the city has sewers. Wastewater and stormwater are discharged untreated to four small rivers, which play a dual role: drainage of wastewater from the city and wastewater supply for reuse in agriculture and aquaculture. Conventional wastewater treatment plants have been constructed but lie idle due to lack of maintenance funds.

Before 1960 the low-lying Tranh Tri district of Hanoi was a sparsely populated swamp where rice was grown with low yields and frequent flooding. Aquaculture began to develop in the early 1960s with the construction of an extensive irrigation and drainage system to facilitate rice cultivation. As farmers began to perceive the benefits of wastewater-fed aquaculture, they started stocking wild fish collected from the river in their rice fields. Following the formation of cooperatives in 1967, land use stabilized into vegetable cultivation on higher land, rice/fish cultivation on midlevel land, and year-round fish pond culture on lower land adjacent to the irrigation and drainage canals. Wastewater-fed aquaculture became the major occupation of six cooperatives with easy access to wastewater and a minor occupation of ten others out of the twenty-five total district cooperatives. The local aquaculture research institute provided exotic fish species and taught farmers how to regulate the introduction of wastewater to produce fish. Three to eight tons of fish per hectare are harvested annually (primarily silver carp, rohu, and tilapia), with lower yields from the mixed rice/fish cultivation and higher yields from the fish pond culture.

The city's master plan for development shows the district retaining the same land use pattern of agriculture and aquaculture through 2010, which should diminish the threat of urban encroachment. An ongoing project to improve Hanoi's wastewater and drainage system has had only marginal impact through loss of a small area to construct a reservoir downstream from the wastewater-fed pond system. A new industrial development is being established outside the district's drainage area, so fish being cultured on city wastewater should be relatively free of contamination. However, one factor that has adversely affected the wastewater-fed aquaculture is the change in land use since the 1980s from cooperative to individual household management. Between 1985 and 1995 the area of rice/fish cultivation declined in area by 36 percent. In contrast to the fish ponds, located adjacent to the main wastewater canals, the midlevel rice/fish farms are unable to obtain sufficient wastewater because of the breakdown in the wastewater distribution system, which was previously operated by the cooperatives.[17]

Other examples of how cities across the Third World have integrated wastewater into food production are given in Hardoy, Mitlin, and Satterthwaite (2001).

Strategy 9: Technology Assessment

Cooperation and sharing ideas is crucial for technological innovation. The concept of environmentally sound technologies is evolving and being refined by UNEP/IETC as a means of assessing technologies for transfer in development. Environmentally sound technologies (ESTs) encompass technologies that have the potential for significantly improved environmental performance relative to other technologies. Broadly speaking, these technologies protect the environment, are less polluting, use resources in a sustainable manner, recycle more of their wastes and products, and handle all residual wastes in a more environmentally acceptable way than technologies for which they are substitutes.

Sharing of information on available technologies and regions is being promoted under the ESTIS program initiated by UNEP/IETC. ESTIS (Environmentally Sound Technologies Information System) is a database tool that allows users to set up databases in their native language and to post technologies in a customized database. Technologies are grouped under the broad headings of Air, Built Environment, Energy, Food, Monitoring, Rehabilitation, Transport, Waste, and Water. The ESTIS concept has been driven by an international group of people dedicated to EST transfer for sustainability.

ESTIS encompasses three integrated components—ESTIS Builder, ESTIS Community, and ESTIS Global—providing a decentralized network for improved access and local control in EST-related information transfer. ESTIS Builder allows users to construct their own customized website in order to manage and disseminate their EST information on the

Table 9.1 **Generic Environmental Criteria and Guidelines for Assessing Environmentally**

Criteria	Guidelines
Sustainable resource development and utilization	• Plans for sustainable resource development and use have been developed • Expenditures on sustainable resource development and utilization have been taken into account • Expenditures on sustainable resource augmentation (e.g., reforestation) have been taken into account
Protection of freshwater quality and supply	• Annual withdrawals of ground- and surface water and water consumption have been determined • Opportunities for water conservation and efficiency improvements have been determined • Potential sources of water pollution have been determined • Plans and facilities for water and wastewater treatment and hydrological monitoring are in place • Expenditures on water and wastewater treatment have been taken into account
Protection of adjacent water bodies and shoreline/coastal resources	• Potential releases of nitrogen, phosphorus, and other contaminants to adjacent water bodies have been identified • Plans for the protection of water bodies and shoreline/coastal resources are in place • Expenditures on protecting water bodies and shoreline/coastal resources have been taken into account
Protection of terrestrial resources	• Population growth and distribution and land use changes have been taken into account, including compatibility of various facilities and systems • Plans for integrated planning and management of terrestrial resources are in place, including consideration of geomorphology and ecohydrology • Decentralized local-level natural resource management is in place • Potential for soil contamination and erosion has been taken into account

Source: Environmentally Sound Technologies for Sustainable Development (2003), UNEP/IETC, http://www.unep.or.jp/ietc/techTran/focus/SustDev_EST_background.pdf

internet. ESTIS Community is populated by technology information from individual ESTIS sites. It allows users of ESTIS Builder to form an internet community to share EST information automatically. ESTIS Global is an internet portal that provides users with a single mechanism to search for selected and approved EST information from ESTIS sites.[18]

Technology assessment can be used by cities. As infrastructure and services are being planned, it is possible to scope the various possibilities and examine them in terms of

Sound Technologies

Criteria	Guidelines
Conservation and biological diversity	• Plans for the protection of biological diversity and preservation of endangered species are in place • Expenditures on the protection and preservation of endangered species and sensitive habitats have been taken into account
Protection of the atmosphere	• Ambient concentrations of pollutants in urban areas have been determined • Potential releases of air emissions have been determined • Plans and equipment for the management of air emissions (e.g., criteria air contaminants, toxics, and GHGs) are in place • Expenditures on air pollution abatement have been taken into account
Environmentally sound management of solid wastes and sewage	• Potential generation of solid waste, industrial waste, and sewage has been determined • Opportunities for waste minimization and material efficiency improvement have been determined • Plans and facilities for waste management and sewage treatment are in place • Waste recycling and reuse plans and facilities are in place • Expenditures on waste management and sewage treatment have been taken into account
Environmentally sound management of toxic chemicals and hazardous wastes	• Potential generation of toxic chemicals and hazardous wastes has been determined • Opportunities for toxic chemical and hazardous waste minimization have been determined • Plans and facilities for the management of toxic chemicals and hazardous wastes are in place • Expenditures on toxic chemicals management and hazardous waste treatment have been taken into account

particular criteria. Table 9.1 sets out the criteria that have been developed by UNEP/IETC for environmentally sound technologies.

These criteria can become integrated into city decision making through:

• Project assessment processes, especially as environmental assessment merges into sustainability assessment where broader resource questions and community scale can be considered (see Pope, Annandale, and Morrison-Saunders 2004 and WA Government 2003)

- Development control in local planning approval processes where a sustainability scorecard approach is now being developed in many cities (see Newman 2006).

Conclusions

Cities have increasingly separated consumption and production activities. In ecosystems, these activities are integrated. Cities need to bring together consumption and production once more so that the scale, type, and processes of production match genuine human needs and bioregional capacities. Reducing resource consumption by technology will not be sufficient unless sustainable consumption patterns are developed in parallel. New technological systems are needed that are bioregional and community scale, and that are linked together by integrated, networked support systems. These systems need to apply the principles of biomimicry and industrial ecology, and meet stringent technology assessment guidelines. Sustainable production and consumption systems can reduce their ecological impact immediately and eventually move to create positive ecologically regenerative cities in their bioregions.

An inspiring demonstration of how we can begin now to have more sustainable production and consumption at the household level, is provided by an American family that has been transforming their suburban block to a productive garden since the mid-1980s. The "organic permaculture garden" that the Dervaes family has created provides them with food all year round. They also run a salad greens business for local restaurants, which helps to fund the purchasing of solar panels, energy-efficient appliances, and other technologies to reduce their dependence on nonrenewable resources. The Path to Freedom project, founded by Jules Dervaes in 2001, aims to promote a "simpler and more fulfilling" way of life. The Path to Freedom website is full of stories, photos, and information about the Dervaes family's journey. The opening page of the website features a stirring call to action:

> Let's face it. Our world is in deep, deep trouble and we are the *"troublemakers."* We have to make real, difficult changes *yesterday*.
>
> Despite the obvious benefits, we are not going to recycle, compost, or talk our way out of this.
>
> Our leaders, being politicians, are not leaders at all but are bound to be followers, who just won't be there for us in a crisis. So, it's up to me and you to make the choice of becoming responsible stewards of the earth.
>
> Let's turn the world right side up as demonstrated through this website. Join us on our journey towards a sustainable present and future. Let's walk the *path to freedom!*[19]

10 | Governance and Hope

PRINCIPLE 10

Enable continual improvement based on accountability, transparency, and good governance.

Elaboration: Good urban governance requires robust processes directed toward achieving the transformation of cities to sustainability through continual improvement. While in some areas gains will be incremental, there are also opportunities to make substantial improvements through innovative strategies, programs, and technologies.

To manage the continual improvement cycle, it is necessary to use relevant indicators, set targets based on benchmarks, and monitor progress against milestones to achieving these targets. This facilitates progress and accountability and ensures effective implementation.

Correlation of Hope and Good Governance

Hope springs from a deep belief in continual improvement—not spectacular achievement, but genuine change. Hope is a shared experience; hence it requires accountability and transparency in communities, business, and government. Hope needs vision and leadership; hence it needs good governance.

The UN Center for Human Settlements (UNCHS) defines urban governance as:

> The exercise of political, economic, social, and administrative authority in the management of a city's affairs. It comprises the mechanisms, traditions, processes, and institutions (whether formal or informal) through which citizens and groups articulate their interests, exercise their rights, meet their obligations, and mediate their differences. It is thus a broader concept than "government," which refers only to the formal and legally established organs of the political structure.[1]

Good governance is critical to moving toward sustainability: "There is an emerging international consensus that good governance is a crucial prerequisite for poverty eradication and for sustainable development."[2]

Strategies for Good Governance and Hope

Natural ecosystems have no central controlling body or organism, but their various parts work together to make them support life at local, bioregional, and global (biosphere) levels. Regulation springs up internally through feedback loops facilitated by proximity and network relationships. The "governance" system is decentralized but strategic for the different levels at which its life forces are dependent and to which they contribute. This allows for flexibility in responses. However, as urban impacts are often complex and occur across scales, it is important to develop coordinated approaches too, especially at the bioregional scale which is so critical for sustainability.

There are five main ways for cities to create good governance and hope. All need to be given the particular flavor of hope that seeks out truly positive, achievable steps that can be taken to launch cities down the path toward sustainability.

1. Structures and processes of urban governance need to be inclusive, cooperative, and empowering in a way that reduces inequities.
2. Governance needs to be matched to local (polycentric) and bioregional scales, but have the ability to address global issues. Governance structure and processes need to facilitate visioning processes (as discussed in chapter 1) and to foster empowerment and partnerships (as discussed in chapters 7 and 8) at these different scales.
3. Sustainability needs to be embedded in the day-to-day operation of government.
4. Indicator projects and reporting need to be developed.
5. Governance structures need to support and facilitate the flourishing of community initiatives for sustainability, providing a wellspring of hope for the future.

Strategy 1: Empowering Citizens and Reducing Inequities
Throughout this book there has been a strong emphasis on empowerment. Sustainability cannot proceed without empowering many different voices, as the solutions to sustainability problems are not found in manuals or in the single-issue orientation of many professions. Broad wisdom is needed, as the issues are ethical and cultural as well as scientific and engineering ones. The book has made less of the need to reduce inequities as part of empowerment, yet if this condition is missing, sustainability is threatened.

Governance to ensure greater social justice is not a new topic for cities to address. It is as old as cities. However, what is new is the awareness that reducing inequities is fundamental to solving sustainability issues and that they are entirely synergistic. The UN's urban governance program makes it very clear that these agendas are closely linked, but the silos of governance still prevail.

Janice Perlman, the director of the Megacities Project, has worked for decades to show that cities, especially megacities, need to be seen as critical to the global environmental agenda, and that reducing inequities is fundamental to how these agendas are linked (Perlman and O'Meara Sheahan 2007). She has established the six Perlman Principles for urban governance and sustainability:

1. There can be no urban environmental solutions without alleviating urban poverty: the urban poor tend to occupy the most ecologically fragile areas of cities and often lack adequate water, sewage, or solid-waste management systems.
2. There can be no solutions to poverty or environmental degradation without building on bottom-up, community-based innovations that are small in scale relative to the magnitude of the problems.
3. There can be no impact at the macro level without sharing what works among local leaders and scaling these programs up into public policy where circumstances permit.
4. There can be no urban transformation without changing the old incentive systems, the "rules of the game," and the players at the table.
5. There can be no sustainable city in the twenty-first century without social justice and political participation as well as economic vitality and ecological regeneration.

Perlman highlights the fact that every First World city has a Third World city within it, and every Third World city has a First World city inside it somewhere. In response, we must produce new governance systems that can generate real change. She concludes: "To plan is human, to implement is divine" (Perlman and O'Meara Sheehan 2007).

The United Nations has initiated a global program, the UN-Habitat's Global Campaign on Urban Governance, to demonstrate how governance of cities can improve sustainability through empowerment and reducing inequities. It was set up in 1999 to support the implementation of the Habitat Agenda goal of "sustainable human settlements development in an urbanizing world." The campaign is based on a growing international consensus that the quality of urban governance is the single most important factor for the eradication of poverty, the facilitation of prosperous cities, and the critical environmental problems that plague the Earth.

The campaign aims to increase the capacity of local governments and other stakeholders to practice good urban governance. It focuses attention on the needs of the excluded urban poor as the mechanism for making a city more sustainable. It recognizes women in particular as one of the biggest levers for positive change in society, and promotes their involvement in decision making at all levels.

The theme of the "Inclusive City" has become the campaign's banner. An Inclusive City promotes growth with equity. It is a place where everyone, regardless of their economic means, gender, race, ethnicity, or religion, is enabled and empowered to fully participate in the social, economic, and political opportunities that cities have to offer—including how to address the deep issues of sustainability. Participatory planning and decision making are the strategic means for realizing this vision.[3]

Strategy 2: Local, Bioregional, and Global Structures

The need for local polycentric and bioregional governance structures has been stressed in several of the ten Melbourne Principles. This insight comes from an understanding of how ecosystems work at both the local and bioregional level. However, ecosystems also work at a global level. As explained in this book's appendixes, ecosystems process carbon, nitrogen, and phosphorus in their local and bioregional economies, but these processes are linked to global cycles in the biosphere. Cities similarly need to address sustainability issues at these three levels as they channel energy and process materials in their local, bioregional, and global contexts. What is interesting is that ecosystems rarely work at national levels but have scales that are both smaller and bigger. Cities are very similar. Their issues are intensely local and bioregional yet also essentially global. Nations can influence the character of cities through the various ways that they fund infrastructure and programs and, at a global level, through their mediation in world politics; but in the end it is the cities that make their own futures. Thus cities need to ensure they have a strong local and bioregional approach to decision making as well as developing new links to emerging global levels of governance.

Local Governance

Community-based decision making in polycentric structures has repeatedly been stressed as critical to engaging cities in their future. It is also the level at which much of the infrastructure of the future should be managed. Municipal approaches to sustainability and the critical role of civil society and business partnerships in local governance are outlined by Roseland (2005, 2007) and Sirolli (1999).

Bioregional Governance

Bioregional structures are rare. Cities in the twentieth century have grown so rapidly that they have engulfed surrounding villages and towns. However, they have generally not created governance structures that can address bioregional issues such as water, food, waste, energy, transport, and biodiversity. The United Nations has recommended that cities form governance structures that cover the full regional extent of the city. CASE would suggest that this should be the bioregion. The UN's Global Campaign on Urban Governance provides the basis of how to develop appropriate polycentric and bioregional urban governance structures.

Regional governance is a genuinely important topic for most cities, as they are often enmeshed in a system of local governments endowed with planning powers yet disposed to fight over regional issues, favoring only what suits their particular area. This lack of regional cooperation usually results in large disparities in wealth and suboptimal solutions to regional transport, water, energy, waste, and biodiversity issues. This is very obvious in the United States, where only in the Portland/Vancouver metropolitan area has a regional governance structure been created with the authority to make key bioregional-scale decisions. Columnist Neal Peirce has been outlining the need for regional governance in US cities for decades, and his arguments are rarely faulted; however, the politics of state and local governments ceding power to regions is very difficult.[4]

Those metropolitan areas with civil and business structures that relate to the bioregion are those that are best able to adapt to the full sustainability agenda, often forcing local governments into being more responsible at a regional level. The New York Regional Plan Association (RPA) has been doing regional planning for the New York/New Jersey/Connecticut metro area for decades, though as an NGO it has no power to implement other than the moral persuasion of its ideas. RPA's America 2050 project sets out a vision of sustainability for large urban regions across the United States which is essentially bioregional in its focus.[5] Although much can be done by NGOs and innovative businesses to set the regional agenda, the significance of regional governance cannot be underestimated as a means of achieving sustainability. It is often the missing part of the tripartite governance partnership, which is needed to make sustainability work.

The need to establish a regional sustainability fund to facilitate regional governance on sustainability issues has been proposed by Lucy and Phillips (2006). It would enable groups of cities to access funds for regional solutions to problems relating to transport, water, waste, energy, and biodiversity—all issues that can be addressed most effectively through a regional planning system that would provide the framework for local communities and business to work together to achieve regional sustainability.

Global Governance

Global governance linking cities is necessary to address sustainability issues such as climate change, oil vulnerability, and the loss of biodiversity. These issues cannot be addressed by cities alone, nor can they be addressed by national or global systems of governance without involving cities.

A range of new global governance groups have established links among cities across the world. These groups come from civil society, business, and local or state governments. Civil society groups like the IUCN (World Conservation Union), WWF (World Wide Fund for Nature), and professional associations of scientists, engineers, planners, and architects all have a global reach in their work and provide cities with a way of tapping the knowledge and expertise required to address sustainability. Global meetings and conferences of such groups increasingly have a focus on cities. The Worldwatch Institute, which publishes an annual State of the World report, has increasingly focused on cities as the "engines of change for sustainability" according to the group's, director, Chris Flavin.[6] The 2007 report was devoted entirely to the future of cities.

Business groups for sustainability are also becoming more global and urban oriented. The World Business Council for Sustainable Development is a consortium of 190 of the world's top companies. They hold conferences, produce papers, and have a very active website to enable business to play its role in sustainability, especially in cities.[7]

Global government-oriented sustainability associations are now creating the linkages that local, city, and state governments need for their sustainability goals. ICLEI (Local Governments for Sustainability) was established in 1990 and continues to grow globally in its mission to help make sustainable development meaningful at the local government level.[8] A similar group was established at the 2002 World Summit in Johannesburg to work at the state and provincial level: the Network of Regional Governments for Sustainable Development (nrg4SD). Based in Spain's Basque Country, it has members from across Europe, Africa, and Australia but has not yet had much impact in the Americas. It has a focus on cities within its state-oriented remit.[9] The Clinton Foundation now works to coordinate global climate change action with the world's biggest cities.

The UN's Global Campaign on Urban Governance is another example of how global links are being established for cities, especially in the Third World. The campaign is being implemented through a combination of strategies and "flagship products" such as policy papers and toolkits. To respond to specific conditions in local cities, national campaigns are underway or planned in Nigeria, Tanzania, Burkina Faso, Senegal, India, the Philippines, Nicaragua, Jamaica, Brazil, Cuba, Peru, and the Balkans. UN-Habitat is providing support to countries seeking to ground their legislation in the principles of good urban governance and to provide policy support on such subjects as the role of gender and youth in good urban governance. It also has set up an emerging network of cities committed to practicing and championing inclusive urban governance.[10]

The UN's Sustainable Cities Program is a joint UN-Habitat/UNEP vehicle for promoting urban environmental governance processes as a basis for achieving sustainable urban growth and development. Established in the early 1990s, the program now operates in over thirty countries worldwide. It helps cities implement Agenda 21 through broad-based stakeholder involvement and bottom-up problem-solving.[11]

The strength of individuals and small groups to influence the sustainability of cities they live in, has been vastly increased by the internet. Paul Hawken believes there are now thousands of globally networked individuals providing informed comment and inspiration on the future direction of their cities. They are emerging as a significant part of global governance for sustainable cities (Hawken 2007).

Strategy 3: Embedding Sustainability in Agencies

The principles of sustainability, like the ten Melbourne Principles, need to be enshrined in some legal sense—whether it be a formal act or an informal code. A Sustainability Code of Conduct should be created to apply to each agency of city government, specifying how the city can lead by example on reducing its ecological footprint and living more closely to the community, bioregional, and global sustainability ideals. The Sustainability Code of Conduct can then be used to examine city agencies' approaches to decision making (their transparency and sustainability), and to such matters as procurement and assessment. Creating partnerships for sustainability can be included in the Sustainability Code. Awards can be given for all the best aspects of sustainability demonstrated by agencies.

Urban governance is critical to how the rapidly growing megacities of the Third World approach their future. Talukder (2006) has developed ten principles for effective governance of megacities based on an analysis of the needs of Dhaka in Bangladesh, a city that has grown from half a million people in 1950 to twelve million in 2000. He has concluded that complex, large cities require these fundamental aspects of governance to be embedded in their approach to future development if they are to ensure sustainable practices. They must have:

1. A **statutory authority** covering a geographical area of responsibility over the extended metropolitan region (i.e., the bioregion).
2. A **strategic planning function** within this authority that can provide a vision for how the city can address its land use problems sustainably.
3. A **statutory planning function** that can control development to ensure common-good outcomes consistent with the strategic plan. This can be devolved to local authorities for most land use decisions but only if they work within the regional framework, and it can be overruled on contentious issues.
4. A **development facilitation function** at regional level that can provide investment coordination and partnerships for infrastructure to attract private-sector involvement in sustainable city visions.
5. A **redevelopment authority** at regional level to enable old areas to be renewed in a more sustainable way, as this is often the most strategic way to make sustainability meaningful.
6. A **transparent local process** that can help define the common-good sustainability outcomes from development with all stakeholders and that can feed into the bioregional goals of the city.
7. A **coordination mechanism** to ensure planning and development are integrated. Sustainability provides the main linking concept for this so that planning isn't just "what not to do" and development isn't only "whatever it takes to get investment."
8. A way of **raising the finance** for the above process from land development and other taxes that can be seen to relate back to sustainability directly.
9. **Strong government links** to enable good political support, as without this a city governance system can be effectively starved of the means to develop sustainably.
10. A **professional development function** to create the required skills in sustainability and local participation at each level of urban governance.

These principles are in fact applicable to cities of all sizes and all wealth levels, to ensure sustainability is translated into planning practice and governance.

Strategy 4: Indicator Projects

Sustainability indicators have attracted growing attention in recent years. They have been formulated at all levels, from international to local and community-based indicators. At the international level, indicators allow comparisons of different countries and help monitor global progress toward sustainability over time. At the national level, indicator programs provide guidelines for action and impetus to implementation. At the community level, indicators not only serve the previous purposes but, if the community is involved in their formulation, this process also serves to stimulate debate about what sustainability means, how we can measure it, and what our goals are. Furthermore, this community process gives people a sense of involvement and ownership rather than leaving the process to decision makers to implement.

Indicator projects are needed in cities, as this regional level is often not included in indicator work. Indicators can be a vehicle for community visioning, learning about sustainability, and demonstrating the value of bioregional governance. They provide communities and governments with a way to monitor progress toward sustainability, keeping both communities and governments accountable. Once a city has developed its indicators, it is very important to report on them regularly. State of Sustainability reporting can enable such indicators to test the ten Melbourne Principles and whether cities are becoming more sustainable ecosystems.

Four examples of indicator-based sustainable city programs follow.

Sustainable Seattle

Seattle was probably the first city to develop a sustainability indicators project. Alan AtKisson (2001)—an international sustainability consultant and key participant in Sustainable Seattle—outlines the project's development and achievements. The process to develop sustainability indicators for Seattle began in late 1990 when seventy Seattle citizens met for a one-day forum to consider the question "What legacy are we leaving to future generations?" (352). The forum was sponsored by several local organizations and a coalition of businesses and environmental groups. While no conclusions were made at this first meeting, it gave birth to an ongoing civic movement called Sustainable Seattle, which established as its first goal the definition, research, and publication of a set of sustainability indicators. This goal was seen as a way of presenting the idea and creating a basis for activism and policy initiatives in the future. The indicators project took five years to complete.

Initially, the city hosted the meetings, but the indicators project was deliberately kept as a volunteer citizens' initiative as it was believed that this approach would have more long-term impact. The group drew on existing literature such as the work of Hazel Henderson, the Oregon Benchmarks program, and Jacksonville, Florida's Quality Indicators for Progress. Three kinds of indicators were identified: key indicators, which were the fundamental measures of sustainability; secondary indicators, which contributed to the first group; and "provocative" indicators, which were nontechnical measures that would attract media attention and public interest (AtKisson 2001, 353). The most famous indicator in this last group was "the extent to which urban streams had salmon returning to spawn in them."

A lengthy community-based process eventually produced a report in 1995 listing forty indicators (AtKisson 2001, 354). The indicators were chosen using the following criteria:

- Reflective of trends that are fundamental to long-term cultural, economic, and environmental health
- Statistically measurable, with data preferably available for one or two decades
- Attractive to the local media
- Comprehensible to the average person.

The indicators were grouped into five categories: Environment, Population and Resources, Economy, Youth and Education, and Health and Community. According to AtKisson the strength of this approach is that it was generated and driven by the community in a lengthy participatory process. Such a process of questioning and reflection was valuable in raising awareness and ecoliteracy. The spirit of cooperation between different organizations was important too. The power of choosing indicators that would inspire debate and action was highlighted by the search for the "provocative" indicators.

Sustainable Pittsburgh

With models created by the consulting firm AtKisson Inc., a group of local leaders and interested citizens known as Sustainable Pittsburgh developed the Southwestern Pennsylvania Regional Indicators Report. What distinguishes this indicators report from many others is that it takes a strongly regional approach, covering the six counties of southwestern Pennsylvania. It identifies the region as a significant unit of organization in ecological, social, and economic terms. Alongside the report, a community handbook was also published to assist local municipalities and neighborhoods in developing their own sustainability goals and measures.

The aim was to produce a set of indicators that was simultaneously comprehensive and reasonably "small, manageable, and easy to communicate." The indicators are grouped into four areas:

1. Nature, which covers "environmental quality, ecosystem health, natural resources, and natural beauty"
2. Economy, which incorporates indicators related to the production of goods and services, including employment, wages, and infrastructure
3. Society, which covers the "collective dimension of human life," including "government, schools, health care systems, public safety, and the web of social relationships called 'social capital'"
4. Well-Being, which refers to individual needs such as good relationships, longevity, and the fulfillment of one's potential[12]

These indicators were aggregated to form a "Compass Index of Sustainability," with each of the above groups representing one of the four points of the compass. The regional focus of this indicator initiative was a strength, giving the city of Pittsburgh a tangible surrounding area to maintain and setting up a tension on how to actually achieve the governance for the implementation of the changes that all participants could see were needed. Use of graphical tools such as the Compass of Sustainability assisted in making the results easier for the wider community to interpret. The community handbook was also a good initiative, encouraging greater community involvement at different levels.

Sustainable Calgary

The Sustainable Calgary "State of Our City" project was started by a group of interested citizens to "re-examine through sustainability indicators reporting, how we define progress, quality of life, and sustainability." Since its inception in 1996, Sustainable Calgary has produced three State of Our City reports.

Its second report, published in 2001, involved almost two thousand people. After forming a project team in 1999, the group held workshops and presentations with citizens, calling for feedback on the first report and for recommendations for new indicators to include in the next report. In 2000, six indicator "think tanks" were formed from previous participants in the process, and they met three times over a six-week period. Following review of all the suggestions for new indicators and further brainstorming, the think tanks nominated five indicators from each of the six established categories—Community, Economic, Education, Natural Environment, Resources Use, and Wellness—to include in the 2001 report. These thirty nominations were voted on, and twelve new indicators were added. Alongside this, a series of task forces conducted research into the "indicators in progress" from the first report, and this research continues on an ongoing basis.

The indicators were selected on the following criteria:

- Is the indicator consistent with our sustainability principles?
- Does the indicator link economic, social, and/or ecological factors?
- Will people understand and care about this indicator?
- Will this indicator trigger action?
- Is this indicator responsive to interventions?
- Is there a way to accurately measure this indicator?
- Are the data for this indicator cost effective to collect?
- Is this indicator comparable to other reference points and standards?

In the introduction to the 2001 report, Sustainable Calgary argues that "we must understand the ends we want to achieve and the means we choose to achieve those ends." The report makes human needs explicit:

> The goal of a sustainable community is to achieve a good quality of life includ-
> ing love, comfort, health, education, physical sustenance, meaningful work,
> spiritual meaning, and a sense of belonging. In a sustainable community, the
> means to attain these qualities is through the most efficient and wise use of
> time, effort, and resources.[13]

The process was seen to be valuable for getting people to reflect on sustainability and notions of progress, for involving people in civic culture, and for ensuring that the outcome is built on diversity and common ground. The explicit statement of a community vision was seen as a strength.

Manchester, England

The sustainability indicators for Greater Manchester were developed as part of a collaborative research partnership between the Town and Country Planning Association (TCPA), Manchester Metropolitan University, and the ten local authorities of Greater Manchester (Ravetz 2000). The TCPA had released the report "Planning for a Sustainable Environment" in the early 1990s, setting out "an agenda for change, based around the concept of 'social city-regions' in which a balanced portfolio of policies could be applied, to help avoid environmental damage, social distress, and economic decline." Greater Manchester was chosen as the city to test the ideas and models that had been presented. Through the research process, an organizing framework was developed.

Using a systems view, an integrated assessment method was devised to examine urban metabolism. It involved mapping the total metabolism, including cultural, social, economic, political, spatial, technological, environmental, and ethical aspects from upstream to downstream. As a result of applying the mapping approach, a prototype package of methods and tools was developed under the title "Sustainable Cities Assessment Method" (ISCAM). It covered a number of applications, including the following (Ravetz 2000, 20):

- Systems mapping, which involves mapping total metabolism
- Accounting, which involves identifying chains of indicators and targets to match the systems mapping, and developing alternative scenarios
- Strategies, which involves devising sets of coordinated actions
- Agencies, which involves identifying appropriate agencies to carry out the strategies
- Appraisal, which involves evaluating the sustainability of systems, projects, or initiatives.

This approach provides a systematic process for analyzing the issues, developing actions, guiding implementation, and assessing overall sustainability.

Viewing the city-region as a "dynamic system," a set of key linked and measurable indicators were identified (Ravetz 2000, 32). The ISCAM software is used to group these indicators together in order to generate two different scenarios: a "business as usual" projection and a "sustainable development" projection. An "aggregate 'trend-target' index of sustainability" is calculated to show the overall trend.

The Core Indicators were grouped into the following categories:

- General, including population and GDP
- Built Environment, including total urban land
- Households, including percentage of energy via direct renewables
- Transport, including total final energy demand
- Open Land and Ecology, including urban open/green space and percentage of food supply organically grown
- Waste and Pollution, including total waste recycled
- Energy and Climate, including total final demand.

Addressing the question of how useful the approach is to other city-regions, Ravetz argued that, while the details were unique to the Manchester region, the principles are generally transferable. The strength of the approach is that it was based on a systems conceptual framework, which assists understanding of the system and the context for the indicators. Such a framework helped not only in the selection of indicators but also in the formulation of responses.

The list is fairly comprehensive, but community and social indicators were not included. Overall this approach provided a useful framework to encourage systematic analysis that can complement or provide input to community-based indicator initiatives.

Strategy 5: Nurturing Sources of Hope

Amid reports of poverty, alienation, and increasing environmental degradation, it is easy to be pessimistic. Yet alongside the challenges there are signs of hope, some of which have already been expressed in the case studies in previous chapters, showing communities, governments, and businesses taking action to improve the quality of life in their cities and developing a more regenerative relationship with their bioregions. Case studies demonstrating how cities generate hope (such as those found in Armstrong, Ruane, and Newman 2002) need to be documented for people to enjoy and to be inspired by.

Examples of sustainability-based hope in cities can be found in education, neighborhood renewal, bioregional voices, the arts, and symbolic sustainability projects.

Education

Ecological and cultural literacy are vital to building hope in sustainability. Programs to increase ecoliteracy in the community, especially among the young, are heartening. These programs counter the lack of immediate experience of nature among urban youth and the lack of awareness of how human activities in cities have an impact on the natural world. Initiatives that take children to wild places in their cities and the wider bioregions, along with community gardens and farms, help reconnect children to land, provide them a sense of belonging and meaning, and enrich their life experiences.

The Center for Education and Research in Environmental Strategies (CERES) is named after the Roman goddess of agriculture. Its Community Environment Park has become a major attraction in Brunswick, Australia (an inner suburb of Melbourne), drawing thousands to its inner-city site to participate in sustainability education programs and events that inspire a sense of place and community.[14]

The CERES project began in the early 1980s, when a group of local citizens acquired a ten-acre site filled with rubbish and turned it into a green urban oasis. The Community Environmental Park is designed to initiate and support environmental sustainability and social equity with an emphasis on cultural richness and community participation. Onsite facilities include community gardens and permaculture demonstration gardens; a nursery, which sells indigenous and permaculture plants; an animal farm; multicultural villages; trails; a popular café and weekend market, which nourish visitors with organic produce; an EcoHouse, with examples of green technology; and displays of household composting, vermiculture, and alternative energy systems.

CERES' annual program of festivals and events celebrates the community's local artistry and sense of place. The award-winning Return of the Sacred Kingfisher Festival and the Autumn Harvest Festival are two highlights in the events calendar. Its education program is a collection of over twenty hands-on programs developed to teach mainly school-age children about energy, water, land, resource conservation, and cultural diversity. The CERES Sustainable Schools Program has been codeveloped with the Gould League as the pilot project of a nationwide program, whereby all schools across Australia commit to becoming centers of environmental technology, design, and behavior, and establish a sustainability curricula while strengthening links with the community.

Hundreds of other programs take place at CERES, including some for older people, diverse ethnicities, the disadvantaged, and the unemployed. Its adult educational courses include accredited horticulture and sustainable agriculture training programs.

One of the key ways of promoting sustainability education is through school food programs. Three such examples are the Edible Schoolyard, Rethinking School Lunch project, and School Lunch Initiative, all in Berkeley, California.

The Edible Schoolyard is a cooking and gardening program that grew out of a conversation between chef Alice Waters and Neil Smith, former principal of the Martin Luther King Junior Middle School in Berkeley. Planning and preparation began in the late 1990s, with the clearing of an asphalt parking lot adjacent to the school, the planting of a soil-enriching cover crop, and the refurbishing of the school's unused 1930s cafeteria kitchen as a kitchen classroom.

Today, the program is integrated into the middle school's daily life. Students work together in their organic garden to plant and tend beds, amend soil, turn compost, and harvest flowers, fruits, and vegetables. In the kitchen classroom, they prepare and eat seasonal dishes from the produce they have grown. Students and teachers gather at the table to share food and conversation during each class.

The Edible Schoolyard is based on Waters' idea that "from the garden and the kitchen and the table, you learn empathy—for each other and all of creation; you learn compassion; and you learn patience and self-discipline."[15] Garden classes teach the principles of ecology, the origins of food, and respect for all living systems. Children learn about the connection between what they eat and where it comes from, with the goal of fostering environmental stewardship and revolutionizing the school lunch program.

The Edible Schoolyard has given rise to school food programs in other cities, such as the one at Collingwood College in Melbourne, Australia. The Edible Schoolyard website provides a wealth of resources to enable schools to start similar programs.[16]

The Rethinking School Lunch (RSL) project, also based in Berkeley, was developed by the Center for Ecoliteracy "to address the crisis in childhood obesity, provide nutrition education, and teach ecological knowledge." The RSL guide, available online, provides a planning framework that schools can follow to improve not only their school lunch programs but also the academic performance, ecological knowledge, and well-being of their students. The guide cover topics such as food policy, curriculum integration, childhood nutrition and health, financing, facilities design, and sustainable waste management. In its chapters, experts and practitioners discuss goals and challenges, showcase success stories, and offer additional resources.[17]

Through the School Lunch Initiative launched by the Berkeley Unified School District, the planning framework of the Rethinking School Lunch project and the methodology and principles of the Edible Schoolyard program are being applied across an entire public school system. The School Lunch Initiative hopes to revolutionize school lunch by making food a central part of the academic curriculum. The initiative includes gardens, kitchen classrooms, and lunchrooms as contexts for learning. It restores connections between what children are taught and what they experience; between nutrition, health, and the ability to learn; and between local communities and the farms that feed them. The project is funded by a public/private partnership of Alice Waters' Chez Panisse Foundation (named after her famous restaurant) and the Berkeley Unified School District, in collaboration with the Center for Ecoliteracy.[18]

Another educational food program, though not school-based, is found across the country in Pittsburgh, Pennsylvania: the Green Harvest sustainable food program.[19] Green Harvest was established by the Greater Pittsburgh Community Food Bank in 1991 to provide nutritious produce to low-income residents and to foster agricultural sustainability, economic development, and urban beautification. The program promotes self-sufficiency in local communities by teaching gardening skills, offering member agencies easier access to locally produced fruit and vegetables, and stimulating the local economy with small-enterprise development. It makes the most of urban/rural linkages and empowers low-income people to move away from dependence on public or private food assistance.

The project has six interrelated components:

- **Gleaning**: Volunteers harvest surplus fruits and vegetables from local farms to eliminate food wastage.

- **Community Gardens**: Over ten community gardens have been set up throughout the area so low-income residents can learn to grow and share their own vegetables. The food bank offers seeds, equipment, and technical support for community gardeners in their first year, with lessening involvement in following years to encourage self-reliance.
- **Longview Food Bank Farm**: The food bank has assumed the operation of a certified organic farm outside Pittsburgh. A farm supervisor is employed to coordinate the planting and harvesting of produce by volunteers. The produce is distributed free to member agencies. Another area of land is used to grow produce for members of a community-supported agriculture program who pay to have weekly deliveries; revenue from this program defers part of Green Harvest's operating expenses. The farm also features a demonstration garden and a venue for school and community workshops.
- **Farm Stand Project**: Fresh produce is made accessible to low-income people through community farm stands. The stands are run by managers from the communities they serve. The produce is supplied by Longview Food Bank Farm and various other local growers. Profits are used to fund the project in future seasons.
- **Market Gardens**: This program helps community gardeners sell some of the vegetables they grow at their own community farm stands.
- **City Parks Farmers Markets**: Unsold produce from farmers' markets is picked up by food bank agencies.

Neighborhood Renewal

Around the world, groups of ordinary people or people in partnership with government and/or business have begun the task of renewing their neighborhoods, reinvigorating a sense of community and place, and making steps toward more sustainable living. Some have revitalized through community gardens, while others have taken this a step further to form cohousing or urban ecovillages. The Green Harvest program outlined above, developed by the Greater Pittsburgh Community Food Bank, is an example of a comprehensive plan to address the root causes of urban poverty and promote sustainable agriculture. This program has achieved neighborhood renewal and enabled a range of other sustainability goals—like reducing travel and fostering a sense of place.

Another initiative, Sustainability Street, assists neighborhoods in starting their own sustainability projects. Described as "an exciting community development and environmental program that is fast gathering momentum across Australia," Sustainability Street aims to bring people together in their local communities to learn about sustainability and to generate their own projects. This community-centered approach was developed by environmental educators Vox Bandicoot in collaboration with Environs Australia.

In Sustainability Street's six-month course, participants initially gain a basic understanding of sustainability. The next stage involves people identifying a vision for their local area and determining how to achieve their goals. The Vox Bandicoot website provides event details, practical information, sustainability tips, community profiles, and an interactive discussion forum.[20]

The program has identified eight guiding principles for promoting sustainability:

1. Biological diversity is precious.
2. No doom and gloom!
3. Imagine the future to be clean, green, and sustainable.
4. Avoid the "holier than thou" soapbox.
5. Enjoy purposeful informality and build "social capital."
6. Celebrating the increasing number of good news stories is critical fuel for the journey.
7. Take baby steps and use common sense.
8. See and revel in the enviro links.

Bioregional Voices

Increasingly indigenous stories and knowledge are being recognized for their wisdom. These and other bioregional voices provide us with another way of seeing the world and relating to place. They challenge the trends of increasing globalization and homogenization. The rich cultural diversity of our world is a wellspring of wisdom. That these voices are becoming louder and that more people are listening is another source of hope. Cities need to tap into this and make these voices more audible.

One effective venue for bioregional, indigenous voices is Kodja Place, a cultural interpretive and visitor center located in the small rural town of Kojonup in Western Australia. The center was developed, and continues to be operated, by the local Kojonup community, a mix of Noongar (local indigenous people), and Wadjela (the Noongar word for white people).

The central theme of the center, "One Story, Many Voices," is an attempt by the Kojonup community to explore and present its common story. The Kodja story, which includes the experiences and aspirations of the Noongar, farmers, settlers, and young people, serves to highlight the diverse cultures involved in the development of Kojonup, especially the three parallel threads of Italian, English, and Aboriginal people. The collection and exhibition of cultural knowledge is based upon the Noongar's way of sharing culture—through stories. This approach was chosen by the community as it departs from the traditional historical "expert" view, which is objective and makes generalizations about the whole community, in favor of multiple present-day, subjective stories about the shared place.

The center has devised a multimedia framework where community stories are displayed. With the assistance of various grants, equipment was purchased and local people were trained in the skills of oral history, video production, photo scanning, and web-page production. Many Noongar elders have told their stories of place on videos produced by Noongar youths. Kodja Place also houses an outdoor maze of Australian-bred roses, which features the stories and cultural experiences of three fictional women—Maria (Italian), Yoondi (Noongar), and Elizabeth (English)—since the time of federation (Waller 2003).

Figure 10.1a–d

Kodja Place is the cultural center and museum of Kojonup in Western Australia.

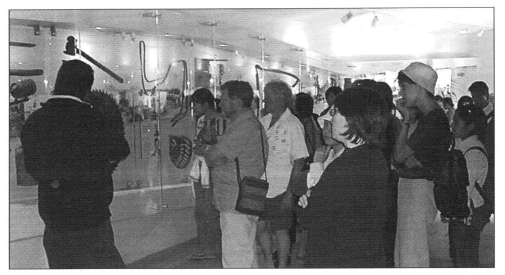

Figure 10.1a

It displays the parallel stories of indigenous, English, and Italian residents in the region.

Photo Gary Burke

Figure 10.1b

Young Noongar people make videos of their elders' stories.

Photo Gary Burke

Kodja Place has achieved many of its goals. People in the community are now better able to understand each other, and the center has won many awards, bringing people from far and wide to enjoy the locals' special story.

The Arts

The arts (including music, dance, storytelling, visual arts, theater, and film) offer an important way to express the creative impulse, which is so vital to human well-being and crucial to finding sustainable ways of living. The arts can inspire and motivate us, teach us to see the world and its challenges differently, and help us to heal and reconnect to each other and the Earth. Through community arts projects, people can give

Figure 10.1c

"Bush tucker" knowledge is passed on.

Photo Gary Burke

Figure10.1d

Kodja Place indigenous art

Photo Gary Burke

expression to their creativity and awaken a deeper sense of community and place. Furthermore, the arts can contribute to all the above sources of hope—in delivering education, enriching neighborhoods, promoting simpler lifestyles, and conveying the wisdom of bioregional voices.

The Santa Monica Festival Environmental Art Project brings art and science into high school and elementary school classrooms for the annual Santa Monica Festival, a celebration of arts and the environment in this California coastal city.[21] Several weeks before the festival, environmentalists from local nonprofit and government agencies give presentations to Santa Monica students on a variety of environmental topics, such as air quality, water quality, urban runoff, and recycling. Following the presentations, resident artists work with the students to help them create artwork for the elementary schools and poetry for the high schools that address environmental topics of interest to the students. The artworks are displayed during the opening procession of the Santa Monica Festival and in a public exhibition and reading at the Santa Monica Place Community Focus Gallery. The project serves not only as an outlet for youth creativity but also as an effective tool for educating students, teachers, and parents about many of the environmental issues faced by the community.

Another initiative that combines art, poetry, and environmental science is the annual River of Words (ROW) contest, conducted by the ROW organization and the Library of Congress, with financial assistance from the Center for Ecoliteracy. The largest youth poetry and art contest in the world, ROW encourages students of all ages to learn more about their local watersheds through careful observation and then express their connections with their environment in art and poetry. Through its Watershed Explorer curriculum, ROW trains thousands of classroom teachers, park rangers, librarians, and others to include nature exploration and the arts in their programs for young people.[22]

The All Species Project (ASP) is a US-based initiative with international outreach seeking to strengthen the sense of community and to reestablish connection to nature through the use of art, pageantry, and science. In 1988 ASP was invited to participate in one of the first big international environmental conferences in Moscow to "lighten up" the serious academic atmosphere. Working with an after-school program for students, the group decided to recruit some of these young Russians to help them put together a final conference event that would convey an "ecosensible" message of hope.

After much hard work, the ASP volunteers and their student recruits presented an afternoon program based on a traditional Native American thanksgiving blessing. About a thousand Russian and international visitors gathered outside the conference center for a processional journey between banners for the earth, water, air, plants, and animals. Punctuating the procession were songs and oratory from Russian children's choirs, recitations of poems from various languages, music from Laplander children playing jaw harps, and a tree blessing performed by a Lakota medicine man with chants, cedar incense, and eagle feathers. The audience crowded around, in awe of the primal act of singing to a tree. As a result of this event and its creative, multicultural expression of gratitude to nature, the All Species Project was presented with a United Nations Environmental Program Award for excellence in education.[23]

The Procession of the Species program in Olympia, Washington, is an example of community arts supporting the sustainability cause.[24] In January 1995, a group of Olympia residents decided to organize an artistic pageant in honor of the twenty-fifth anniversary of Earth Day and the renewal of the US Endangered Species Act. The event would have only three simple rules: no written words, no live pets, and no motorized vehicles.

Each year on procession day, Olympians put on their creative expressions and proceed through the streets of the city in animal masks and costumes, carrying banners and giant puppets, and playing or dancing to music. In recent years, the procession has drawn several thousand participants and over thirty thousand onlookers. The procession program includes seven weeks of art, music, and dance workshops that inspire a better understanding of nature and the need for wildlife protection.

Of course such a project, whose roots and ongoing commitment come from civil society, requires the oversight of local government and participation of local businesses. Together, these groups have created a celebration of the bioregional environment that provides hope for the future.

Symbolic Sustainability Projects

One of the key ways that governance can provide hope for the residents of cities trying to be more sustainable is through symbolic sustainability projects. There are many examples in this book of how that is being done. Examples can often be quite small—like a neighborhood permaculture park, a demonstration sustainable home, a traffic-calmed street, or an ecotourism project involving indigenous people describing an ancient "song-

Figure 10.2a

A six-kilometer freeway in central Seoul is removed and an important river has a chance to be restored.

Photo Jeff Kenworthy

Figure 10.2b

Seoul now has a restored river, a public park, and forty thousand less vehicles per day in the central city.

Photo Tim Newman

line" through the city. Often the symbols that mean the most are high-quality public transport systems, especially if they simultaneously replace hated, noisy freeways. Projects like this are evident in Curitiba, Bogotá, San Francisco, Milwaukee, Strasbourg, Delhi, Toronto, Aarhus, and Perth.

Perhaps the most spectacular example of a sustainable project is the removal of a highway in Seoul (figure 10.2). The large highway had completely covered a river and an ancient historic bridge. The Cheonggyecheon project has demolished the road, begun the restoration of the river and its foreshores, renewed the bridge as a heritage icon, and replaced the traffic with an underground rail line, a bus rapid transit, and overall reductions in mobility. Significant cost returns have been made from real estate along the new prestigious reclaimed area. The whole project was envisioned by a local NGO that lobbied all mayoral candidates; the candidate who committed to the project won the election and has implemented the dream of these committed citizens.

Conclusions

Hope emerges out of good governance, but it is also the quality that gives rise to good governance. By taking organic steps toward a long-term vision, a city can build on its history and culture and move toward a sustainable future. Cities need to create sources of hope, embed sustainability in government agencies, and create indicators for sustainability reporting. Symbolic projects are important for generating hope. Hope is the beacon that shines on the city, shading the parts that must one day change, but giving urban dwellers a glimpse of what can be. For any city, one can hope that it will someday become a source of ecological and social regeneration within its whole fabric and out into its bioregion.

Conclusions

The world is on an unsustainable path; setting a new direction for cities is a major part of turning the world to a new path, where cities first begin to mitigate their impacts and then become a source of regeneration as in natural ecosystems.

Cities as Sustainable Ecosystems can assist in charting how this can be done. Building on the ten Melbourne Principles, this book has elaborated what a sustainable path for cities could look like. All the principles bring us back to a central truth—that the best human innovations mimic and learn from natural systems. Cities need to reflect this approach to innovation in their planning, design, production, consumption, and governance.

An important insight presented in the book is the need to counter the trend toward increasing globalization of city economies by focusing on the local and bioregional scales at which feedback loops can operate more effectively, and where consumption and production can be better matched to bioregional capacities. Nutrient cycling and integration of processes operate better at these scales. Global feedback on issues like the carbon cycle is also shaping the way cities relate more responsibly to the economic globalization phenomenon.

Ecological footprints can be reduced by use of more environmentally sound technologies along with a focus on meeting human needs and reducing consumption in the developed world. Transportation priorities are an important factor in shaping urban form and thus the amount of land taken up for housing and energy usage and thus reducing ecological footprint. Bioregional and local economies cut down the amount of fuel used to transport food, water, and other essential materials. Ecological regeneration can become the operational focus for cities as they mimic ecosystems in terms of their infrastructure, buildings, industry, community, and governance.

Traditional wisdom and eco-city social movements are providing a revitalized sense of place and demonstrating new ways of living, from simplicity circles to urban ecovillages. These voices demonstrate the concept of environmental citizenship, whereby people take responsibility for caring for their "life-places" and communities. Leadership is needed to create more polycentric, participatory forms of governance, from the local to bioregional scale. Informed, active citizens and supportive, effective governance are elements of sustainability. The path ahead is a challenging one, but the examples of innovation presented throughout this book give cause for hope.

In summary, Cities as Sustainable Ecosystems can be described as cities that embody the following principles:

- Urban values respect the intrinsic value of all life
- Urban lifestyles are equitable, conserving, varied, and enriched by a strong sense of place and community
- Urban institutional structures are polycentric and bioregional as well as being linked globally, involving processes that are participatory, cooperative, and based on adaptive management
- Urban production and consumption activities focus on meeting genuine human needs (especially those of the poor), rely less on globalization and more on integration at local and bioregional scales, and employ environmentally sustainable technologies
- City form is designed to encourage human interaction in walkable spaces, and to restore and maintain ecological processes and links to the bioregion
- Urban infrastructure support systems are integrated into the urban fabric, are designed to mimic or use natural processes, and are linked to support systems
- Urban mobility infrastructure maximizes positive social interactions and minimizes land and energy use
- Urban bioregional processes and biodiversity are maintained and enhanced through a system of reserves throughout the bioregion, with the city acting as an "ark"
- Urban systems progressively reduce their impact and begin to form ecologically and socially regenerative systems
- Urban governance is based on creating hope through leadership, innovation, participation, and the demonstration of practical and symbolic sustainability projects.

Jane Jacobs (1961, 1984) saw cities as being crucibles for innovation and the source for global change. She showed that in various stages of history, innovations from one city have been rapidly copied and improved by other cities in a constant struggle to see who has the edge. At a certain point the innovation becomes accepted by the main agents of change within the city, and it is then rapidly adopted and universalized. Thus the innovation does not need mass acceptance before it becomes critical enough to create change.

This book has gathered enough evidence from around the world to show there is a profound change challenging civilization and its cities: the challenge of sustainability. Perhaps a threshold is being passed in this era in which cities are beginning to respond at a much deeper and faster rate to issues of sustainability.

Cities may want to do an audit of where they stand in terms of sustainability by examining their activities and policies in relation to the ten Melbourne Principles. These CASE cities can see how well they are doing in each area; few cities examined in this book were innovative in all ten areas. CASE cities can then compare themselves with others and share innovations, leading to further change. The checklist in table 11.1 can guide this audit.

Table 11.1 **Sustainability Checklist Based on the Ten Melbourne Principles**

Principle	Criteria	Yes/No
Vision	Does your city have a vision statement based on sustainability principles?	
Economy and Society	Does your city have an economy and society that recognize sustainability goals?	
Biodiversity	Does your city have a biodiversity strategy?	
Ecological Footprints	Does your city know its ecological footprint, and does it have a strategy to reduce it?	
Model Cities on Ecosystems	Does your city model itself on sustainable ecosystems by having • visibility of processes and functions? • bioregional and local economic processes? • renewable energy systems? • ecological architecture? • support systems that mimic ecosystem patterns (cyclical, functional diversity, integrated, etc.)? • polycentric and adaptive institutions? • neighborhood and urban renewal processes? • decoupling processes for energy and material from urban growth? • built-form diversification processes? • participatory governance structures? • transportation infrastructure and urban design that favor sustainable modes of transport?	
Sense of Place	Does your city have a "sense of place" strategy?	
Empowerment	Is your city committed to empowerment and participation for sustainability?	
Partnerships	Does your city have sustainability networks involving all sectors: citizens, business, academia, government? Is your city part of a bioregional sustainability network?	
Sustainable Production and Consumption	Is your city committed to achieving more sustainable production and consumption patterns?	
Governance and Hope	Does your city create hope for the future through good governance at local, bioregional, and global scales? Does your city have a sustainability assessment program to monitor change? Does your city have an arts program to celebrate and promote sustainability?	

As cities begin to embrace sustainability and to use ideas such as those found in the ten Melbourne Principles, they may produce a range of powerful innovations and changes that go well beyond any of the examples in this book. Cities of the world now need to prioritize their agendas so that urban innovations and change for sustainability become a driving force, linking governments, business, and communities. Government officials increasingly will not get elected unless they can show such leadership; businesses will get left behind unless they can find a niche in this "green New Deal" (Friedman 2007); and communities will become more and more alienated unless they can see progress on this agenda. As cities share their inspiration, their ideas, and their implementation, the world will change.

Who will lead the world in this new direction? Will it be American cities with all their business resources, education, and risk-taking ability, or will they succumb to the powers of SUVs and gated suburbs? Will it be European cities which have the urban form and history of sustainability to build on, or will they focus too much on the past rather than envisioning an innovative sustainability agenda? Maybe it will be the cities in emerging economies like China, India, and Brazil with their huge growth potential which can adapt to sustainability, or will their cities just try to copy the fading Western model? Will they glimpse the possibilities for cities to be sources of regeneration within their bioregions? Will any of them see enough of the underlying deeper messages of caring and commitment to make the necessary changes?

> For the Children
> The rising hills, the slopes,
> of statistics
> lie before us.
> the steep climb
> of everything, going up,
> up, as we all
> go down.
> In the next century
> or the one beyond that,
> they say,
> are valleys, pastures,
> we can meet there in peace
> if we make it.
> To climb these coming crests
> one word to you, to
> you and your children:
> *stay together*
> *learn the flowers*
> *go light*
>
> —Gary Snyder (1974)

A

Extracts from the "Local Government Declaration to the World Summit on Sustainable Development," 2002

We the Mayors, Leaders, and representatives of the cities and local governments of the world, and of their international and national associations, meeting in Johannesburg on the occasion of the 2002 World Summit on Sustainable Development (WSSD), agree to the following Declaration:

Welcoming the initiative of the United Nations and its Member States in convening the World Summit on Sustainable Development, which meets at a crucial time in the life of our planet;

Committed to the goals and targets of Agenda 21, the Habitat Agenda, and of the UN Millennium Declaration, in the struggle against global poverty and for sustainable development;

Reaffirming our commitment to the principles of sustainable development, including solidarity, transversality (integrating the economic, social, and environmental dimensions), participation of civil society in decision making, and responsibility toward future generations and disadvantaged populations;

Aware that, despite many successes and much commitment (in particular by local governments) in relation to Agenda 21, we remain far from achieving a sustainable future for humankind;

Gravely concerned at the ongoing process of depletion of the earth's resource base and degradation of the global environment;

Convinced that, if we are to resolve the challenges facing the world, a strong partnership between all spheres of government (from international to local) is essential. . . .

The Context

With half of the world's population now living in urban settlements, and with the world's population due to grow to eight billion by 2025, the issue of sustainable urban management and development is one of the critical issues for the twenty-first century. National states cannot, on their own, centrally manage and control the complex, fast-moving cities and towns of today and tomorrow—only strong decentralized local governments, in touch with and involving their citizens, and working in partnership with national governments, are in a position to do so. The future of rural settlements is also of vital importance, with urban/rural linkages and interdependence becoming key issues for the future of sustainable development. . . .

Commitments by Local Governments

Arising from the above, we reaffirm our strong commitment to Agenda 21, and further commit ourselves:

> . . . To develop a new and deeper culture of sustainability in our cities and localities, including a commitment to socially and environmentally sound procurement policies and consumption patterns, sustainable planning, investment and management of resources, and promotion of public health and of clean energy sources; to this end we ask all local governments to discuss endorsement of the Earth Charter;

> To develop effective and transparent local governance, including a proactive leadership role, working with the local organizations of civil society and the private sector, and ensuring the equal participation of women and men, and the active involvement of disadvantaged sectors. . . .

Source: International Development Research Center archive,
http://www.idrc.ca/en/ev-95049-201-1-DO_TOPIC.html.

B | *The Carbon Cycle*

Plants photosynthesize glucose from carbon dioxide gas and water, and in turn more complex organic matter is synthesized. Plants are consumed by plant-eating animals, which in turn are consumed by meat-eating animals. Organic carbon compounds are digested by these animals and resynthesized into other forms, which are useful for energy, cell growth, and cell multiplication. Carbon dioxide is released into the atmosphere during the process of respiration. The respiration process releases energy for the organism through oxidizing the organic carbon. Plants and animals produce waste materials and will eventually die. Leaf litter, animal wastes, and dead organic matter are decomposed by bacteria and other decomposers releasing the carbon as carbon dioxide, thus completing the carbon cycle. Oxygen is required in the process of respiration and oxidation of organic carbon, and this is the reason for the oxygen demand of organic wastes. Some organic matter from dead animals and plants is, however, stored in nature, particularly in sediments, and slowly turns into peat or more stable carbon-rich materials (see figure B.1).

In the process of decomposition, not only is carbon released as carbon dioxide, but other minerals are released. These minerals are involved in other cycles, such as the nitrogen cycle (appendix C) and phosphorus cycle (appendix D).

Source: Ho 2002

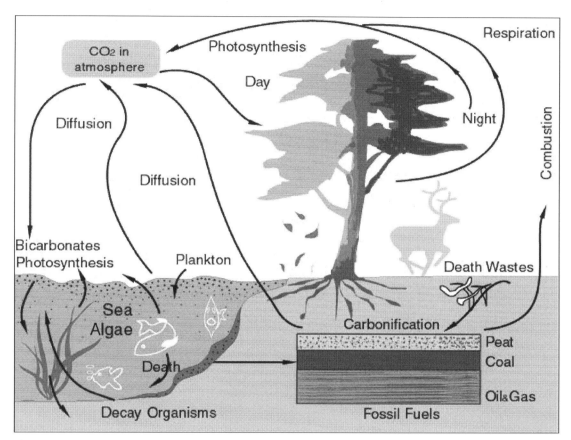

Figure B.1

Carbon cycle

Ho 2002

C | *The Nitrogen Cycle*

R elatively small amounts of nitrogen are converted into forms that can be utilized by plants. This conversion occurs through the activity of nitrogen-fixing bacteria in the root nodules of some plants, through nitrogen-fixing blue-green algae, or through lightning. Volcanic eruptions also contribute. Therefore, the amount of nitrogen cycled in natural ecosystems is relatively small and is absorbed rapidly by plants.

Generally, the decomposition of organic wastes releases nitrogen in the form of ammonia. In the presence of oxygen (aerobic conditions), the ammonia is oxidized by a group of bacteria (termed "nitrifiers") to nitrate. This is another process that places oxygen demand on the environment. Plants normally take up nitrogen in the form of nitrate in order to synthesize protein. On the other hand, under conditions devoid of oxygen (anaerobic conditions), nitrate may be converted to nitrogen gas by a group of bacteria (termed "denitrifiers"). Generally, denitrification occurs in sediments, where anaerobic conditions and availability of organic carbon facilitate the process.

Humans add nitrogen to the cycle through the use of nitrogen fertilizers and dumping of wastewaters into waterways. This can lead to excessive buildup in water bodies causing eutrophicaton, which involves the overgrowth of algae. The decay of this algae produces high biological oxygen demand, which deoxygenates the water, causing death of fish and other organisms.

Source: Ho 2002; http://www.greenfacts.org/glossary/def/environmental-cycles.htm#3

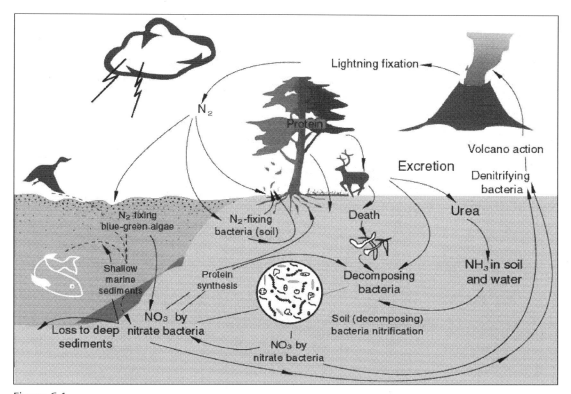

Figure C.1

Nitrogen cycle

Ho 2002

APPENDIX

D | *The Phosphorus Cycle*

The phosphorus cycle is driven by organisms and natural weathering processes. Natural weathering of phosphorus deposits, mostly found in rocks, makes phosphorus available to organisms in the form of phosphates. Animals take up phosphorus by eating plants or other animals. It is returned to the soil or sediments eventually through the excretion of wastes, along with the decomposition of dead plants and animals.

Phosphates also enter waterways from human inputs such as fertilizer runoff (fertilizer is mined from phosphate rock), sewage seepage, and wastes from other industrial processes. These phosphates tend to form sediments in oceans and lakes, and if sediments are stirred up, phosphates may reenter the phosphorous cycle. Excessive concentrations of phosphates in surface waterways can lead to eutrophication.

Source: Ho 2002; GreenFacts, http://www.greenfacts.org/glossary/def/environmental-cycles.htm#3

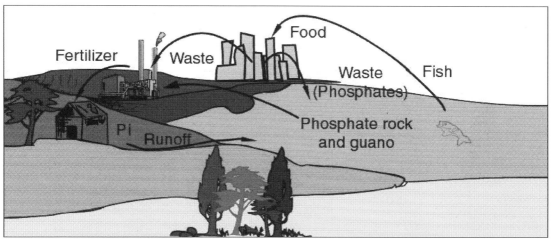

Figure D.1

Phosphorus cycle

Ho 2002

E | *The Hydrological Cycle*

The hydrological cycle recycles and purifies water. It involves seven main processes:

1. **Evaporation**, whereby water in the oceans and terrestrial water bodies is converted to water vapor by incoming solar energy
2. **Transpiration**, whereby water is lost from plants that have taken up water through their roots
3. **Condensation**, whereby water vapor is converted into droplets
4. **Precipitation**, whereby rain, sleet, hail, and snow fall
5. **Infiltration**, whereby water moves into the soil
6. **Percolation**, whereby water flows downward through the soil and possibly permeable rock layers to the groundwater aquifer
7. **Runoff**, whereby water runs off the land into the ocean or terrestrial water bodies

This cycle is driven largely by direct solar energy and gravity. However, plants play a crucial role in this cycle, affecting condensation, infiltration, percolation, and runoff patterns.

Source: Tyler-Miller 1996, 43; Ho 2002

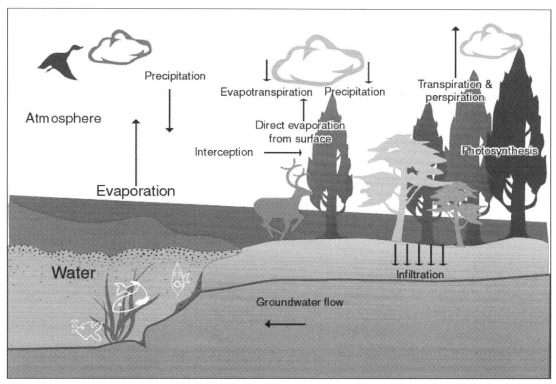

Figure E.1

Hydrological cycle

Ho 2002

Notes

Introduction

1. L. Sweet, Room to live: Healthy cities for the urban century, International Development Research Center Briefing No. 4, http://www.idrc.ca/wuf/ev-25775-201-1-DO_TOPIC.html.
2. Defining an ecosystem approach to urban management and policy development (2003), United Nations University/Institute of Advanced Studies, http://www.ias.unu.edu /binaries/UNUIAS_UrbanReport1.pdf.
3. K. Töpfer, address to World Council of Churches (1999), United Nations Environment Program/New York Office, http://www.nyo.unep.org/eaf/intro.pdf.

Chapter 1

1. Where do we want to be?, Green Communities program, US Environmental Protection Agency, http://www.epa.gov/greenkit/intro3.htm.
2. Corvallis 2020 vision statement (1997), City of Corvallis, Oregon, http://www.ci.corvallis.or.us/index.php?option=content&task=view&id=234&Itemid=188.
3. Dialogue with the City [Perth]: Visions and objectives, Department for Planning and Infrastructure, Government of Western Australia, http://www.dpi.wa.gov.au/dialogue/1668.asp.
4. Imagine Chicago, http://www.imaginechicago.org/about_us.html.
5. For more on the Burlington Legacy Project, see http://www.cedo.ci.burlington.vt.us/legacy /documents.html.
6. Indigenous and Tribal Peoples Center, http://www.itpcentre.org/env_index.htm.
7. Earth Charter, p. 6 , http://www.earthcharter.org/files/charter/charter.pdf.
8. Qualities of a healthy city, World Health Organization, http://www.euro.who.int /healthy-cities/introducing/20050202_4.
9. Child-Friendly Cities, UNICEF, http://www.childfriendlycities.org.
10. M. Bloomberg, Long-term planning in New York City: Challenges and goals (12 Dec. 2006), *Gotham Gazette*, http://www.gothamgazette.com/article/searchlight/20061212/203/2059.
11. Citizens' Bioregional Plan for Northeast Ohio, p. 25, EcoCity Cleveland, http://www.ecocitycleveland.org/smartgrowth/bioplan/pdfiles/cbp_full.pdf.

Chapter 2

1. Earth Charter, p. 1, http://www.earthcharter.org/files/charter/charter.pdf.
2. Chevron Corporation, http://www.willyoujoinus.com.

3. PLANYC, Government of New York City, http://www.nyc.gov/html/planyc2030/html/about/10-goals.shtml.

4. William J. Clinton Foundation, http://www.clintonfoundation.org.

5. Oil Depletion Analysis Center, http://www.odac-info.org.

6. Transition Towns Wiki, http://www.transitiontowns.org.

7. ConservationEconomy.net (a project of Ecotrust), http://www.conservationeconomy.net/conservation_economy.html.

8. Ibid.

9. Business Alliance for Local Living Economies, www.localeconomies.org.

10. Sirolli Institute, http://www.sirolli.co.uk.

11. Global Ecovillage Network, http://gen.ecovillage.org.

12. Online communities directory, Intentional Communities (a project of Fellowship for Intentional Community), http://www.directory.ic.org.

13. SomerVille Ecovillage, http://www.somervilleecovillage.com.au.

14. Los Angeles Ecovillage, http://www.laecovillage.org/brochure.html.

15. For information on community land trusts, see the Institute for Community Economics website at http://www.iceclt.org.

16. Sampling of goals for '06 –'07, Los Angeles Ecovillage, http://www.laecovillage.org/Goals.htm.

17. L. Sweet, Room to live: Healthy cities for the urban century, International Development Research Center Briefing No. 4, http://www.idrc.ca/wuf/ev-25775-201-1-DO_TOPIC.html#FarmingCity.

18. Food gardens in South Africa: The Food Gardens Foundation (1995), *City Farmer*, Canada's Office of Urban Agriculture, http://www.cityfarmer.org/s.africa.html; Food Gardens Foundation, http://www.foodgardensfoundation.org.za/about.html.

19. Annual reports: Soweto 2001, Food Gardens Foundation, http://www.foodgardensfoundation.org.za/annual_reports_anglo.html.

20. M. Haldane, Edible urban landscape, (2004) *McGill Reporter*, http://www.mcgill.ca/reporter/37/05/bhatt.

21. M. Linton, LETSystems, http://www.gmlets.u-net.com.

22. Crystal Waters Permaculture Village, http://www.ecologicalsolutions.com.au/crystalwaters/index.html.

23. B. Lietaer and A. Warmoth, Designing bioregional economies in response to globalization (1999), http://ceres.ca.gov/tcsf/pathways/chapter2.html#building.

24. Ibid., http://ceres.ca.gov/tcsf/pathways/chapter2.html#curitiba.

25. The Village of Arts and Humanities, http://www.inliquid.com/organizations/village.shtml.

Chapter 3

1. United Nations Environment Program, *State of the Environment and Policy Retrospective: 1972–2002*, http://www.unep.org/geo/geo3/english/pdfs/chapter2-4_biodiversity.pdf.

2. Strategic Plan (2002), Convention on Biological Diversity (UNEP), http://www.biodiv.org/sp.

3. Convention on Biological Diversity (UNEP), http://www.biodiv.org/doc/publications/guide.asp.

4. World Resources Institute, *World Resources 1996–97: The Urban Environment*, http://www.wri.org/wr-96-97; http://pubs.wri.org/pubs_content_print.cfm?ContentID=798.

5. Millennium Ecosystem Assessment, http://www.maweb.org.

6. ConservationEconomy.net (a project of Ecotrust), http://www.conservationeconomy.net/connected_wildlands.html.

7. Ibid.

8. Gondwana Link, http://www.gondwanalink.org; Bush Heritage Australia, http://www.bushheritage.asn.au.

9. Lady Bird Johnson Wildflower Center, http://www.wildflower.org.

Chapter 4

1. The ecological footprints of Tokyo, Global Development Research Center, http://www.gdrc.org/uem/tokyo-fprint.html.

2. On component methodology, see C. Simmons and K. Lewis, Two feet—two approaches: A component-based model of ecological footprinting, Best Foot Forward, http://www.bestfootforward.com/articles/twofeet.htm.

3. Regional Governance for Sustainability Pre-Conference Workshop, Perth, Western Australia, 2003.

4. Living Planet Report 2002, WWF, http://assets.panda.org/downloads/LPR_2002.pdf.

Chapter 5

1. US Long-Term Ecological Research Network, http://www.lternet.edu/sites; Central Arizona—Phoenix Long-Term Ecological Research, http://www.lternet.edu/sites/cap; Baltimore Ecosystem Study, http://www.lternet.edu/sites/bes.

2. Defining an ecosystem approach to urban management and policy development (2003), United Nations University/Institute of Advanced Studies, http://www.ias.unu.edu/binaries/UNUIAS_UrbanReport1.pdf.

3. *BedZED—Beddington Zero Energy Development, Sutton: General Information Report 89* (2002), BioRegional Development Group, http://www.bioregional.com/programme_projects/ecohous_prog/bedzed/BedZED%20Best%20Practice%20Report.pdf.

4. Planet Drum Foundation, Eco Ecuador works, http://www.planetdrum.org/eco_ecuador.htm.

5. P. Berg, lecture at University of Montana–Missoula (10 April, 2001), http://www.planetdrum.org/Post-Enviro.htm.

6. Christie Walk, Urban Ecology Australia, http://www.urbanecology.org.au/christiewalk; Australian Greenhouse Office, http://www.greenhouse.gov.au/yourhome/technical/fs73.htm.

7. E. Peñalosa, report to United Nations Asia-Pacific Leadership Forum: Sustainable Development for Cities (2004), http://www.susdev.gov.hk/html/en/leadership_forum/enrique_penalosa_paper.pdf.

Chapter 6

1. Five principles of ecological design, Ecological Design Institute, http://www.ecodesign.org/edi/ecodesign.html.

2. Sim Van der Ryn, Ecological Design Institute, http://www.ecodesign.org/edi/aboutedi.html.

3. Wonga Wetlands, City of Albury (NSW), http://www.wongawetlands.nsw.gov.au/wetlands/overview.htm.

4. Ecotrust, http://ecotrust.org/toolkit; http://ecotrust.org/knowledgesystems.

5. N. Logan, Sharing ethnoecological information using Internet technology: Bioregional ethnographic collectivism, restoration ethnography, and oral history on the web, http://www.fortlewis.edu/anthro/ethnobotany/Dbase/images/Documents/Outline.htm.

6. Ethnoecology Database of the Greater Southwest, Anthropology Department, Fort Lewis College, http://www.fortlewis.edu/anthro/ethnobotany/database.htm.

7. Trails and greenways, Metro (Portland regional government), http://www.metro-region.org/article.cfm?ArticleID=3418.

8. Putah-Cache Bioregion Project, University of California–Davis, http://bioregion.ucdavis.edu/what/artlit.html.

Chapter 7

1. Office of Citizens and Civics, Government of Western Australia, Department of the Premier and Cabinet, http://www.citizenscape.wa.gov.au/index.cfm?event=aboutCivic.
2. 21st Century Dialogue, http://www.21stcenturydialogue.com.
3. Case studies on sustainable development, World Health Organization, Regional Office for Europe, http://www.euro.who.int/healthy-cities/introducing/20050202_4.
4. These are summarized from the 21st Century Dialogue website, which sets out deliberative democracy approaches on twenty-two separate projects (http://www.21stcenturydialogue.com), from Carson and Hartz-Karp (2005), and from Sarkissian, Cook, and Walsh (1994–2005).
5. Poverty alleviation through community participation—UBSP India, United Nations Educational, Scientific, and Cultural Organization (UNESCO), http://www.unesco.org/most /asia12.htm.
6. Child-Friendly Cities, UNICEF, http://www.childfriendlycities.org.
7. UN-Habitat's new focus on youth empowerment and its global partnership program, UN-Habitat (United Nations Human Settlements Program), http://ww2.unhabitat.org/programmes /safercities/documents/PRESS%20RELEASE.PDF.
8. T. Atlee, Ways to make a community stronger, wiser, more resilient, and engaged, The Co-Intelligence Institute; http://www.co-intelligence.org/CIPol_CSWM.html.
9. J. Hartz-Karp, 21st Century Dialogue, http://www.21stcenturydialogue.com.
10. See the publications listed at Murdoch University's Institute for Sustainability and Technology Policy website, http://www.sustainability.murdoch.edu.au.
11. Green Communities program, US Environmental Protection Agency, http://www.epa.gov/greenkit/index.html.

Chapter 8

1. See, for example, The new science of networks, *The Science Show* (19 June 2004), hosted by Robyn Williams, http://www.abc.net.au/rn/science/ss/stories/s1127796.htm.
2. H. Srinivas, The role of local governments in fostering business partnerships for environmental sustainability, Global Development Research Center, http://www.gdrc.org/sustbiz/bizpartnerships.html.
3. Bremen Initiative, http://www.bremen-initiative.de/index2.html; Bremen Declaration (1997), adopted at the International Conference on Business and Municipality, http://www.bremen -initiative.de/lib/declarations/engl/bremen_decla_gb.pdf.
4. Environs Australia, http://www.environs.org.au.
5. World Business Council for Sustainable Development, http://www.wbcsd.org.
6. Surface Transportation Policy Partnership, http://www.transact.org.
7. GreenCityBlueLake (a project of EcoCity Cleveland), http://www.gcbl.org.
8. Objectives, GreenCityBlueLake, http://www.gcbl.org/about/objectives.
9. WA Collaboration, http://www.wacollaboration.org.au.
10. Global Ecovillage Network, http://gen.ecovillage.org.
11. Urban Ecovillage Network, http://urban.ecovillage.org/index.shtml.
12. M. Gamble, Urban community food systems and the role of permaculture design (2002), Sustaining our communities (International Local Agenda 21 Conference, Adelaide), Regional Institute, http://www.regional.org.au/au/soc/2002/3/gamble.htm.
13. Programs, ICLEI, (Local Governments for Sustainability) http://www.iclei.org/index.php?id =global-programs.
14. PLUS Network, http://plusnetwork.org.
15. C40 Cities (Large Cities Climate Leadership Group), http://www.c40cities.org.

16. Aalborg Charter and Aalborg +10 Commitments, European Commission, Environment Directorate-General, http://europa.eu.int/comm/environment/urban/aalborg.htm.

17. Aalborg Commitments, Aalborg +10 Conference, http://www.aalborgplus10.dk/default.aspx?m=2&i=307.

Chapter 9

1. See, for example, What is a simplicity study group (a.k.a. study circles)?, Simple Living Network, http://www.simpleliving.net/studygroups/default.asp.

2. L. B. Pierce, Simplicity Resource Guide, http://www.gallagherpress.com/pierce.

3. J. O'Neill, Affluenza Project, http://www.affluenza.com.

4. TravelSmart, Government of Western Australia, Department for Planning and Infrastructure, http://www.dpi.wa.gov.au/travelsmart/14890.asp.

5. Sustainable living, Government of Western Australia, http://www.sustainableliving.wa.gov.au.

6. EcoSmart, http://www.ecosmart.com.au.

7. Living Smart—for a sustainable community, Fremantle Focus (city of Fremantle, Western Australia), http://www.freofocus.com/projects/html/living_smart.cfm.

8. EU directive on sustainable procurement, http://ec.europa.eu/internal_market/publicprocurement/legislation_en.htm.

9. History, Slow Food, http://www.slowfood.com/about_us/eng/manifesto.lasso.

10. A. Abbona and P. Nano, undated interview with S. Cimicchi (trans. John Irving), Cittaslow International, http://www.cittaslow.net/pagine.asp?idn=998.

11. LessTraffic.com (a project of Creative Communities International), www.lesstraffic.com.

12. M. Schulz, European cities do away with traffic signs (16 Nov. 2006), *Spiegel Online*, http://www.spiegel.de/international/spiegel/0,1518,448747,00.html.

13. Examples of biomimicry, Biomimicry Institute, http://www.biomimicry.net/casestudiesB.htm.

14. Cleaner production, United Nations Environment Program, http://www.uneptie.org/pc/cp/understanding_cp/related_concepts.htm#2.

15. C. Murphy, Cultivating Havana: Urban agriculture and food security in the years of crisis (1999), Development Report No. 12, Institute for Food and Development Policy (Food First), http://www.foodfirst.org/dr12.

16. Case study 2 (section 9.3.2), *International Source Book on Environmentally Sound Technologies for Wastewater and Stormwater Management* (2002), ed. G. Ho, United Nations Environment Program/International Environmental Technology Center (UNIEP/IETC), http://www.unep.or.jp/ietc/Publications/TechPublications/TechPub-15/2-9/9-3-2_2.asp.

17. Case study 1 (section 9.3.1), ibid., http://www.unep.or.jp/Ietc/Publications/TechPublications/TechPub-15/2-9/9-3-1.asp.

18. ESTIS (Environmentally Sound Technologies Information System), http://www.estis.net.

19. Path to Freedom, http://www.pathtofreedom.com.

Chapter 10

1. *Tools to Support Participatory Urban Decision Making* (2001), UN Center for Human Settlements, publications, UN-Habitat, http://www.unhabitat.org/pmss/getElectronicVersion.asp?nr=1122&alt=1.

2. H. Srinivas, The role of local governments in fostering business partnerships for environmental sustainability, Global Development Research Center, http://www.gdrc.org/sustbiz/bizpartnerships.html.

3. Global Campaign on Urban Governance, UN-Habitat, http://www.unhabitat.org/categories.asp?catid=25.

4. The Citistates Group, http://www.citistates.com.

5. America 2050 (a project of the New York Regional Plan Association), http://www.america2050.org.

6. Flavin made this claim at the launch of *State of the World 2007: Our Urban Future*. For more information about the Worldwatch Institute, visit the group's website, http://www.worldwatch.org.

7. World Business Council for Sustainable Development, http://www.wbcsd.org.

8. ICLEI (Local Governments for Sustainability), http://www.iclei.org.

9. Network of Regional Governments for Sustainable Development, http://www.nrg4sd.net.

10. *The Global Campaign on Urban Governance* (2002), UN-Habitat, http://www.unhabitat.org /pmss/getElectronicVersion.asp?nr=1537&alt=1.

11. Sustainable Cities Program, UN-Habitat, http://www.unhabitat.org/categories.asp?catid=369.

12. Southwestern Pennyslvania Regional Indicators Report (2002), Sustainable Pittsburgh, http://203.147.150.6/docs/swpaindicators2002.pdf.

13. State of Our City Report (2001), Sustainable Calgary, http://www.sustainablecalgary.ca /documents/SOOC2001.pdf.

14. CERES (Center for Education and Research in Environmental Strategies), http://www.ceres.org .au/about/about.htm.

15. A. Waters, remarks at a conference promoting the integration of garden-based education, cooking and nutrition, and sustainable agriculture awareness in schools (14 Mar. 1997), Edible Schoolyard, http://www.edibleschoolyard.org/ppl_aw.html.

16. Edible Schoolyard, http://www.edibleschoolyard.org.

17. Rethinking School Lunch, Center for Ecoliteracy, http://www.ecoliteracy.org/programs /rsl.html; Rethinking School Lunch guide, Center for Ecoliteracy, http://www.ecoliteracy.org /programs/rsl-guide.html.

18. School Lunch Initiative (a project of Berkeley Unified School District), http://www.schoollunchinitiative.org.

19. Green Harvest Program, case studies, Sustainable Communities Network, http://www.sustainable.org/casestudies/SIA_PDFs/SIA_Pennsylvania.pdf; Greater Pittsburgh Community Food Bank, http://www.pittsburghfoodbank.org.

20. Sustainability Street, Vox Bandicoot, http://www.voxbandicoot.com.au/sustainability_street.html.

21. Santa Monica Festival Environmental Art Project for SMMUSD, City of Santa Monica, Environmental Programs Division, http://www.smgov.net/epd/residents/Education/festival.htm.

22. Education for sustainability: Exemplars, Center for Ecoliteracy, http://www.ecoliteracy.org /education/exemplars.html; River of Words, http://www.riverofwords.org.

23. C. Wells, Making ecology make sense: The six disciplines of All Species Project (1999), All Species Project, http://www.allspecies.org/aspint/wellsart.htm.

24. Procession of the Species Celebration, http://www.procession.org.

Glossary

adaptive management

Learning by doing is the essence of adaptive management of the natural environment and its resources. . . . There is often great uncertainty regarding future conditions of the ecosystems, the relationships among the different components in the systems, the management objectives, and how abundant the resources really are. Adaptive management is aided by researchers as well as local users, takes onboard new information regarding natural systems, and adapts to new situations and disturbances. According to a growing number of ecologists such flexible management that is open to learning stimulates sustainable development by enhancing resilience in coupled human and natural systems.

Source: Sustainability School, Albaeco, http://www.albaeco.com/ss/text.htm

appropriated carrying capacity

Another name for the ecological footprint. "Appropriated" refers to captured, claimed, or occupied. Ecological footprints remind us that we appropriate ecological capacity for food, fibers, energy, waste absorption, etc. In industrial regions, a large part of these flows is imported.

Source: Sustainability indicators program, glossary, Redefining Progress, http://www.redefiningprogress.org/programs/sustainabilityindicators/glossary/terms.html

autotrophic

Self-feeding. The term is applied to organisms that produce their own food (such as plants, through photosynthesis) and to ecosystems that produce enough energy internally to meet their own needs (as in forests or savannas, where plants capture sufficient energy to drive the system).

biodiversity

Ecosystem, species, and genetic diversity. *The term "biological diversity," or "biodiversity," refers collectively to the full range of species, genes, and ecosystems in a given place.*

Source: Cities, glossary, People and the Planet, http://www.peopleandplanet.net/section.php?section=5&topic=8

biomimicry

The use of natural patterns as the basis for design. *Biomimicry (from* bios, *meaning life, and* mimesis, *meaning to imitate) is a design discipline that studies nature's best ideas and then imi-*

tates these designs and processes to solve human problems. Studying a leaf to invent a better solar cell is an example of this "innovation inspired by nature."

Source: Introduction to biomimicry, Biomimicry Institute, http://www.biomimicry.net/biomimicryintroduction.htm

bioregion

A distinct area with coherent and interconnected plant and animal communities, and natural systems, often defined by a watershed. A bioregion is a whole "life-place" with unique requirements for human inhabitation so that it will not be disrupted and injured.

Source: Planet Drum Foundation, http://www.planetdrum.org

A territory defined by a combination of biological, social, and geographic criteria, rather than geopolitical considerations; generally, a system of related, interconnected ecosystems.

Source: Glossary of biodiversity terms, UNEP World Conservation Monitoring Center,
http:/www.unep-wcmc.org/reception/glossaryA-E.htm

biosphere

The zone of the Earth and its atmosphere that supports life or is capable of supporting life.

Source: Greenfacts, glossary, http://www.greenfacts.org/glossary/abc/biosphere.htm.

biosphere reserve

Established under UNESCO's Man in the Biosphere Program, biosphere reserves are sites which show and foster innovative approaches to conservation and sustainable development.

Source: UNESCO, MAB, http://www.unesco.org/mab/BRs.shtml

carrying capacity

The maximum sustainable size of a resident population in a given ecosystem.

Source: Reproductive health, glossary, People and the Planet,
http://www.peopleandplanet.net/section.php?section=4&topic=8

city

A city is generally understood to be a relatively large or important urban center. In some nations, an urban center's designation as a city brings a higher political and administrative status. Most large cities are made up of many different local government areas, and this often leads to the designation of a metropolitan area encompassing these, and some administrative or political system to promote coordination between them. A local government area is considered to be part of the city if more than 15 percent of the residents work in the city.

Source: Cities, glossary, People and the Planet, http://www.peopleandplanet.net/section.php?section=5&topic=8

community

A group of ecologically related populations of various species occurring in a particular place and time. . . . A human community is a social group of any size whose members reside in a specific locality or have particular shared interests.

Source: Glossary of biodiversity terms, UNEP World Conservation Monitoring Center,
http:/www.unep-wcmc.org/reception/glossaryA-E.htm

ecological footprint

The land and water area that is required to support a defined human population and material standard indefinitely, using prevailing technology.

Source: Sustainability indicators program, glossary, Redefining Progress,
http://www.redefiningprogress.org/programs/sustainabilityindicators/glossary/terms.html

ecological overshoot

The situation when humanity consumes more resources than nature can regenerate and creates more wastes than nature can recycle.

Source: Ecological footprint analysis, Redefining Progress,
http://www.rprogress.org/newprojects/ecolFoot/concepts/overshoot.html

ecosystem

A dynamic complex of plant, animal, fungal, and microorganism communities and their associated non-living environment interacting as an ecological unit.

Source: Glossary of biodiversity terms, UNEP World Conservation Monitoring Center,
http:/www.unep-wcmc.org/reception/glossaryA-E.htm

ecosystem services

The benefits people obtain from ecosystems. These include provisioning services such as food, water, timber, and fiber; regulating services that affect climate, floods, disease, wastes, and water quality; cultural services that provide recreational, aesthetic, and spiritual benefits; and supporting services such as soil formation, photosynthesis, and nutrient cycling.

Source: MEA 2005, v

ecovillage

Ecovillages are urban or rural communities of people, who strive to integrate a supportive social environment with a low-impact way of life.

Source: Global Ecovillage Network, http://gen.ecovillage.org

embodied energy

The energy that is used during the entire life cycle of [a] commodity for manufacturing, transporting, and disposing of the commodity.

Source: Sustainability indicators program, glossary, Redefining Progress,
http://www.redefiningprogress.org/programs/sustainabilityindicators/glossary/terms.html

empowerment

The expansion of people's capacities and choices; the ability to exercise choice based on freedom from hunger, want, and deprivation; and the opportunity to participate in or endorse decision making that affects their lives.

Source: Governance for sustainable human development (1997 policy document), glossary of key terms,
United Nations Development Program, http://mirror.undp.org/magnet/policy/glossary.htm

Factor Four

The idea that resource productivity should be quadrupled so that wealth is doubled, and resource use is halved. The concept has been summed up as "doing more with less."

Source: Instruments for change, definitions and concepts, International Institute for Sustainable Development,
http://www.iisd.org/susprod/principles.htm

Factor Ten

The idea that per capita material flows caused by OECD [Organization for Economic Cooperation and Development] countries should be reduced by a factor of ten. Globally, claim proponents, material turnover should be reduced by 50 percent, but because OECD countries are responsible for material flows five times as high as developing countries, and world population is inevitably increasing, the OECD has to set long-term targets well beyond the more conservative Factor Four target.

Source: Instruments for change, definitions and concepts, International Institute for Sustainable Development,
http://www.iisd.org/susprod/principles.htm

governance

The exercise of political, economic, and administrative authority in the management of a country's affairs at all levels. Governance is a neutral concept comprising the complex mechanisms, processes, relationships, and institutions through which citizens and groups articulate their interests, exercise their rights and obligations, and mediate their differences. Governance is a confluence between government, civil society, and business.

Source: Governance for sustainable human development (1997 policy document), glossary of key terms, United Nations Development Program, http://mirror.undp.org/magnet/policy/glossary.htm

government

Governance applied to state responsibility.

heterotrophic

"Other-feeding." A term applied to an organism that cannot make its own food—for example, animals—or an ecosystem that cannot produce sufficient energy internally from photosynthetic processes to meet its own metabolism (that is, it needs external inputs of energy besides sunlight)—for example, deep ocean, and streams.

Source: Luck et al. 2001

industrial ecology

Industrial ecology uses the metaphor of metabolism to analyze production and consumption by industry, government, organizations, and consumers, and the interactions between them. It involves tracking energy and material flows through industrial systems (e.g., a plant, region, or national or global economy) and usually involves the sharing of wastes as resources between industries.

Source: Instruments for change, definitions and concepts, International Institute for Sustainable Development, http://www.iisd.org/susprod/principles.htm

organic farming

Production system that avoids or largely excludes the use of synthetically produced fertilizers, pesticides, growth regulators, and livestock feed additives. As far as possible, it relies on crop rotations, crop residues, animal manures, legumes, green manures, off-farm organic wastes, and aspects of biological pest control to maintain soil productivity and tillage, to supply plant nutrients, and to control insects, weeds, and other pests.

Source: Food and agriculture, glossary, People and the Planet, http://www.peopleandplanet.net/section.php?section=3&topic=8

natural capital

An extension of the economic notion of capital (manufactured means of production) to environmental "goods and services." It refers to a stock (e.g., a forest) which produces a flow of goods (e.g., new trees) and services (e.g., carbon sequestration, erosion control, habitat). Natural capital can be divided into renewable and nonrenewable; the level of flow of nonrenewable resources (e.g., fossil fuels) is determined politically.

Source: Instruments for change, definitions and concepts, International Institute for Sustainable Development, http://www.iisd.org/susprod/principles.htm

panarchy

The hierarchical set of adaptive cycles at different scales in a social-ecological system, and their cross-scale effects (i.e., the effects of the state of the system at one scale on the states of the sys-

tem at other scales) This nesting of adaptive cycles—from small to large—and the influences across scales is referred to as a panarchy.

Source: Walker and Salt 2006, 164

permaculture

Originally coined in the 1970s by Bill Mollison and David Holmgren to refer to an *integrated, evolving system of perennial or self-perpetuating plant and animal species useful to man.*

A more current definition of permaculture reflects the expansion of focus implicit in *Permaculture 1: Consciously designed landscapes which mimic the patterns and relationships found in nature, while yielding an abundance of food, fiber, and energy for provision of local needs. People, their buildings, and the ways in which they organize themselves are central to permaculture. Thus, the permaculture vision of permanent or sustainable agriculture has evolved to one of permanent or sustainable culture.*

More precisely permaculture is a "design system based on ecological principles" *which provides the organizing framework for implementing the above vision.*

Source: http://www.holmgren.com.au/html/About/aboutpermaculture.html; Mollison and Holmgren 1978.

photosynthesis

The biological process in chlorophyll-containing cells that transforms sunlight into plant matter (or biomass). All food chains that support animal life—including our own—are based on this plant matter.

Source: Sustainability indicators program, glossary, Redefining Progress, http://www.redefiningprogress.org/programs/sustainabilityindicators/glossary/terms.html

place

The intersection of people's physical, biological, social, and economic worlds. Usually about local geography and what makes it distinctive. Hence "sense of place" is how people belong because of their feelings about and commitment to the distinctive features of their place.

Source: S. Moore 1997

polycentric

Polycentric systems are the organization of small-, medium-, and large-scale democratic units that each may exercise considerable independence to make and enforce rules within a circumscribed scope of authority for a specified geographical area. . . . The strength of polycentric governance systems in coping with complex, dynamic biophysical systems is that each of the subunits has considerable autonomy to experiment with diverse rules for using a particular type of resource system and with different response capabilities to external shock but still within the constraints of the broader system rather than being independent.

Source: Ostrom 2001

resilience

Ecosystem resilience is the capacity of an ecosystem to tolerate disturbance without collapsing into a qualitatively different state that is controlled by a different set of processes. A resilient ecosystem can withstand shocks and rebuild itself when necessary. Resilience in social systems has the added capacity of humans to anticipate and plan for the future and thus to adapt to disturbance.

Source: Resilience, Resilience Alliance, http://www.resalliance.org/576.php

social capital

Features of social organization—such as networks and values, including tolerance, inclusion, reciprocity, participation, and trust—that facilitate coordination and cooperation for mutual benefit.

Social capital develops from the relations between and among actors in a particular place from government, business, and most of all civil society.

Source: Governance for sustainable human development (1997 policy document), glossary of key terms, United Nations Development Program, http://mirror.undp.org/magnet/policy/glossary.htm

sustainability

Sustainability is meeting the needs of present and future generations through an integration of environmental protection, social advancement and economic prosperity.

Source: Government of Western Australia 2003

A dynamic state in which system needs are being met. A sustainable ecosystem is one that is healthy (effective), zero-waste-producing, self-regulating, self-renewing, resilient, and flexible. A sustainable social-ecological system will have those same characteristics as well as being ethical, psychologically fulfilling, and coexisting (cooperative).

Source: Adapted from Bossel 1998

The ability of giving and receiving sustenance. Thus, sustainability can be thought of as the capacity to nourish humans and the wider life community over the long term.

Source: Davison 2001, 206

Online Resources

Introduction

Best Practices for Human Settlements (Together
  Foundation and UN-Habitat)
  http://www.bestpractices.org

CASE—Cities as Sustainable Ecosystems
  (UNEP/IETC)
  http://www.unep.or.jp/ietc/Activities
  /Cross-Cutting/CASE.asp

Cities in a Globalizing World: Global Report on
  Human Settlements
  http://www.unchs.org/Istanbul+5
  /globalreport.htm

Melbourne Principles for Sustainable Cities
  http://www.unep.or.jp/ietc/Focus
  /MelbournePrinciples/English.pdf

United Nations University/Institute of Advanced
  Studies, Urban Program
  http://www.ias.unu.edu/research
  /urbaneco.cfm

Vision

Community Visioning (Ames 1997)
  http://www.design.asu.edu/apa
  /proceedings97/ames.html

Dialogue with the City, Perth, Western Australia
  http://www.dpi.wa.gov.au/dialogue

Earth Charter
  http://www.earthcharter.org/files
  /charter/charter.pdf

EcoCity Cleveland
  http://www.ecocitycleveland.org

Healthy Cities (World Health Organization)
  http://www.euro.who.int
  /healthy-cities/introducing/20050202_4

US Environmental Protection Agency, Green
  Communities Program
  http://www.epa.gov/greenkit

Western Australian State Sustainability Strategy
  http://www.sustainability.dpc.wa.gov.au

Economy and Society

Bioregional Economies
  http://www.conservationeconomy.net
  /bioregional_economies.html

Complementary Currencies and Curitiba (Lietaer
  and Warmoth 1999)
  http://ceres.ca.gov/tcsf/pathways
  /chapter2.html#building

City Farms
  http://journeytoforever.org/cityfarm.html

Cities Feeding People (International Development
  Research Centre)
  http://network.idrc.ca/en
  /ev-81979-201-1-DO_TOPIC.html

Community Sustainability Assessment
  http://ecovillage.org/gen/activities/csa
  /pdf/CSA-English.pdf

Ecolabels (Consumers Union Guide, USA)
  http://www.eco-labels.org/home.cfm

Ecotrust and the Conservation Economy
  http://www.ecotrust.org/about

LA Ecovillage
  http://www.laecovillage.org/brochure.html

LETS Initiatives
  http://www.gmlets.u-net.com/faq.html
  #whatis

LETS Schemes and Cooperatives in Maleny, Australia
http://www.feasta.org/documents
/shortcircuit/index.html?epilogue.html

Trust for Public Lands—City Farms
http://www.tpl.org

Village of Arts and Humanities
http://www.inliquid.com/organizations
/village.shtml; http://www.villagearts.org

Biodiversity

Biosphere Reserves (Douglas and Box 2000)
http://www.ukmaburbanforum.org.uk
/Publications/Cities_rep/Changing_rep.pdf

Connected Wildlands
http://www.conservationeconomy.net
/connected_wildlands.html

Global Biodiversity Assessment
http://www.unep-wcmc.org/assessments
/index.htm

Millennium Ecosystem Assessment
http://www.millenniumassessment.org

The Nature Conservancy
http://www.nature.org

Ecological Footprints

Best Foot Forward
http://www.bestfootforward.com/cities.html

Ecological Footprint Calculators
http://www.earthday.net/footprint/index
.asp; http://www.epa.vic.gov.au
/ecologicalfootprint/calculators/default.asp

Ecological Footprints: Making Tracks toward
Sustainable Cities (Rees 2001)
http://www.iisd.ca/consume/brfoot.html

Redefining Progress
http://www.rprogress.org;
http://www.redefiningprogress.org

Urban and Ecological Footprints
http://www.gdrc.org/uem/footprints

Modeling Cities on Ecosystems

Bahía de Caráquez, Ecuador
http://www.planetdrum.org/eco
_ecuador.htm

Beddington ZeroEnergy Development, London
http://www.bedzed.org.uk

Capra, Fritjof
http://fritjofcapra.net/summary.html

Center for Ecoliteracy
http://www.ecoliteracy.org

Ecological Cities Project
http://www.ecologicalcities.org

Resilience Alliance
http://www.resalliance.org/ev_en.php

Urban Ecology
http://www.urbanecology.org

Your Home (Australian Greenhouse Unit)
http://greenhouse.gov.au/yourhome

Sense of Place

Arcata Marsh and Wildlife Sanctuary
http://www.humboldt.edu/~ere_dept/marsh

Ecological Design Institute
http://www.ecodesign.org/edi/aboutedi.html

Ecotrust GIS
http://ecotrust.org/knowledgesystems

Ethnoecology Database of the Greater Southwest
http://www.fortlewis.edu/anthro
/ethnobotany/database.htm

Portland Metropolitan Region Trails System
http://www.metro-region.org/article
.cfm?ArticleID=3418

Putah-Cache Bioregion Project
http://bioregion.ucdavis.edu

Wonga Wetlands
http://www.wongawetlands.nsw.gov.au

Empowerment and Participation

Anti-Freeway Movement
http://www.newint.org/issue313/exit.htm

Child-Friendly Cities (UNICEF)
http://www.childfriendlycities.org

Co-Intelligence Institute (Ways to Make a
Community Stronger . . .)
http://www.co-intelligence.org/CIPol
_CSWM.html

Community-Based Watershed Management Project
http://www.chs.ubc.ca/brazil/Outputs
/CBWM_Project_Overview.pdf

Urban Basic Services for the Poor
http://www.unesco.org/most/asia12.htm

Partnerships

Community-Supported Agriculture
http://umassvegetable.org/food
_farming_systems/csa

Environs Australia
http://www.environs.org.au

The Food Project
http://www.thefoodproject.org

Global Development Research Center
http://www.gdrc.org/sustbiz/index.html

Global Ecovillage Network
http://gen.ecovillage.org

ICLEI—Local Governments for Sustainability
  http://www.iclei.org

Northey Street City Farm, Brisbane, Australia
  http://www.regional.org.au/au/soc/2002
  /3/gamble.htm;
  http://www.northeystreetcityfarm.org.au/

Permaculture International Limited
  http://www.permacultureinternational.org

Robyn Van En Center for Community-Supported
  Agriculture
  http://www.csacenter.org

Sustainable Communities Network
  http://www.sustainable.org

WA Collaboration
  http://www.wacollaboration.org.au

Sustainable Production and Consumption

APEC Virtual Center for Environmental Technology
  Exchange
  http://www.apec-vc.or.jp

Energy Efficiency and Renewable Energy (CADDET)
  http://www.caddet.org

Environmentally Sound Technologies for
  Sustainable Development (UNEP/IETC)
  http://www.unep.or.jp/ietc/techTran/focus
  /SustDev_EST_background.pdf

ESTIS—Environmentally Sound Technologies
  Information System
  http://www.estis.net

Natural Step—Sustainability Training and
  Consultation
  http://www.naturalstep.org

Organic Farming in Havana, Cuba
  http://www.foodfirst.org/dr12

Path to Freedom—Urban Homesteading
  http://www.pathtofreedom.com

Simple Living Network
  http://www.simpleliving.net

Youth and Sustainable Consumption
  (UNEP/UNESCO)
  http://www.uneptie.org/pc/youth_survey

ZERI Brewery (Zero Emissions Research and
  Initiatives)
  http://www.zeri.org/case_studies_beer.htm

Governance and Hope

All Species Project
  http://www.allspecies.org

Center for Ecoliteracy
  http://www.ecoliteracy.org

City-Regions (Center for Urban Regional Ecology,
  University of Manchester)
  http://www.sed.manchester.ac.uk/research
  /cure/research

Edible Schoolyard
  http://www.edibleschoolyard.org

Global Campaign on Urban Governance (UN-
  Habitat)
  http://www.unhabitat.org/categories.asp
  ?catid=25

Greater Pittsburgh Community Food Bank: Green
  (Healthy) Harvest Program
  http://www.pittsburghfoodbank.org
  /programs/healthyharvest.htm

Procession of the Species Celebration
  http://www.procession.org

Sustainable Calgary
  http://www.sustainablecalgary.ca

Sustainable Cities Program (UN-Habitat)
  http://www.unhabitat.org/categories
  .asp?catid=369

Sustainable Pittsburgh
  http://www.sustainablepittsburgh.org

Sustainable Seattle
  http://www.sustainableseattle.org

Understanding Urban Governance (Global
  Development Research Center)
  http://www.gdrc.org/u-gov/ugov-define.html

References

Abram, D. 1997. *The Spell of the Sensuous: Perception and Language in a More-Than-Human World*. New York: Vintage Books.

Alberti, M. 2002. The effects of urban patterns on ecosystem function. Paper presented at symposium on Smart Growth and New Urbanism, National Center for Smart Growth, University of Maryland.

Alexander, C. 1979. *The Timeless Way of Building*. New York: Oxford Universty Press.

_____. 1987. *New Theory of Urban Design*. New York: Oxford Universty Press.

Ames, S. 1997. Community visioning: Planning for the future in Oregon's local communities. In *Contrasts and Transitions: Conference Proceedings of the American Planning Association*. http://www.design.asu.edu /apa/proceedings97/ames.html.

Anderson, E. 1996. *Ecologies of the Heart: Emotion, Belief, and the Environment*. New York: Oxford University Press.

Armstrong, R., S. Ruane, and P. Newman. 2002. *Case Studies in Sustainability: Hope for the Future in Western Australia*. Perth: Murdoch University, Institute for Sustainability and Technology Policy. CD-ROM. http://www.sustainability.murdoch.edu.au/casestudies/Hope4future/start.htm.

Arnold, M. B., and R. B. Day. 1998. *The Next Bottom-Line: Making Sustainable Development Tangible*. Washington, DC: World Resources Institute.

Ashton-Graham, C., and G. John. 2005. TravelSmart + TOD = synergy and sustainability. Paper presented at Transit Oriented Development: Making it Happen, PATREC Conference, Fremantle, Western Australia, 5–8 July. http://www.patrec.org/conferences.

AtKisson, A. 2001. Developing indicators of sustainable community: Lessons from Sustainable Seattle. In *The Earthscan Reader in Sustainable Cities*, ed. D. Satterthwaite, 352–63. London: Earthscan.

Beatley, T. 2005. *Native to Nowhere: Sustaining Home and Community in a Global Age*. Washington, DC: Island Press.

Beatley, T., and K. Manning. 1997. *The Ecology of Place: Planning for Environment, Economy, and Community*. Washington, DC: Island Press.

BedZED. 2002. *BedZED—Beddington Zero Energy Development, Sutton. General Information Report 89*. BioRegional Development Group, http://www.bioregional.com/programme_projects/ecohous_prog/bedzed /BedZED%20Best%20Practice%20Report.pdf.

Bengtsson, J., P. Angelstam, T. Elmqvist, U. Emmanuelson, and C. Folke. 2002. Reserves, resilience and dynamic landscapes. Discussion paper, Beijer Institute, Royal Swedish Academy of Sciences. http://www.beijer.kva.se/publications/pdf-archive/Disc157.pdf.

Benyus, J. 1997. *Biomimicry: Innovation Inspired by Nature*. New York: Morrow.

Berg, P., and R. Dasmann. 1978. *Reinhabiting a Separate County*. Planet Drum Foundation. http://www.planet-drum.org.

Berkes, F., and C. Holling. 2002. Back to the future: Ecosystem dynamics and local knowledge. In *Panarchy: Understanding Transformations in Human and Natural Systems*, ed. L. Gunderson and C. Holling, 121–46. Washington, DC: Island Press.

Berry, W. 1991. Out of your car, off your horse: Twenty-seven propositions about global thinking and the sustainability of cities. *Atlantic Monthly* 267 (2): 61–63.

_____. 2001. The whole horse. In *The New Agrarianism: Land, Culture, and the Community of Life*, ed. E. Freyfogle, 63–79. Washington, DC: Island Press.

Best Foot Forward. 2002. *City Limits: A Resource Flow and Ecological Footprint Analysis for Greater London*. http://www.citylimitslondon.com/downloads/Complete%20report.pdf.

Bossel, H. 1998. *Earth at a Crossroads: Paths to a Sustainable Future*. Cambridge: Cambridge University Press.

Boyden, S. 1992. *Biohistory: The Interplay Between Human Society and the Biosphere—Past and Present*. Paris: UNESCO/Parthenon Publishing Group.

Butler, D. 2006. Urban agriculture: A growing opportunity takes root. *The Ottawa Citizen*, 18 June.

Calthorpe, P., and W. Fulton. 2001. *The Regional City*. Washington, DC: Island Press.

Capra, F. 1996. *The Web of Life: A New Understanding of Living Systems*. New York: Anchor/Doubleday.

_____. 2002. *The Hidden Connections*. London: Flamingo.

_____. 2005. Preface to *Ecological Literacy: Educating Our Children for a Sustainable World*, ed. M. Stone and Z. Barlow. San Francisco: Sierra Club Books; Berkeley: Produced and distributed by University of California Press

Carson, L., and J. Hartz-Karp. 2005. Adapting and combining deliberative designs: Juries, polls, and forums. In *The Deliberative Democracy Handbook: Strategies for Effective Civic Engagement in the Twenty-First Century*, ed. J. Gastil and P. Levine. San Francisco: Jossey-Bass.

Casanova, L. 2003. *Environmental Citizenship: An Introductory Guidebook on Building Partnerships between Citizens and Local Governments for Environmental Sustainability*. Osaka: UNEP/IETC. http://www.unep.or.jp/ietc/publications/integrative/ims5/index.asp.

Chambers, N., C. Simmons, and M. Wackernagel. 2000. *Sharing Nature's Interest: Ecological Footprints as an Indicator of Sustainability*. London: Earthscan.

Clarkson, L., V. Morrisette, and G. Regallet. 1992. Our responsibility to the seventh generation: Indigenous peoples and sustainable development. International Institute for Sustainable Development. http://www.iisd.org/7thgen/default.htm.

Corbett, J., M. Corbett, and R. L. Thayer. 2000. *Designing Sustainable Communities: Learning from Village Homes*. Washington, DC: Island Press.

Daly, H. 1997. *Beyond Growth: The Economics of Sustainable Development*. Boston: Beacon Press.

Davison, A. 2001. *Technology and the Contested Meanings of Sustainability*. Albany: State University of New York Press.

de Castro, E., and A. McNaughton. 2003. Bioregional mapping as a participatory tool in the community based watershed management project in Santo André, Greater São Paulo, Brazil. Paper presented at a meeting of the Latin American Studies Associations, Dallas. http://www.chs.ubc.ca/brazil/Outputs/Bioregional_Mapping.pdf.

de Duve, C. 1995. *Vital Dust: Life as a Cosmic Imperative*. New York: Basic Books.

Dent, M. 2003. *Saving Our Children from Our Chaotic World*. Dunsborough, Western Australia: Pennington Publications.

Desai, P., and S. Riddlestone. 2002. *Bioregional Solutions for Living on One Planet*. Foxhole: Green Books Ltd.

Devall, B., and G. Sessions. 1985. *Deep Ecology: Living as if Nature Mattered*. Salt Lake City: Gibbs M. Smith.

Diamond, J. 2005. *Collapse: How Societies Choose to Fail or Succeed*. New York: Viking.

Douglas, I., and J. Box. 2000. The changing relationship between cities and biosphere reserves. Report prepared for the Urban Forum of the UK Man and Biosphere Committee. http://www.ukmaburbanforum.org.uk/Publications/Cities_rep/Changing_rep.pdf.

Earth Charter. 2000. Global consensus statement on sustainability. http://www.earthcharter.org/files/charter/charter.pdf.

Eisenstein, W. 2001. Ecological design, urban places, and the culture of sustainability. San Francisco Planning and Urban Research Association Report 399. http://www.spur.org/documents/ecodesign.pdf.

Elgin, D. 1981. *Voluntary Simplicity: Toward a Way of Life That Is Outwardly Simple, Inwardly Rich*. New York: William Morrow.

_____. 2003. Garden of simplicity. The Simple Living Network. http://www.simpleliving.net/content/custom_garden_of_simplicity.asp.

Feiner, J., D. Salmeron, E. Joos, and W. Schmid. 2002. Priming sustainability: The Kunming region development project. *DISP* 151 (4): 59–67.

Folke, C., S. Carpenter, T. Elmqvist, L. Gunderson, C. Holling, B. Walker, J. Bengtsson, F. Berkes, J. Colding, K. Danell, M. Falkenmark, L. Gordon, R. Kasperson, N. Kautsky, A. Kinzig, S. Levin, K. Maeler, F. Moberg, L. Ohlsson, P. Olsson, E. Ostrom, W. Reid, J. Rockstroem, H. Savenje, and U. Svedin. 2002. Resilience and sustainable development: Building adaptive capacity in a world of transformation. Paper for the World Summit on Sustainable Development, Johannesburg. http://www.sou.gov.se/mvb/pdf/resiliens.pdf.

Friedman, T. 2007. A green New Deal. *New York Times Magazine*. 15 April.

Frumkin, H. 2001. Beyond toxicity: Human health and the natural environment. *American Journal of Preventive Medicine*, 20 (3): 23440. http://www.sciencedirect.com

Girardet, H. 1992. *The Gaia Atlas of Cities: New Directions for Sustainable Living*. London: Gaia Books Ltd.

_____. 2001. *Creating Sustainable Cities: Schumacher Briefings 2*. Foxhole: Green Books Ltd.

Golany, G. S. 1995. *Ethics and Urban Design: Culture, Form and Environment*. New York: John Wiley & Sons.

Gough, I. 2003. Lists and thresholds: Comparing the Doyal-Gough theory of human need with Nussbaum's capabilities approach. WeD Working Paper No. 1, University of Bath, UK.

Government of Western Australia. 2003. *Hope for the Future: The Western Australian State Sustainability Strategy*. Perth: Government of Western Australia, Department of Premier and Cabinet. http://www.sustainability.dpc.wa.gov.au/docs/Strategy.htm.

Grimm, N., J. Grove, S. Pickett, and C. Redman. 2000. Integrated approaches to long-term studies of urban ecological systems. *BioScience* 5 (7): 571–85.

Hall, P. 1998. *Cities in Civilization: A Study of Creativity in Cities Down the Ages*. London: Weidenfeld and Nicolson.

Hallsmith G., 2005. *The Key to Sustainable Cities: Meeting Human Needs, Transforming Community Systems*. Vancouver: New Society Publishers.

Hamilton, C. 2003. *Growth Fetish*. Sydney: Allen and Unwin.

Hamilton, C., and R. Denniss. 2005. *Affluenza: When Too Much Is Never Enough*. Sydney: Allen and Unwin.

Hargoves, K., and M. H. Smith, eds. 2005. *The Natural Advantage of Nations* London: Earthscan.

Hardoy, J., D. Mitlin, and D. Satterthwaite. 2001. *Environmental Problems in an Urbanising World*. London: Earthscan.

Hawken, P. 2007. A global democratic movement is about to pop. *Orion Magazine*. 1 May. http://www.alternet.org/story/51088.

Hawken, P., H. Lovins, and A. Lovins. 2000. *Natural Capitalism: The Next Industrial Revolution*. London: Earthscan.

Hawkins, C. 2003. How indicators can inform policies and practices for sustainability. Sustainable Community Roundtable, City of Olympia, Washington. http://www.olywa.net/roundtable/psip/inform.html.

H. M. Treasury. 2006. *Stern Review on Economics of Climate Change*. London: H. M. Treasury.

Hartz-Karp, J. 2004. Harmonising Divergent Voices: Sharing the Challenge of Decision-Making. Keynote address, IPAA New South Wales State Conference.

Hartz-Karp, J., P. W. G. Newman. 2006. The Participative Route to Sustainability. In *Communities Doing it for Themselves: Creating Space for Sustainability*, ed. S. Paulin. Perth: University of Western Australia Press.

Heath, J. 1999. Why save orchids under threat? *Orchids Australia* October.

Ho, G., ed. 2002. *International Source Book on Environmentally Sound Technologies for Wastewater and Stormwater Management*. Osaka: UNEP/IETC; London: International Water Association Publishing. http://www.unep.or.jp/ietc/Publications/TechPublications/TechPub-15/main_index.asp.

Holling, C. S. 1973. Resilience and stability of ecological systems. *Annual Review of Ecology and Systematics* 4:1–23.

———. 1998. The renewal, growth, birth, and death of ecological communities. *Whole Earth Review* (Summer). http://www.wholeearthmag.com/ArticleBin/120.html.

Holling, C., and L. Gunderson. 2002. Resilience and adaptive cycles. In *Panarchy: Understanding Transformations in Human and Natural Systems*, ed. L. Gunderson and C. Holling. Washington, DC: Island Press.

Holmgren, D. 2002. *Permaculture: Principles and Pathways Beyond Sustainability*. Hepburn: Holmgren Design Services.

Hopkins, R. 2000. The food producing neighbourhood. In *Sustainable Communities: The Potential for Eco-Neighbourhoods*, ed. H. Barton, 199–215. London: Earthscan.

Howard, E. 1965. *Garden Cities of To-morrow*. London: Faber and Faber.

Husar, R. 1994. Ecosystem and the biosphere: Metaphors for human-induced material flows. In *Industrial Metabolism: Restructuring for Sustainable Development*, ed. R. Ayres and U. Simonis. Tokyo: United Nations University Press.

IUCN, UNEP, WWF. 1991. *Caring for the Earth*. Gland, Switzerland: IUCN, UNEP, WWF.

Jackson, H., and K. Svensson. 2002. *Ecovillage Living: Restoring the Earth and Her People*. Foxhole: Green Books Ltd.

Jacobs, J. 1961. *The Death and Life of Great American Cities*. Repr., New York: Vintage Books, 1992.

———. 1984. *Cities and the Wealth of Nations*. Harmondsworth, UK: Penguin Books.

Johnson, C. 2003. *Greening Sydney*. Sydney: Government Architect Publications.

Kay, J., and H. Regier. 2000. Uncertainty, complexity, and ecological integrity: Insights from an ecosystem approach. In *Implementing Ecological Integrity: Restoring Regional and Global Environmental and Human Health*, ed. P. Crabbe, A. Holland, L. Ryskowski, and L. Westra. Dordrecht: Kluwer Academic Publishers.

Kenworthy, J., and F. Laube. 2001. *The Millennium Cities Database for Sustainable Cities*. Brussels and ISTP: International Union of Public Transport (UITP), Murdoch University.

Kinnane, S. 2002. Recurring visions of Australindia. In *Country: Visions of Land and People in Western Australia*, ed. A. Gaynor, M. Trinca, and A. Haebich. Perth: Western Australian Museum.

Kinsley, D. 1995. *Ecology and Religion: Ecological Spirituality in Cross-Cultural Perspective*. Englewood Cliffs: Prentice-Hall.

Knudtson, P., and D. Suzuki. 1992. *Wisdom of the Elders*. St. Leonards: Allen & Unwin.

Korten, D. 1999. *The Post-Corporate World: Life after Capitalism*. West Hartford: Kumarian Press.

Krebs, C. 1988. *The Message of Ecology*. New York: Harper & Row.

Landry, C. 2000. *The Creative City: A Toolkit for Urban Innovators*. London: Earthscan.

———. 2006. *The Art of City Making*. London: Earthscan.

Lawton, R. 1989. *The Rise and Fall of Great Cities*. London: Belhaven Press.

Lewan, L., and C. Simmons. 2001. The use of ecological footprint and biocapacity analyses as sustainability indicators for sub-national geographical areas: A recommended way forward. Final Report. 27 August. www.bestfootforward.com/downloads/Use of EF for SGA - Main Report.PDF.

Lietaer, B., and A. Warmoth. 1999. Designing bioregional economies in response to globalization. In *Pathways to Sustainability: The Age of Transformation*, ed. A. Cohill and J. Kruth. http://ceres.ca.gov/tcsf/pathways/chapter2.html#building.

Lilburne, G. 1989. *A Sense of Place: A Christian Theology of the Land*. Nashville: Abingdon Press.

Lister, N., and J. Kay. 1999. Celebrating diversity: Adaptive planning and biodiversity conservation. In *Biodiversity in Canada: An Introduction to Environmental Studies*, ed. S. Bocking, 189–218. Peterborough; Orchard Park: Broadview Press.

Lopes, D., and C. Rakodi. 2002. Community empowerment and social sustainability in Florianopolis, Brazil. In *Building Sustainable Urban Settlements: Approaches and Case Studies in the Developing World*, ed. S. Romaya and C. Rakodi, 120–34. London: ITDG Publishing.

Loreau, M. 2000. Biodiversity and ecosystem functioning: Recent theoretical advances. *Oikos* 91:3–17.

Luck, M., G. D. Jenerette, J. Wu, and N. Grimm. 2001. The urban funnel and the spatially heterogeneous ecological footprint. *Ecosystems* 4:782–96.

Lucy, W. H., and D. L. Phillips. 2006. *Tomorrow's Cities, Tomorrow's Suburbs*. Washington, DC: Planners Press, American Planning Association.

Lyle, J. 1994. *Regenerative Design for Sustainable Development*. New York: John Wiley & Sons.

MacTiernan, A. 2004. Harmonising divergent voices: Sharing the challenge of decision-making. Keynote address at the IPAA New South Wales State Conference.

Maffi, L. 1999. Linguistic diversity. In *Cultural and Spiritual Values of Biodiversity: A Complementary Contribution to the Global Biodiversity Assessment*, ed. D. Posey, 21–56. Nairobi: UNEP.

Marten, G. 2001. *Human Ecology: Basic Concepts for Sustainable Development*. London: Earthscan.

Maslow, A. H. 1954. *Motivation and Personality*. New York: Harper & Row.

_____. 1968. *Toward a Psychology of Being*. New York: Van Nostrand.

_____. 1996. A theory of human motivation. In *Classics of Organization Theory*, 4th ed., ed., J. Shafritz, and J. Ott, 163–75. New York: Harcourt.

Mastny, L. 2003. *Purchasing Power: Harnessing Institutional Procurement for People and the Planet*. Worldwatch Paper 166. Washington, DC: Worldwatch Institute. http://www.worldwatch.org/node/824.

Max-Neef, M. 1992. Development and human needs. In *Real-Life Economics: Understanding Wealth Creation*, ed. P. Ekins and M. Max-Neef. London: Routledge.

Maybury-Lewis, D. 1992. *Millennium: Tribal Wisdom and the Modern World*. New York: Viking.

McDonough, W. 1992. The Hanover Principles. Charlottesville, VA: McDonough Consultants.

McDonough, W., and M. Braungart. 2002. *Cradle to Cradle: Remaking the Way We Make Things*. New York: North Point Press.

McHarg, I. 1969. *Design with Nature*. New York: Natural History Press.

McManus, P., and G. Haughton. 2006. Planning with ecological footprints: A sympathetic critique of theory and practice. *Environment and Urbanization* 18 (1): 113–27

MEA (Millennium Ecosystem Assessment). 2005. *Ecosystems and Human Well-Being: Synthesis*. Washington, DC: Island Press.

Meadows, D. H., J. Randers, and D. Meadows. 2005. *Limits to Growth: The 30-Year Update*. London: Earthscan.

Melbourne Principles for Sustainable Cities. 2002. Osaka: UNEP/IETC. http://www.unep.or.jp/ietc/focus /MelbournePrinciples/English.pdf.

Mollison, B. 1988. *Permaculture: A Designer's Manual*. Tyalgum, NSW: Tagari Publications.

Mollison, B., and D. Holmgren. 1978. *Permaculture 1: A Perennial Agricultural System for Human Settlement*. Melbourne: Corgi.

Moore, J. 1997. Inertia and resistance on the path to healthy communities. In *Eco-City Dimensions: Healthy Communities, Healthy Planet*, ed. M. Roseland. Gabriola Island: New Society Publishers.

Moore, S. 1997. "Place" and sustainability: Research opportunities and dilemmas. Paper presented at the Conference of the Australian Association for Social Research, Wagga Wagga, NSW.

Moroney, J., and D. Jones. 2006. Biodiversity space in urban environments: Implications of changing lot size. *Australian Planner* 43 (4): 22–27.

Morris, A. 1994. *History of Urban Form: Before the Industrial Revolutions*. Harlow: Longman Scientific & Technical.

Mumford, L. 1961. *The City in History: Its Origins, Its Transformations, and Its Prospects*. London: Secker & Warburg.

Nabhan, G. 1998. *Cultures of Habitat: On Nature, Culture, and Story*. Washington, DC: Counterpoint.

Newman, P. 1975. An ecological model for city structure and development. *Ekistics* 239:258–65.

_____. 1999. Exit from auto hell. *New Internationalist* 313. http://www.newint.org/issue313/exit.htm.

_____. 2001. Railways and Reurbanism in Perth. In *Case Studies in Planning Success*, eds. J. Williams and R. Stimson. New York: Elsevier..

_____. 2006. The environmental impact of cities. *Environment and Urbanization* 18 (2): 275–95.

_____. 2007. Does new urbanism really overcome automobile dependence: Some evidence from Australia. In *New Urbanism and Beyond*, ed. T. Haas. London: Rizzoli.

Newman, P., and J. Kenworthy. 1999. *Sustainability and Cities: Overcoming Automobile Dependence*. Washington, DC: Island Press.

————. 2007. Greening urban transportation. In *State of the World 2007*, ed. M. O'Meara Sheehan. New York: Norton.

Newman, P., and Suriptono. 2000. Community scale domestic waste water treatment systems in large third world cities: A case study in Malang, East Java. In *Sustainable Development Case Studies*. Perth: Murdoch University, Institute for Sustainability and Technology Policy. CD-ROM. http://www.sustainability.murdoch.edu.au/casestudies/Case_Studies _Asia/cww/cww.htm.

Nussbaum, M. 2006. *Frontiers of Justice: Disability, Nationality, Species Membership*. Cambridge, MA: Belknap Press of Harvard University Press.

Odum, E. 1997. *Ecology: A Bridge Between Science and Society*. Sunderland: Sinauer.

OECD (Organization for Economic Cooperation and Development). 2003. *Metropolitan Region of Melbourne, Australia: OECD Territorial Reviews*. Paris: OECD.

O'Meara Sheehan, M., ed. 2007. *State of the World 2007*. New York: Norton.

Ostrom, E. 2001. Vulnerability and polycentric governance systems. *Update: Newsletter of the International Human Dimensions Program on Global Environmental Change*. March. http://www.ihdp.uni-bonn.de/html/publications/update /update01_03/IHDPUpdate01_03_ostrom.html.

Paulin, S. (ed.) 2006. *Community Voices: Creating Sustainable Spaces*. Perth: University of Western Australia Press.

Peacock, K. 1999. Staying out of the lifeboat: Sustainability, culture, and the thermodynamics of symbiosis. *Ecosystem Health* 5 (2): 91.

Pearce, D., and E. Barbier. 2000. *Blueprint for a Sustainable Economy*. London: Earthscan.

Perlman, J., and M. O'Meara Sheehan. 2007. Fighting poverty and environmental injustice in cities. In *State of the World 2007*, ed. M. O'Meara Sheehan. New York: Norton.

Pope J., D. Annandale, and A. Morrison-Saunders. 2004. Conceptualising sustainability assessment. *Environmental Impact Assessment Review* 24: 595–616.

Posey, D., ed. 1999. *Cultural and Spiritual Values of Biodiversity: A Complementary Contribution to the Global Biodiversity Assessment*. Nairobi: UNEP.

Princen, T. 2005. *The Logic of Sufficiency*. Cambridge, MA: MIT Press.

Putnam, R. 1993. *Making Democracy Work: Civic Tradition in Modern Italy*. Princeton: Princeton University Press.

Raphael, C., S. Richardson-Newton, L. Sheehy, and S. Jennings. 2003. Living Smart—for a sustainable community: An innovative and collaborative approach to sustainable living in the city of Fremantle. In *Proceedings of the International Sustainability Conference, 2003*. Perth: Government of Western Australia, Regional Government Network for Sustainable Development. CD-ROM. http://www.livingsmart.org.au/pdfs/CRaphaelRegGovforSustDevfinal.pdf.

Ravetz, J. 2000. *City Region 2020: Integrated Planning for a Sustainable Environment*. London: Earthscan.

Rees, W. 1992. Ecological footprints and appropriated carrying capacity: What urban economics leaves out. *Environment and Urbanisation* 42:121–30.

————. 2001. Ecological footprints of the future. *People and the Planet*, 12 June. http://www.peopleandplanet.net/doc.php?id=1043. (Also appears under the alternate title "Ecological footprints: Making tracks toward sustainable cities" at http://www.iisd.ca/consume/brfoot.html.)

————. 2003. A blot on the land. *Nature*, 27 February.

Reid, W., N. Ash, E. Bennett, P. Kumar, M. Lee, N. Lucas, H. Simons, V. Thompson, and M. Zurek. 2002. *Millennium Ecosystem Assessment Methods*. Penang: MA Secretariat.

Riley, A. 1998. *Restoring Streams in Cities: A Guide for Planners, Policy Makers, and Citizens*. Washington, DC: Island Press.

Robinson, L. 2002. Public outrage and public trust: A road map for public involvement in waste management decision-making. Keynote address to Waste and Recycle Conference, Perth. http://media.socialchange.net.au/people/les /Public_outrage_public_trust.pdf.

Rodgers, R. G. 1997. *Cities for a Small Planet*. London: Faber & Faber.

Rose, D., and S. D'Amico. 2002. *Country of the Heart: An Indigenous Australian Homeland*. Canberra, Australia: Aboriginal Studies Press.

Roseland, M. 1997. Dimensions of the future: An Eco-city overview. In *Eco-City Dimensions: Healthy Communities, Healthy Planet*, ed. M. Roseland. Gabriola Island, BC: New Society Publishers.

———. 2005. *Towards Sustainable Communities*. 3rd ed. Vancouver: New Society Publishers.

———. 2007. Strengthening local economies. In *State of the World 2007*, ed. M. O'Meara Sheehan. New York: Norton.

Roszak, T. 1992. *The Voice of the Earth*. New York: Simon & Schuster.

Sahtouris, E. 1998. The biology of globalization. Adapted from first publication in *Perspectives in Business and Social Change* (Sep. 1997). http://www.ratical.org/LifeWeb/Articles/globalize.html#p6.

Sandercock, L. 2003. *Cosmopolis II: Mongrel Cities of the 21st Century*. London: Continuum.

Sarkissian, W., A. Cook, and K. Walsh. 1994–2005. *Community Participation in Practice* series (five books). Perth: Murdoch University, Institute for Sustainability and Technology Policy.

Sarkissian, W., A. Hirst, and B. Stenberg. 2003. New directions. In *Community Participation in Practice Series*. Perth: Murdoch University, Institute for Sustainability and Technology Policy.

Scheurer, J. 2001. Urban ecology, innovations in housing policy and the future of cities: Towards sustainability in neighbourhood communities. PhD diss., Murdoch University, Institute for Sustainability and Technology Policy.

Schumacher, E. F. 1973. *Small Is Beautiful: A Study of Economics as if People Mattered*. London: Abacus.

Sewall, L. 1999. *Sight and Sensibility: The Ecopsychology of Perception*. New York: Jeremy P. Tarcher/Putnam.

Sheehy, L., and P. Dingle. 2003. Goal setting, education, and sustainability: Living smart in the city of Fremantle. In *Proceedings of the International Sustainability Conference, 2003*. Perth: Government of Western Australia, Regional Government Network for Sustainable Development. CD-ROM.

Shuman, M. 2000. *Going Local: Creating Self-Reliant Communities in a Global Age*. New York: Routledge.

———. 2006. *The Small-Mart Revolution: How Local Businesses Are Beating the Global Competition*. San Francisco: Berrett-Koehler.

Sirolli, E. 1999. *Ripples from the Zambezi: Passion, Entrepreneurship and the Rebirth of Local Economies*. Vancouver: New Society Press.

Smil, V. 1997. *Cycles of Life: Civilization and the Biosphere*. New York: Scientific American Library.

Snyder, G. 1974. *Turtle Island*. New York: New Directions.

Spretnak, C. 1999. *The Resurgence of the Real: Body, Nature, and Place in the Hypermodern World*. New York: Routledge.

Srinivas, H. n.d. The role of local governments in fostering business partnerships for environmental sustainability. Global Development Research Center. http://www.gdrc.org/sustbiz/bizpartnerships.html.

Stiglitz, J. 2006. *Making Globalization Work*. New York: Norton.

Strang, V. 1997. *Uncommon Ground: Cultural Landscapes and Environmental Values*. Oxford; New York: Berg.

Sweet, L. n.d. Room to live: Healthy cities for the urban century. International Development Research Center Briefing No. 4. http://www.idrc.ca/wuf/ev-25775-201-1-DO_TOPIC.html#FarmingCity.

Takano, T., K. Nakamura, and M. Watanabe. 2002. Urban residential environments and senior citizens' longevity in megacity areas: The importance of walkable green spaces. *Journal of Epidemiology and Community Health* 56:913–18.

Talukder, S. 2006. Managing megacities: A case study of metroplitan regional governance for Dhaka. PhD diss., Murdoch University, Institute for Sustainability and Technology Policy.

Thayer, R. 2003. *LifePlace: Bioregional Thought and Practice*. Berkeley: University of California Press.

Thorpe, A. 2006. *Designer's Atlas of Sustainability*. Washington, DC: Island Press.

Tranter, P., and K. Malone. 2003. *Out of Bounds: Insights from Children to Support a Cultural Shift Towards Sustainable and Child-Friendly Cities*. State of Australian Cities Conference, University of Western Sydney. http://www.uws.edu.au/download.php?file_id=5009&filename=6.2_FINAL_TranterMalone.pdf&mimetype=application/pdf.

Turner, N. 2005. *The Earth's Blanket: Traditional Teachings for Sustainable Living*. Seattle: University of Washington Press.

Tyler-Miller, G. 1996. *Sustaining the Earth: An Integrated Approach*. Belmont: Wadsworth Publishing Company.

UNEP (United Nations Environment Program). 2002. *Global Environment Outlook 3: Past, Present and Future Perspectives*. Nairobi: UNEP; London: Earthscan.

————. 2003. Weather related natural disasters in 2003 cost the world billions: Press release, UNEP, Nairobi, 10 Dec.

UNEP/IETC. 2002. *Melbourne Principles for Sustainable Cities*. Integrative Management Series No. 1. Osaka: UNEP-IETC.

————. 2003. *Energy Savings in Cities: Issues, Strategies, and Options for Local Governments*. IETC Urban Management Series 1. Osaka: UNEP/IETC. http://www.gdrc.org/uem/energy/cd-contents/ietc-energysavingsincities.html.

UNEP Interfaith Partnership on the Environment. 2000. *Earth and Faith: A Book of Reflection for Action*. New York: UNEP.

UN-Habitat. 2006. *The State of the World's Cities*. London: Earthscan.

Van Der Ryn, S., and S. Cowan. 1996. *Ecological Design*. Washington, DC: Island Press.

Verstegen, P. 2003. Capacity building and resource exchange: Kwinana industries—a Western Australian contribution to industrial ecology. In *Proceedings of the International Sustainability Conference, 2003*. Perth: Government of Western Australia, Regional Government Network for Sustainable Development. CD-ROM. http://www.sustainability.dpc.wa.gov.au/docs/BGPapers/Verstegen%20P%20-%20Kwinana.pdf.

von Weizsäcker E., A. B. Lovins, and L. H. Lovins. 1997. *Factor Four: Doubling Wealth, Halving Resource Use*. London: Earthscan.

Wackernagel, M., and W. Rees. 1996. *Our Ecological Footprint: Reducing Human Impact on the Earth*. Gabriola Island, BC; Philadelphia, PA: New Society Publishers.

Wackernagel, M., N. Schulz, D. Deumling, A. Linares, M. Jenkins, V. Kapos, C. Monfredo, J. Loh, N. Myers, R. Norgaard, and J. Randers. 2002. Tracking the ecological overshoot of the human economy. *Proceedings of the National Academy of Sciences of the United States of America* 99 (14): 9266–71.

Wakely, P. 1997. From participation to partnership: Who does what to build the capacity to build capacity? *Habitat Debate* 3 (4). (UN-Habitat quarterly, Dec. 1997.)

Walker B., S. Carpenter, A. Anderies, N. Abel, C. Cumming, M. Janssen, L. Lebel, J. Norberg, G. D. Peterson, and R. Pritchard. 2002. Resilience management in social-ecological systems: A working hypothesis for a participatory approach. Conservation Ecology 6 (1): 14. http://www.consecol.org/vol6/iss1/art14.

Walker, B., and D. Salt. 2006. *Resilience Thinking: Sustaining Ecosystems and People in a Changing World*. Washington, DC: Island Press.

Walker, L. 2005. *Ecovillage at Ithaca: Pioneering a Sustainable Culture*. Vancouver: New Society Publishers.

Waller, S. 2003. Story-telling and community visioning: Tools for sustainability. Background paper for the state sustainability strategy, Department of Premier and Cabinet, Perth, Australia. http://www.sustainability.dpc.wa.gov.au.

Wallington, T., R. Hobbs, and S. Moore. 2005. Implications of current ecological thinking for biodiversity conservation: A review of the salient issues. *Ecology and Society* 10 (1): 15. http://www.ecologyandsociety.org/vol10/iss1/art15.

Water Sensitive Urban Design Research Group. 1990. *Water Sensitive Residential Design*. Perth: WA Water Resources Council.

Wines, J. 2000. *Green Architecture*. Cologne: Taschen.

WCED (World Commission on Environment and Development). 1987. *Our Common Future* [The Brundtland Report]. Oxford; New York: Oxford University Press.

World Council for Renewable Energy. 2005. Renewable Energy and the City. World Renewable Energy Policy and Strategy Forum. Bonn, Germany: 13-15 June.

WWF–UK. 2006. Taking the first step: A "how to" guide for local authorities. Surrey: WWF–UK. http://www.wwf.org.uk/filelibrary/pdf/takingfirststep_ef.pdf.

WWF, ZSL, and Global Footprint Network. 2006. *Living Planet Report 2006*. http://www.wwf.org.au/publications/living-planet-report-2006.

Yamamura, N., S. Yachi, M. Higashi. 2001. An ecosystem organization model explaining diversity at an ecosystem level: Coevolution of primary producer and decomposer. *Ecological Research* 16 (5): 975–82.

Young, J. 2006. Black water rising. *World Watch*, Sept./Oct., 26.

Index

Note: *Italicized page numbers* indicate illustrations.

Island Press Board of Directors